March into My Heart

March into My Heart

A Memoir of Mothers, Daughters, and Adoption

Patty Lazarus

SURAZAL PRESS

First Edition, 2013

Permission for epigraph courtesy of Gracie Harmon from her collection, *A Life Full of Poems.*

Cover Design: Jessika Merrill

ISBN-10: 0615776450
ISBN-13: 9780615776453

Dedicated with love
to my daughter, Sophia Mariel,
and to the memory of my dear mother,
Shirley Merielle (1934–1994)

My mom is a never-ending song in my heart
of comfort, happiness and being.
I may sometimes forget the words but I always
remember the tune.

—Gracie Harmon, *A Life Full of Poems*

CONTENTS

Introduction.........1
My Loss.........3
Missing a Girl.........26
Working with Science.........36
Considering Our Options.........48
Moving Forward.........58
March 1.........73
The First Call.........83
The Lawyers.........100
The Decision.........117
Diving In.........127
The Stop in Phoenix.........138
Our Adventure Begins.........149
St. Patrick's Day Visit.........159
The Legal Business.........168
The Panicking.........176
The Waiting.........188
The Birth.........197
The Countdown.........208
The Final Day.........221
Weekend Between Two Worlds.........235
Going Home.........251
Epilogue.........255

ACKNOWLEDGMENTS

A few dear friends of mine read this story in different phases of completion. I deeply appreciate them for their encouragement, time, advice, and challenging questions. Thanks, in particular, to Karen, Ellen, Sharon, Linda, and Jennifer. In addition, I want to thank my friend Dale Behar for his insight, perspective, and loving friendship. Dale passed away just two months after reading my story, and the precious time he spent helping me with my book was just one example of the constant compassion and goodwill he showed to all of his friends and family. It was one of the last good deeds accomplished in a life full of generosity. I also appreciate many other friends, too numerous to mention, who have helped me along the way.

I thank my copy editors Heather Miller and Mark Berens, as well as proofer Dan Janeck, for their tedious and quality work on my manuscript. I also thank my team at Girl Friday Productions for their efforts to help publish my book. Thanks to Jessika Merrill for her cover design and my friend Michael Longacre for his expert advice.

My children deserve credit for their emotional support and patience during the many hours I spent writing and editing this story. My husband, Jon, deserves a huge thank-you for his devotion to my emotional needs throughout the journey we took together ten years ago and more recently, for his insight and support. I thank my loving father and most of all, my dearly departed mother for being such an amazing role model and for giving me the strength and life skills to become the mother I always wanted to be.

INTRODUCTION

I finally opened the envelope my father handed me shortly after my mother's death. Over the years, I had kept the envelope in a safe place and would frequently pick it up, consider whether it was a "good time," and put it back. I remember when my mother was writing her autobiography, just months before her death, as the cancer infiltrated her body and the chemotherapy permanently damaged her heart, at only sixty years old. I had asked several times to read it in draft form. She politely declined and said she was writing it for her grandchildren, but that I could read it when it was finished. She enjoyed writing and doing something meaningful, after years of lying on the couch recuperating from chemotherapy treatments.

When she died, I wondered if she had ever finished her autobiography and if I would ever recover. It took me eighteen years to gather the courage to face my grief over her death again. Somehow, I finally realized that I would never feel strong enough to read about the incredible woman who left me too soon. She had been my best friend and I heard her loving voice through her written words. Even though I had given myself that many years to prepare, I was in tears as I read it for the first time.

My mother's life story was brief, both on paper and in years, but she managed to support the decisions her children had made before she died, compliment her husband of almost forty years, and give words of wisdom to her grandchildren. Reading her autobiography brought back many memories of her intelligence, strong will, kindness, and unwavering love for her family.

Her loss almost two decades ago was devastating to me, her only daughter, and left a vast hole in my life that even a wonderful husband and three incredible children could never completely fill. Even more upsetting has been recognizing that her grandchildren will never truly understand what a fantastic grandmother they might have had. My two sons don't remember her, but at least I feel heartened that she had met them. She never met my daughter, who was named after her and whom she would have loved wholeheartedly.

This story is about the adoption of my daughter ten years ago. At first, I wrote this story for her, Sophia Mariel. I wanted to tell her all the details about where she came from and why she is so important to our family and me. After I gave birth to my two sons, I struggled with infertility. Eventually, my husband and I adopted Sophia. It was a remarkable journey.

The excellent relationship I had with my mother played a fundamental role in my desire to have a girl. I wished to share the joy of a flourishing mother-daughter relationship with a daughter of my own and to give her the same quality of life and words of wisdom my mother had given me. It had always been my dream to have a daughter and after my two sons were born, I felt incomplete without a girl. At times, I felt selfish about being unsatisfied with my life when I had so much to be grateful for, but I gave myself permission to reach for my dream.

I published this story to encourage other women discouraged by infertility to consider adoption as a way to fulfill their dreams of a family. I hope to give back to others for the blessing I was lucky enough to realize. Although my daughter is not biologically related to me, Sophie reminds me of my mother. She has the same zest for life, the same patient disposition, the same kind heart, and most of all, the same love for her mother as I had for mine.

MY LOSS

I remember as if it were yesterday—the Tuesday morning that I heard the worst news I had ever received. I was twenty-three years old, going about my life, while my mother underwent yet another biopsy. It was not her first. Almost five years earlier, she had found a lump, and I remember being worried sick. That tumor was benign, as were the two others that quickly followed. After the second, I stopped taking time off from work and let my father sit and wait alone at the hospital. Each time, I worried about it less when I knew she was under the scalpel. I assumed that that Tuesday morning's test would have the same outcome as the others and half wondered why my mother was going through the same procedure each time she felt something abnormal in her breast.

At the time, my mother was working as an administrative secretary at the same hospital at which she had her procedures done. It was close to my office in Redmond, Washington. Every day at work, my mother saw people who were either patients themselves or visitors, so naturally, she heard a lot about disease. I often wondered how she could work there—to me it seemed depressing.

Maybe because of what she was exposed to at work, my mother had always been extra careful to follow up on every health issue, real or perceived. As a teenager, I had given her many an eye roll in response to what seemed like her "fear of the week," as I referred to them. My now dearly departed grandfather had always been a hypochondriac, yet he and my grandmother had smoked cigarettes since their teens and were still smoking, and healthy, at eighty years old. It never occurred to me that one of those frightening and depressing diseases would strike someone in our family. I was convinced that we had longevity in our genes, so I tolerated what seemed to me to be excessive fear and discussion of scary diseases.

My father called my office late that fateful Tuesday and asked me to sit down. His voice was very quiet, which was not typical. I swallowed hard. Because I had someone in my office at the time, I put the call on hold, excused myself, and stepped into an empty conference room across the hall. I closed the door and braced myself as I picked up the phone. "Dad, are you okay?" I said.

"It's breast cancer," he said before he broke into sobs.

I remember standing up and screaming "NO!" loud enough for several of my coworkers to rush out of their offices. Tears ran down my face as I nodded and waved them away, still holding the phone. My mother was only fifty years old. I thought about my mother's best friend who had died the previous year of breast cancer. The sudden fear felt like a cage I knew I couldn't escape from.

I tried to get more information from my father, hoping to hear something positive in the diagnosis, but he could barely speak. All he managed to say was, "Please come to the hospital, and you can talk to the doctors and see your mother." I could still hear him sobbing as we said good-bye.

My life changed forever at that moment.

I had always felt comfortable talking to my mother about everything: the men in my life, work issues, friends, and goals for my future. She knew me well and was good at getting me to make decisions without making them for me, even when I asked her to. She was tricky that way. She never took credit for my successes although she was often more responsible than she would admit for the good things in my life.

My mother's cancer treatments seemed to go reasonably well for the first five years. Life went along with some normalcy, even though her answers to the question "How are you?" held new meaning for my father, my brother, and me when we spoke with her. The initial medication had few side effects, and she continued working, but her concern for her own health consumed her. She had less energy and diminished interest in the activities I knew she enjoyed. I watched her struggle through social events with reduced enthusiasm; even just shopping with me took days of recovery.

We tried to enjoy more time together as a family during those days, and my mom took more hours off work each week, as well as more vacation time. My father took her on cruises to Mexico and the Caribbean, and a trip to Europe, with her doctor's blessing. I missed them terribly when they were away and I could see how the illness was pulling her away from me mentally and physically. I was starting to lose the supportive friend and advisor I had learned to count on.

At the hospital where she worked, the doctors checked her blood levels every month and never found anything to worry about—until it was too late.

She was fifty-five years old when the doctors realized the cancer had been secretly metastasizing. They had only been checking her blood, which remained healthy and cancer free. But the cancer had spread through her skin and into her bones, which they hadn't been checking regularly via scans of her body since her blood tests were negative. We were all stunned.

The doctors found the cancer after they biopsied a seemingly minor bump on Mom's head. She had been frustrated that the doctors not only couldn't explain the bump but also refused to take it seriously for over three months. My mother kept pushing different specialists on the issue, and finally found a doctor who agreed to do a biopsy. Bad news followed that test, and a subsequent full body scan uncovered the devastating news. Her prognosis was suddenly much worse.

I couldn't believe that she had been working at that same hospital and getting checked frequently, but the doctors didn't notice that the cancer was taking control. We were beyond disappointed in her doctors and the overall care she had received, but even more shocked that her health could have declined so quickly. How could this have happened? How did the doctors miss it? Why hadn't they listened to her? Why hadn't I convinced them to test her sooner?

After five relatively good years, we prayed that she would beat the cancer and that our family would remain intact. Again, we were sorely disappointed. Our lives changed dramatically with the new cancer treatment she endured. The radiation and chemo treatments were brutal, and the next three years were excruciating for my mother.

My father, brother, and I spent a lot of time worrying and caring for her. She unselfishly managed to ask about me whenever we were together, but my life seemed so unimportant compared to what she was dealing with. I couldn't decide if talking about good things in my life helped take her mind off her troubles or made her feel worse about spending so much time in bed. She missed so many activities with her friends and family. She had to quit her job, which she loved, and was too weak to travel. I started to lose sight of the woman I had known and cherished all my life. Her energy and zest for life started to fail and I panicked. She was slipping away from me in every way, slowly but steadily, every day.

ꟹ

I had always felt like I was in complete control over my life and my future. I thought I had things all planned out. I thought I knew what my life was going to look like as early as second grade when my teacher asked the class to draw a picture of each major event or important stage of our life on an index card, creating a string of cards to represent our life plan. There they were in bold Crayola color: each important event in my life detailed on a 3" x 5" card. Along with my birth and childhood, the cards included college, career, marriage, giving birth to a son, giving birth to a daughter, and my death (seventy-six seemed *so* old then). I didn't plan for the death of my parents, whom I expected to be alive through all the big events of my life, except for my own death. I still remember that art project and am amazed at how easy adult life seemed when I was a kid.

Things appeared to go as planned through high school and college, and I was confident that my future would play out according to plan. Was I ever wrong.

Life was generally good as I was nearing thirty years old. I had graduated from the University of Washington when I was twenty-two—right on schedule—and before I could worry about finding my first job out of college, my mother had suggested that I look into a new local company called Microsoft. My decision to apply there was yet another occasion when my mother's advice and encouragement made a monumental difference in my life. I was confident about everything I did in my life, thanks to my mother. Somehow, she was able to give me advice in a way that I could hear at an age when most young adults ignore advice from their parents. I respected her in so many ways, and our relationship was excellent.

My mother and I were best friends, even though we were very different. I was less patient and put more demands on myself and those around me than she did. She watched my father and me have heated arguments or get upset over silly things, all the while knowing that we'd quickly get over it. She handled her family—and life in general—with remarkable aplomb. She was amazing with schedules and details, and even though she worried excessively about everything, we all knew we could rely on her in every way.

I always wanted to be just like my mother—to build a satisfying life for myself just as she had done, even if it was the more difficult path. I worked hard at school and then at my career to become a person she could be proud of. She never pressured me. I always thought I had it easier than she did, so success seemed simply the only obtainable goal.

As a teenager, my mother had moved away from her family and home in Canada to attend college in Seattle. She graduated from the business school at University of Washington—only one of two women in that program at the time—started a youth center on campus that still exists today, and became a US citizen. Her accomplishments followed her and were reflected in the people she befriended and worked with along the way. She always saw the good side of people and wasn't afraid of hard work or being the first one to do something difficult, especially as a woman.

My mother was a strong woman, and yet selfless, caring, and loving with family and friends. After college, she married a man who traveled for business Monday through Friday every week and raised two kids virtually by herself for many years. I remember her trying to be the disciplinarian with my brother and me while my father was away. She got her point across successfully but failed when it came to being upset with us. We usually ended up laughing together, which made learning lessons easier for all of us. She was a wonderful role model as I grew from a student into a professional woman.

In July 1983, one month after my college graduation and after an hour-long interview (thanks to my mother's suggestion), I was hired into an entry-level position at Microsoft. I was thrilled but not surprised. I had always set my sights on goals—grades, college, and sorority choices, for example—and accomplishing them. I was willing to work hard and getting that job was, to me, a predictable achievement. After all, I was my mother's daughter.

Back in 1983, I could barely find the power switch on a personal computer, which sat on every desk at Microsoft, let alone use one. I quickly learned as much as I could about computers and the budding Microsoft business. I worked on various projects for several different departments in the company and listened carefully to those smart computer science graduates. I had no trouble asking for help, and as a result, I quickly learned the basics of hardware and software. I even received a short tutorial from Bill Gates.

After only a couple months, I set my sights on a job in the sales department, and within a year, I got my chance. As a member of the Original Equipment Manufacturer sales force, I spent a lot of time with marketing and program managers at Microsoft. I enjoyed being exposed to the brainpower working at Microsoft and the constant energetic flow we had at work. Most of the people working there were from the East Coast, and they seemed to run at faster speeds than Seattleites, both functionally and intellectually. I worked hard and went from managing small start-ups building computers in their home garages to managing giant corporate accounts. Microsoft was becoming a powerhouse in the software world, and it was exciting to be part of it, despite the frequent cross-country travel that was required of me.

Although the early Microsoft was mostly full of shy computer "geeks" from MIT and other technology schools, I met several great people who were focused on marketing, including my future husband. I met Jon at a party given by a Microsoft coworker and common friend on the Fourth of July in 1990. Jon was a vice president and had been working for Microsoft from New York for a few years. He managed a Microsoft office in Manhattan and had just moved to Seattle when we met. He had an incredibly funny sense of humor that caused me to ignore the date I had come to the party with for most of the afternoon.

Jon and I were different in many ways, especially because he grew up on the East Coast. However, we realized over the course of subsequent dates that we had similar goals in life, along with other connections, and quickly fell in love.

Jon and I traveled together a good bit for business and for pleasure the first few months of our relationship. For vacations, we visited Greece, France, and Italy, staying in incredible hotels and eating amazing food. We also went to San Francisco and Los Angeles for parties given by friends in the software industry and to Aspen for skiing. My favorite times were weekends we spent together in New York City after working in New Jersey during the week. Having lived there for twenty years after college in Philadelphia, Jon knew the city well. He took me to all the great sights, museums, theaters, and restaurants. It was a fascinating and fun courtship.

After dating for six months, we agreed to live together with the caveat that after six months, we would either get engaged or break up. I wasn't willing to wait too long to get my life on track, since I was behind on my life plan at nearly thirty years old. It wasn't an ultimatum; it was "the deal."

Three months later, we met in New York after a week of working on separate business trips. I was tired as I stepped into the hotel room but excited about another fabulous New York weekend. There were two dozen red roses waiting for me. Jon was very romantic and always celebrated the first of each new month together by sending me a bouquet of flowers. That was March 1, and it turned out to be a magical date as Jon asked me to marry him at dinner in uptown Manhattan later that same evening. I was completely surprised when he handed me a loose diamond resting in a small Tiffany silver box. He was delighted when I said yes.

"You are so tricky," I said. "This is only March. You had until the end of June to ask me this question. Why did you ask me so soon?"

"I'm a businessman, a *good* businessman. When I see a good deal, I close the deal as soon as possible," Jon explained with a big smile. "It isn't necessary to wait another three months. We belong together. We'll go find a setting for that diamond tomorrow."

He knew me well enough to resist picking out a ring on his own, and I appreciated that, as well as the beautiful diamond he gave me. We spent the rest of the weekend shopping for diamond settings, calling our families, and picking a wedding date. I agreed we were a perfect fit and the wedding planning could not have gone easier. We organized the event ourselves and seemed to agree on everything. It was the first sign that as a couple we made quick decisions, even about lifelong issues.

Jon and I made a good team. Since we were from opposite coasts, we had grown up very differently, but we had similar values from traditional backgrounds and loving parents. He went to private schools growing up while I was a public school kid. He spent many years in New York hailing cabs everywhere while I never stopped driving after age sixteen; consequently, I drove no matter where we went. He makes decisions from a logical standpoint while I rely on my emotions. He's always had more patience than I have, especially in traffic, but I'm not as picky about food. We have similar tastes in almost everything and he always knows when to let me decide. Most importantly, we both always knew we wanted kids.

I had been working for Microsoft for eight years when Jon and I were engaged, and I was thrilled to be getting married at a time when I felt I had accomplished a lot in my career. I had traveled extensively and was quite successful. I had met some amazing people, both inside and outside Microsoft. I didn't feel the need to move up in the corporation beyond my current department. Although I enjoyed working, I was ready to be a full-time mother, which had always been my plan.

The wedding took place on a glorious, sunny Sunday in July 1991, and my mother was well enough that day to walk me down the aisle with my father. Our close friends and family sat in white chairs on either side of the aisle, which ran across the patio and deck outside our home on the lake. My mother looked beautiful, despite the recent weight loss, and she kept smiling, despite the pain we all knew she suffered.

After the ceremony, we all walked down to our dock where Jon and I boarded our small boat for a romantic champagne cruise down the lake to the reception at a waterfront hotel. Even though I was deliriously happy at that moment, I remember looking at my mother waving to me as the boat pulled away from the dock. I was thinking how sad it felt to be leaving her, when in reality she was leaving me. The boat was taking me away for a few minutes, but the cancer would ultimately take her away forever.

Everyone who had attended the ceremony, plus another large group of friends, met us at the reception. It was a wonderful afternoon full of good cheer, warm wishes, and a bright outlook for our future as a couple. I delighted in the fact that we had given my mother something to look forward to, and now that the wedding was over, I was determined to give her a grandchild as quickly as possible.

The day I married Jon was not only a happy day because we made a great pair and I loved him so much but also because I knew that someday he would be a great father to the son I looked forward to and I would be a great mother for our daughter. Perhaps it was a strange way to look at it, especially now that we have two beautiful boys and I love them as much as Jon does, but that's how I had always thought about it. I had known that in addition to a son, I wanted a daughter. I had known this since I was a little girl myself. It was my plan.

It wasn't that I didn't want sons. I did, and I looked forward to the sports teams, roughhousing, and other boy-related activities that I had learned about from my brother growing up. We used to play "army" with the neighborhood kids, and one of my best friends growing up was a boy. I still love playing and watching sports. Having a son was going to be a blessing, but it had always been my dream to have a daughter too.

I loved my "girly" childhood and I had good girlfriends, but my mother was the most important person in my life. I remember sitting in the bathroom with her almost every evening while she took a bubble bath, talking about friends, boys, school, and life. I admired everything about her; she struck the perfect balance between friendly and motherly advice. We loved shopping and cooking together, and she taught me how to play golf, one of my favorite hobbies now. She encouraged me to learn to ski, which I fought as a teenager and is now my favorite sport, especially with my own kids. I was amazed at her strength as a mentor and her compassion as a friend.

Our relationship was similar to the one my mother had with her mother, my grandmother Pearl, another remarkable woman. My mother chose the name Patricia when I was born to honor my grandmother Pearl. Choosing a baby name with the same first letter as a parent or grandparent was a tradition in our family; my brother's middle name is Lee for Grandpa Leo. When we visited Pearl in Vancouver, Canada, or when she came to Seattle, the three of us had an unbelievable connection and rapport. We spent entire days shopping and enjoyed long lunches together. Like my mother, my grandmother always had excellent advice for me, no matter what topic was at hand. She was a smart businesswoman who helped her husband run a women's clothing store. She dressed her petite physique impeccably, and although she was small in stature, she had a knack for getting people to follow her directions. We always knew that she was looking out for us in every way, and everyone in the family respected her immensely. I remember holding my grandmother's hand when I was about ten years old and thinking I wanted to be just like her. I always tried to live up to her expectations, even after she was gone. I looked forward to being that kind of a role model and enjoying happy memories and warm relationships. I was confident that it would happen, and I couldn't wait.

My desire to have a child increased considerably when my mother became ill. I knew it would give my mother great pleasure to become a grandmother. My older brother was not at all close to marriage at that time. I was already thirty years old and Jon was forty, so we felt that it was time to get started. We had no idea how long it would take to conceive, so we decided that we would let pregnancy happen naturally. Shortly after our wonderful honeymoon in the Caribbean, it did.

Our first son Jake was born in May 1992, exactly ten months after our wedding. We had just added an entire floor to our house, including two bedrooms, a bathroom, and a playroom—it was finally a family home rather than a bachelor pad. They were still working on the landscaping when I went into labor.

"The rockery along the driveway is almost finished, honey," Jon whispered in my ear when I awoke from one of many post-delivery naps in the hospital, "and I've emailed all our friends and family about Jake with a picture."

Jake was a beautiful baby, even as a newborn. He looked up at me as I held him for the first time, and my heart exploded. I instantly loved him more than anything, and I could already tell he looked like my side of the family.

My mother and father appeared by my bedside at the hospital with a beautiful blue hydrangea plant to commemorate their first grandchild's birth. I remember how good my mother looked that day with her sweet smile of genuine happiness and caring concern. She held her new grandson proudly. She looked vibrant as ever that day, despite the changes she had suffered from the cancer treatments. She had beautiful hazel eyes and a light brown wig made from her own hair. I had always wished I had her eyes, rather than my father's dark features.

I cherished my mother's approval on everything, including the birth of our son, which I felt was my biggest accomplishment. My mother's approval wasn't hard to come by. She had always been supportive and proud of me: when I became a cheerleader in junior high school, when I graduated with honors from high school, when I earned a scholarship for my last year in college, when I was promoted at Microsoft, and of course, when I married one of the handsome vice presidents, whom she liked very much. My mother knew Jon was right for me the minute they met. She liked his strong, vibrant personality and his smart sense of humor. She knew he adored me but that he would never let me take full control, even when I tried. She could tell our relationship would last.

At thirty-one years old, I had done exactly as my mother had done thirty-one years earlier, given birth to a son. I was certain a daughter would come next, just as it had happened for my mother.

My mother and father were in love with Jake and he was a bright spot in their dark struggle with cancer. Jon frequently traveled for business, leaving Jake and me at home, so my dad spent time helping me with Jake, especially at night when I was exhausted. He was amazing with Jake, even after spending most of the day taking care of my mother. I figured that taking care of Jake was a good distraction for both of us, as we watched my mother's health decline. The relationship Jake has with his grandfather to this day is due, in part, to the nights those two spent together early in Jake's life.

My second pregnancy came as a surprise. Flying home after a ski trip when Jake was eighteen months old, I started feeling queasy, which never happened to me on airplanes. I looked at the calendar and realized that I had miscalculated and missed my period. Sure enough, when I did a pregnancy test the next morning, the test was positive.

I studied the dates again and concluded that the timing might have been good for conceiving a daughter. I had read books about timing, foods, and positions that might increase the odds of having a girl. Although we didn't get a chance to employ all the suggestions I had read about, I was confident I had been successful. After all, I was following my life plan. During the first month or so, I noted differences between this pregnancy and the first one. I felt queasier the second time around and my confidence about carrying a girl this time was boosted.

I was thrilled to be able to bring some good news to my mother's bedside when I told my parents I was expecting for the second time. She had gotten much sicker by then and was rarely well enough to leave the house. She was in the hospital that day and a smile spread across her face when I told her. I thought it would give her another reason to fight the battle that had now been going on for nine years. I was certain I was pregnant with a girl, even though it was early, and knew my mother would be thrilled to have a granddaughter.

"I'm so happy for you, honey," she said in a low tone. Each word seemed to drain her of more energy. "Congratulations to you and Jon." My father was also thrilled for us, but his concern for my mother's failing health understandably overshadowed everything.

I imagined she would feel better when she had a baby girl to hold. A new baby is such an incredible blessing to a family, and we all needed a joyful distraction at that time in our lives. Seeing Jake with a little sister would surely remind my mother of fun memories of my brother and me growing up.

When I had the ultrasound during the second trimester of my pregnancy, I was sure the technician was wrong when she said she saw a penis. All the early signs had pointed to a girl. I asked myself how I could have been wrong. Maybe it had just been wishful thinking. I made the technician look at the ultrasound screen again extra carefully and show me what she saw. Indeed, we were having another boy.

I tried not to overreact, but a second son wasn't in my plan. I had been so convinced that I knew exactly how my life would go, and suddenly it seemed like everything was going in the wrong direction. I didn't hate the idea of another boy; I just had never considered the possibility. I was supposed to be having a girl. Was I supposed to have three children? I had never considered that possibility either.

My mother gave birth to my brother two years before she had me, and the timing would be nearly the same between my two children. My mother was also born a few years after her brother, and my grandmother Pearl was born a few years after her brother. I was certain it had to be a genetic birth pattern in our family that my generation was sure to continue.

I was devastated. I wasn't sure if my reaction was to the loss of "my daughter" or the loss of control I thought I had over my life, including what was happening to my mother. I was an emotional wreck and unsure how to cope. I remember sitting in my car one day sobbing uncontrollably about everything I was dealing with. Pregnancy hormones coupled with my mother's illness had brought me down to a dark place. I forgot about how much joy a baby brings to your life and started dreading the pregnancy, which suddenly seemed like it would go on forever. I wondered why I had been so convinced it was a girl.

Logically, I knew I would have to find a way to enjoy the remaining months, just like I enjoyed the first pregnancy. I decided not to tell my parents that we were having a boy. I knew I was the only person who would feel any disappointment, but I realized I had to keep it to myself until I resolved my feelings. That decision made my situation even more difficult, because I had always told my mother everything. She would have told me how ridiculous I was acting and how much I would love another little boy. Deep down inside I knew that too and longed to hear it from her.

But adding to my mother's stress was not an option. Her condition wasn't improving, and she didn't need to worry about my problems. Plus, my parents loved Jake so much that I really didn't expect them to feel any disappointment at all. They would undoubtedly love another little boy who would bring just as much joy to their world as Jake did. It was the first time I would have to deal with a major troubling issue without my mother's help, and I recognized that this was the beginning of many solitary challenges for me.

The guilt I felt about dreading my pregnancy complicated the situation even more. As crazy as it may seem, I felt as if I was being punished. I knew I should have felt blessed to be having another child when so many couples remained childless, but I didn't care. I knew I was being unreasonable; Jon didn't have to tell me that repeatedly, but he did. I tried to mask the disappointment with him, but I was clearly unconvincing. He was thrilled that we were pregnant again and didn't care what the sex was. That might have made me feel better, but he had told me after Jake was born that he wanted only one more child and that comment had stayed with me.

How would I ever convince him (and myself) to have a third child? Three seemed like such a handful, especially to my husband who was an only child. Every day, I came up with rational reasons to keep our family limited to four, just as my family had been. It was so much easier to get a table for four in restaurants. Most chairlifts at ski resorts were built for four skiers back then. Airplane seating works well with four travelers. Our home lacked a bedroom for a third child. Everything in our lives would be simpler if we had a family of four. So I tried, unsuccessfully, to convince myself that I could be happy without a daughter.

But the truth was that I couldn't imagine not having a daughter—I knew it would always be my biggest regret. I wished we had used a technological sex-selection method that I had read about in the *New York Times*, but I had been so convinced that we'd have a daughter naturally based on our family history, and my life plan, that I didn't think it was necessary. Clearly, it was too late to do anything about it, and eventually, I hoped, I would be able to cope.

To reduce my anxiety throughout the pregnancy, we elected not to tell anyone the sex of the baby. Over the months, as I grew bigger and more uncomfortable, I tried to appear happy when I was with friends and family, knowing that I would still be longing for a girl at the end of it. I felt sorry for the baby I was carrying and prayed he wasn't picking up on my bad attitude toward having a second son. I assured him aloud that I would be able to love him as much as I loved Jake, or would have loved a daughter.

The rest of my pregnancy was depressing, but our friends knew what our family was going through with my mother's illness, so they understood that I had reason to be unhappy. I spent my spare time helping my mother through chemo treatments, trying to figure out how I was going to care for another baby while dealing with Jake's "terrible twos" without my mother's help, and wondering how I was going to convince my husband that we needed a third child.

When Micah was born a week before his due date in August 1994, my disappointment almost completely disappeared. He looked so much like Jon with his big dark brown eyes, curly dark hair, prominent nose, and sweet face. I loved him just as much the first minute I held him as I had loved Jake when he was born. It was both a beautiful moment and an emotional relief. He looked at me innocently as if to say, "Mom, you are going to be very happy that I'm part of your life." Tears streamed down my face. I wasn't sure if they were tears of happiness about Micah, tears of guilt about hating the pregnancy, or simply a result of postpartum hormones.

Once again, my parents brought a beautiful hydrangea plant to my hospital room. I thought how different my mother looked as she entered the room. She was not nearly as vibrant as she had been when Jake was born. She had a big smile on her face that reflected the joy she felt, but she walked gingerly and needed to sit down right away. My dad helped her to the chair and beamed at his new grandson while holding the pretty plant. It was a pink hydrangea this time, not blue. Perhaps my mother knew my feelings and had picked it out in anticipation of a baby girl. I have always wondered about that detail and regretted not asking her.

Our family felt blessed now that we had two beautiful little boys. Even new big brother Jake, who gave Micah a hug at the hospital, was excited, although he managed to smack Micah before we could get him out of the car seat when we brought him home. I think Jake was convinced Micah was staying in the hospital for good rather than actually coming home to live with us.

Micah was a sweet pleasure and very different from Jake. Although he had colic and didn't sleep as well at night as Jake did as an infant, he was a sensitive boy and his expressions seemed to communicate that he understood everything going on around him. He reacted to us lovingly right away, and the joy we felt when he smiled back at us was deeply rewarding.

We picked the name Jake for many reasons, both because we liked it and also to give him a J name for Jon and my father, Joseph. When we chose the name Micah, it was one of many M names we had considered to honor my mother. She had liked the name Micah when we talked about our final list of boy (and girl) names. She said to me, "If this is a boy, he will need a strong name like Micah to compete with his strong big brother." I was happy that we chose a name that she liked.

My mother, whom Jake referred to as "Nammy," was a different woman by the time Micah was born. The chemo treatments were much more toxic and she had fewer good days. She tried hard to be attentive to my boys, but she didn't have much energy by then and spent most of her time resting. I knew she was frustrated at not being able to be more hands-on with my children. I had always imagined her happily spending time reading and playing with her grandchildren. It was a big disappointment for both of us.

My father was an excellent, committed grandfather, however, and made as much time for our boys as possible. Jake had trouble finding a name he could pronounce easily for Grandpa Joe, so he called him "Poppy." We constantly thanked Poppy for being so involved with our boys while he was going through so much at home.

I remember sitting with my family at my parents' house on Sunday, October 16, 1994. I was exhausted and overwhelmed with a busy two-year-old and a demanding infant. My parents loved having the boys over, and it was heartwarming to see their joy when we were all together on Sunday nights. I was so exhausted during the week when Jon was working and traveling that I thought I would never be able to handle a third child, ever. If my mother had been healthy and able to help me more, I knew it would have been more sensible to consider more children. I envied my friends whose mothers were available to help them with their young children. I tried to ignore the feelings of disappointment day after day.

After our weekly dinner that Sunday evening, while we were still sitting at the table, my mother held Micah in her arms. He was two months old. He cried almost every evening at dinnertime and that day was no exception, until my mother held him. He stopped crying and just looked at her with his big brown eyes. Looking at her with him made all my emotional pain, lack of sleep, and exhaustion worth it. She loved him thoroughly and it gave her such joy to hold him, even though she was by that time very weak. That moment was memorable to both of us.

Just two days after that dinner, the phone rang in the middle of the night. My father had called 911 and my mother had been rushed to the hospital. I panicked. "The doctor here at the hospital said the recent chemo treatments really affected her heart and the damage is making her heart very weak," he said on the phone, trying to control his emotions. "She was struggling to breathe all evening and then just collapsed. I felt so helpless. You need to come soon."

As I dressed to leave for the hospital, I stopped for a minute to collect myself. I wondered if this was as serious as it sounded. Heart damage sounded frightening. I wondered if I would be able to handle this unexpected turn for the worse. I took a deep breath and rushed to the hospital with trepidation, leaving the boys with Jon.

As I drove to the hospital, I wondered how this could have happened to my mother. She had discovered the disease early and taken care of herself. She had endured all the recommended treatments just like so many women who survived breast cancer. Why was my mother heading down this perilous path? The cancer was in her bones and had now spread to her liver. Just recently, she had been given roughly six months to live. The chemo was supposed to stop the cancer, but the side effects were lethal. How could the doctors have continued the treatments given the risk to her heart? We had trusted their advice, as well as the second opinion doctors' advice that I had insisted upon. Clearly, they had all been wrong.

On previous occasions, the doctors had always said to us, "This isn't the last hospital visit. She has more time." I wondered if I would get that reassurance again.

I arrived at the hospital and checked with the front desk. It was very quiet in the halls of the hospital at that hour and the smell of disinfectant was strong. I glanced at all the medical equipment lining the halls of the corridor and felt very alone as I looked for my mother's room number.

As I walked into the hospital room, the look on my father's face was grim. I hugged him and apprehensively looked toward the bed. My mother was asleep and struggling for every breath. She looked pale and vulnerable from the weight loss. I hadn't seen her with her wig off for quite some time and she barely looked like herself.

The doctor beckoned us into the hallway so my father and I could speak with him outside her room. The news wasn't good, and as I had dreaded, there was no reassurance from the doctor. In fact, the doctor seemed as helpless as I felt. I wanted to scream at him, blaming him for her situation, but he clearly felt terrible. We needed him to continue helping us in every way possible, so I held my tongue.

I stayed with my father in her room until dawn and then returned home briefly to help Jon with the kids. I moved around the house in a fog. Nothing seemed real and I felt relieved that my children were too young to ask unanswerable questions. My father called to tell us that she was awake, so I showered quickly and returned to the hospital.

My mother seemed stronger when I arrived. I spent that day talking to her about happy topics like the kids, our travel plans, and good things in the news that day. We didn't talk about the cancer. I tried to keep her mind off how terrible I'm sure she felt. She smiled and tried to show interest in life, but I could see she was tired of fighting. I wished I could take her place so she wouldn't have to deal with this disease, even if it was just for a day.

It broke my heart to leave her but my children were small and needed me. When I kissed her good-bye at the end of the long day, I didn't know that it would be the last chance I had to talk to her. I thought I had weeks or at least days.

After putting the kids to bed that evening, I thought about all the things I could have said to her earlier that day—important things. I promised myself I would tell her everything on my mind the following day. I never got the chance.

My mother's doctors put her into a pain-medication-induced coma that night and said the outlook was bleak. When my father called us at dawn with the grave news, I rushed to her bedside. He also called my brother, Murray, who had just left on a business trip to North Carolina that morning, not knowing she was in such danger. When he got my father's message later that afternoon, he immediately flew all the way home. The grim developments were a shock to all of us.

I spent the entire day, Wednesday, sitting by my mother's bedside and watching her fighting to breathe. She was unconscious and her hands were cold, symptoms of a weak heart. I prayed for her to wake up. I couldn't believe this was the same woman who had held my baby boy just three days before. We kept receiving phone messages about my brother's return flight to Seattle, praying he would arrive before her strength ran out.

Jon asked our sitter to watch the boys and came to the hospital. The three of us, my father, Jon, and I, sat in my mother's room, quietly reminiscing about good times we had shared. We chuckled at times, but my mother's heavy breathing interrupted any happy moments. We told her Murray was on the way, not knowing if she could hear us. I prayed she knew we were with her.

A couple hours before midnight, a nurse gave my mother what turned out to be her final dose of morphine. She awoke briefly just before it started to work. My father rushed to her side. She looked at him lucidly and said, "I love you." My heart ached. He responded with the same loving phrase, tears streaming down his face. I stood next to him, trying to tell her how much I loved her, but she fell into a deep sleep almost immediately. By then, our extended family had arrived at the hospital and none of us were able to speak to her. I begged the nurse to wait before giving her more morphine the next time she woke up, but she didn't want to risk her feeling any pain. I agreed with the nurse.

A few minutes before midnight, my brother appeared in the doorway of the hospital room. He looked exhausted, but it was a relief to see him. He was shocked when he saw my mother's condition. I gently grabbed her weak, cold hand and said, "It's okay, Mom. Murray is here now. We are all here with you now. We love you." Again, I had no idea if she could hear me.

It was almost as if she was waiting for Murray's arrival. We sat at her bedside hoping for another brief awakening when the morphine wore off, but her breathing suddenly became erratic. She opened her eyes, looking toward the ceiling for the first time in hours. I stood up and leaned in close to her, hoping she could see my face or hear my voice, but she was not awake and her eyes were not focusing on anything. Not more than thirty seconds later, she took her last breath. The nurse came rushing in to take her pulse. She shook her head as she took her hand away from my mother. No pulse. She was gone. My mother died just before midnight on October 19, 1994, at the age of sixty.

I remember the profound pain I felt when I hugged her for the last time. I remember putting my head on her chest, begging, "Don't leave me alone," through my tears. It now seems that it was an odd thing to say, given that I was surrounded by family members who loved me, but I was alone. She was the only woman I could talk to about my secrets, hopes, and insecurities. The relationship we had was irreplaceable. It was the worst night of my life.

My father and I had discussed my mother's situation just hours before her death in another hospital room. We really didn't know how much pain she was in and wondered how she could go on in her condition. We had reached the point where we felt so bad for her that we wished for God's compassionate relief. Neither of us could believe we felt that way. After she died, neither of us felt better, even though she was no longer in pain. I immediately regretted wishing for her death, as selfish as that was, and regret it to this day.

I didn't get to tell her what an incredible woman she was to her family, her friends, and everyone she knew. I didn't get to tell her how I would try to raise my children as well as she had raised my brother and me. I didn't get to thank her for all the wonderful traits and life lessons she had given me. Most of all, I didn't get to tell her that no one would ever replace her in my heart.

For weeks after her funeral, I felt guilty about feeling sorry for myself. I felt jealous of the mothers who still had their mothers to help them with their children. The postpartum depression, not having a daughter, and the incredible sorrow of losing my mother was a toxic combination that seemed like it would never go away. I thought about going to a grief counselor, but I was convinced that no one would understand my "double depression," as I called it.

I'm not sure I fully understood how depressed I was. On the surface, I was functioning well, coping with the daily details of being a wife and mother of two. But after my mother died, the need to have a girl grew stronger. I saw TV shows featuring mothers and daughters and turned them off. I saw families in commercials that had a boy and a girl and thought about how unfair life was. I brought my boys to the park and watched mothers with their little girls enjoying each other. Even taking Jake to his preschool classes was painful for me.

The boys brought me joy and kept me so busy that I wondered if I could do it again. Could I be the mother of three kids? I literally thought about it every day—it seemed like I thought about it hourly. I knew it wasn't the right time, just after my mother's death, but when I thought I was ready, would Jon ever agree? Could I manage it if he did agree? Even worse, what if he didn't want to do it?

I didn't think my disappointment and angst showed to other people and I tried not to talk about it all the time with Jon, but I was suffering. I woke up with it every morning and went to sleep with it every night. I didn't feel like I could talk about it with anyone, not even my good friends. I felt angry all the time.

I was secretly despondent for at least a year after my mother's death until Jon surprised me. "Let's get through the second set of terrible twos and then talk about a third baby—a girl," he said. I guess my secret wasn't such a secret.

MISSING A GIRL

The toddler years went by fast. As our boys grew into preschoolers and then went to kindergarten, our life was busy with T-ball, soccer, and Y-Guide campouts. I was almost too busy even to think about another child long after the terrible twos passed, but the emptiness was still there. I felt like I was part of a "no-girl club." I had several friends who, like me, had two boys. I wondered if they longed for a girl as I did. Most of them still had the supportive love of mothers who lived nearby. None of those friends ever mentioned wanting a girl, so I figured they were happy with their families the way they were.

Jon and I were happy, too, watching the boys play sports, teaching them to ski, and taking them on trips to Aspen, Hawaii, and California. It was a great life, but for me, there was something missing. Someone missing. I missed my mother desperately. I thought about college, and how I used to count down the days until her return from a long vacation with my father. I had thought those were the hardest times. Even though I had my sorority sisters and other friends, I couldn't share with them what I could share with my mother. When she died, I thought I couldn't make it through life. Her "never coming back" was impossible. How could she really be gone forever?

Everything I read in magazine articles and books said the pain of her loss would get easier, but I never found that to be the case. Watching my boys grow up without her only made it worse. She would have been a fantastic grandmother and I felt sorry for my boys that they missed out on that. I remembered so much about my grandmothers, who both lived to age ninety-three. They enriched my childhood and were wonderful role models as I became an adult. I felt cheated and lonely. Even though I had good girlfriends, I missed the family relationship I had with my mother.

In 1994, the same year that Micah was born and my mother passed away, my brother got married. Murray and I hung out together as kids and as adults. We even lived together in an apartment for a year while we were both in college. We agreed on everything, except occasionally about who got the living room TV on Saturday nights. When he bought a house in the suburbs after graduation, I moved in as his roommate while I worked at Microsoft. We were extremely close, especially after our mother got sick, and I cherished our relationship.

I always expected that anyone who my brother chose to marry would become a sister to me. I figured she would be someone I could get along with simply because he and I got along so well. I looked forward to that new relationship. After I married Jon, my brother still asked for my opinion on his dates and the long-term girlfriends he had well into his thirties. My brother dated many women and had been very close to several of them, but for one reason or another, the relationships ended. In hindsight, I thought any of those women would have made a wonderful sister-in-law.

He met the woman he married, Michele, in a bar, and they dated for a long time before I met her. I was optimistic since she only had brothers in her family as well. I thought it was hopeful that we had something in common—never having had a sister. She, however, wasn't like any of his previous girlfriends and had grown up differently from us. My adult life had included college and a career, while she had left high school to have a son before age nineteen. When we were finally introduced, we had little to talk about and our relationship was soon strained. I tried to find some common ground on which to build a relationship but it just seemed impossible. She misinterpreted my well-meaning comments as offensive remarks. My brother felt he had to defend her and the relationship between us disintegrated.

I really tried to like her, despite our differences, but after she gave birth to my nephew in 1995, our relationship got worse. She acted like there was a competition between us. She became overly sensitive around me and convinced my brother that I was malicious toward her. Family events became uncomfortable, so eventually we started having separate celebrations and holiday dinners. Even though we tried to be "family" for several years, I finally gave up entirely on the relationship. I had wanted us to connect as sisters but it became clear that that would never happen.

I tried to maintain a relationship with my brother. I was willing to do anything to make that relationship work, but Murray quickly learned that crossing his wife only led to useless arguments, and because he was conflict averse, he gave way every time. Instead of continuing to argue when we tried to discuss the relationship issues between Michele and me, we stopped speaking to each other altogether.

And so the year I lost my mother was essentially the year I also lost my brother, as well as any hope of a meaningful woman-to-woman relationship with my sister-in-law. For someone who had lived most of her life happily ensconced in healthy family relationships, it was tragic. I again wondered what happened to the good luck I thought I had in life. I knew my mother would never have allowed her family to become estranged and I never felt more alone.

My relationship with my mother-in-law, Lucille, was geographically challenged, because she and my father-in-law, Earl, lived across the country in Philadelphia. I met Lucille and Earl at a dinner in Seattle soon after Jon and I started dating seriously. While they were quite different from my parents, there were many similarities. Both of our mothers had gone to college, held full-time jobs while raising their children, and were active in civic and charitable groups. Over the years, we had some wonderful conversations about being Jewish, and what Jon was like growing up. But their visits to Seattle were brief and far between. When they came west in their motor home, we were just one stop on a long trip. Their visits were also shortened as Jon's father loved taking day or weekend trips to the San Juan Islands, to Portland, Oregon, or to Vancouver, BC. Consequently, our family spent very little time with Jon's parents.

Soon after our engagement in 1990, we visited Lucille at a hospital near Philadelphia after she suffered her first stroke. Jon said she was never the same woman again after the stroke, so I never really knew the real Lucille. His stories of growing up with her convinced me that she and I would have been close. She volunteered for many of the same charities in Philadelphia that I volunteered for in Seattle, so we had similar interests and sense of civic duty.

Apparently, Lucille was a wonderful woman when Jon was growing up, but she seemed somewhat cranky and self-centered in her later years. I attributed all of that to her health issues and tried to be patient when she visited; even when she forgot the word "please," our sons were quick to point that out to her. Jon loved his mother and she taught him to be loving, as well as strong and independent. She also taught him how to treat and respect women. I admired her for that.

Lucille was suffering from diabetes and had just recovered from a second stroke shortly before their visit in the summer of 1996. The boys were only two and four years old and they barely knew their paternal grandmother, but they loved the fun stories she told them on the phone. She and Earl had driven across the country in their motor home that summer. As usual, they stopped in various places along the way, enjoying the country and its sights. After spending two wonderful weeks with us in Seattle and the surrounding areas, one of their longest visits ever, they started their journey back to Philadelphia near the end of August.

Earl called us just a week after they left Seattle with horrible news. Lucille had been cooking dinner in their motor home while Earl was taking one of his famous afternoon naps a few feet away on the couch. She got distracted and used spray cooking oil on a pan sitting on a lit gas burner and set herself on fire. It took some time for Earl to wake up and realize what she was screaming about before he could get up and extinguish the fire. Earl and several people in the motor home park cared for Lucille until the medics arrived by helicopter. Lucille had been horrifically burned and at her age, with all her other medical issues, she was in deep trouble.

To further complicate matters, the medics airlifted her to the burn unit in a Salt Lake City hospital because of their location. Each hospital has a designated territory for traumas; if they had been a couple hundred miles closer to Washington State, she would have been brought to Harborview Hospital's burn unit in Seattle instead. It was a stroke of bad luck for all of us, in so many ways.

Jon and I were completely distraught. Watching both of our mothers suffer from health-related disasters, less than two years apart, was more than we could bear. Jon was an only child and his father needed him in Salt Lake City for comfort and to sit at Lucille's bedside. The distance created a hardship on our family that we didn't need while we were so concerned for her grave condition.

Over the next few months, Jon went to Salt Lake City alone several times, but we also visited Lucille together as often as we could, given the distance from Seattle and having to leave the boys at home. Scary even for adults, the burn unit was no place for our children. Lucille was severely injured and barely recognizable. She couldn't speak due to the respirator helping her breathe and she was bandaged head to toe. Any remaining healthy skin was used for grafting onto burned areas on her body. It was a devastating sight. A medical crane lifted her gingerly into a sterile tank for baths. During our visits, we heard horrible stories about other victims in the burn unit—from infants to the elderly. Their families, like us, miserably watched their loved ones suffer terrible pain.

Lucille struggled through painful skin grafts and many other operations. It had been a long road for both of Jon's parents by the time we took the boys to see them just after Thanksgiving. The skin grafts had healed, the pain subsided, and Lucille could finally sit up. She was still unable to breathe on her own and the respirator still made it impossible for her to talk to us. She wrote notes to the boys on a little whiteboard and hugged them. We ached for the day she would be able to leave the hospital.

Given her condition and the likelihood that she would not be able to breathe without the respirator anytime soon, Lucille was moved from the burn unit to a long-term care facility nearby in early December. We all thought it was a good sign that she could finally leave the burn unit, but on the day she was moved, a day before Earl's eightieth birthday, Lucille died without any of us by her side. The doctors at the care facility clearly didn't understand that she was at risk and did not properly monitor her. Earl had been moving the motor home to the new facility, so he could remain close to her. Like my own mother, Lucille died of heart failure.

The news came as a complete shock. She had been doing so well and had fought so hard for so long. We wondered if she had panicked when she found herself in a new place with no familiar faces. We would never know and we were devastated.

Her doctors had discharged her from the hospital without proper supervision or monitoring instructions. We considered legal action for negligence but decided it would be too much to put Jon's father through in addition to his grief. Earl and Lucille had been married for almost fifty years and he took her loss incredibly hard. It was another case of unbelievably bad luck for our family. She had made so much progress and we were so optimistic when we took the boys to see her. At least they were able to see her shortly before she died and, like all of us, they were unaware that it was their last visit with her. Just like my mother's death, none of us had the opportunity to say good-bye to Lucille.

After her funeral in Philadelphia, my depression over the loss of another grandmother for my boys and another woman in our family deepened. I tried talking to a psychologist or two about the losses I had suffered. I also talked to them about not having a female family member anymore and how much that bothered me. My dear aunts offered to help me but they had their own daughters and grandchildren, and I didn't want to burden them.

One psychologist seemed shocked that I could be depressed about "only having boys" and showed no compassion for my whole situation. She seemed to believe that if we had enough money for traveling and private schools, I didn't really have cause for depression. I couldn't believe what I was hearing. She was definitely the wrong counselor for me and I almost lost hope in finding someone who could help.

She wasn't the only bad fit, though. Months later, my doctor referred me to another psychologist. When he found out I had started working for Microsoft in 1983, he only wanted to talk about Bill Gates and the early days at Microsoft. I couldn't understand why I was paying him when I was doing all the talking and not about anything helpful to me. It was a waste of time. I knew there had to be good psychologists out there; I just didn't know how to find one. Jon did what he could but I continued to suffer silently without anyone to talk to. I didn't feel comfortable sharing my pain with my friends. Sometimes, I wonder how I ever got through those years.

I remember wondering if I would have felt such a tremendous need for a daughter had my mother remained alive through my thirties. Even though I had always wanted a daughter, it was the close female family relationship that I really missed. I truly loved my boys and the joy they brought to our lives, but I was missing a daughter to love, cherish, get dressed up with, and most important, talk to and spend time with, like my mother and I had done.

My everyday reality was that I was jealous of every woman who had a mother, a daughter, or a sister. I saw happy mother-daughter or sister pairs everywhere, older mother-daughter couples who played golf together at our country club, younger mother-daughter couples who walked into preschool together, and sisters who were in each other's weddings or raising their kids together. Every mall restaurant seemed to have cute little girls eating lunch with their mothers. Every toy store I went to displayed dolls that I couldn't buy. I felt "stuck" on the boys' side of the Nordstrom children's department and couldn't bear to glance at the pink frilly clothes on the other side of the floor.

I felt like I belonged to an unofficial "mothers with boys only" club, especially when I caught snippets of strangers' and friends' conversations around me. I overheard remarks from other women who clearly felt cheated too: "I sit at basketball games and you get girly tea parties," and "You are so lucky you get to shop for prom dresses." At one of the boys' baseball games, I overheard an acquaintance say, "I have this great skill of French braiding that I'll never get to use with my three boys." I understood exactly why they were complaining. There wasn't an outlet for us "boy-only" mothers to console each other, but I knew there were other mothers suffering like me. I loved motherhood, but I wanted the entire experience, not just the boy half. I had seen how short life could be and someday dying without fulfilling my dreams seemed heartbreaking.

The worst part of that time in my life was that I had no one to talk to about my emotions. My husband listened to me when he wasn't working, but certainly not as often as I needed to complain. I woke up thinking about a girl and went to sleep thinking about a girl. My need for a daughter consumed me.

I felt guilty complaining when I knew there were many couples who couldn't have any children at all. Infertility seemed much more prevalent than ever before and I heard about it often from friends, relatives, and casual acquaintances, and in the news. Although I was grateful that infertility was not one of my problems at that moment, my depression ensued. I hid my feelings from my family and friends because I knew no one would understand. Gender differences would probably seem like a petty issue to people who weren't in my shoes.

I had always been one of those perfectionists who sees what life should be like and pursues it. I had control over most of my life and everything seemed to go my way in high school, in college, and in my career. I got good grades, met a wonderful man, and succeeded in a software company without any previous computer or sales experience. Dealing with my mother's death, my brother's marriage, and motherhood changed all that. I felt like I had no control over anything anymore. As I looked down the road at my life, I knew there was work to do to ensure both my family's happiness and my own.

I was thirty-seven and the boys were both in elementary school, which finally left me some time to contemplate another child. Life had become easier as the boys achieved some independence and everything required less effort from me. Traveling, supplying the boys' basic needs, and making sure they were safe had all gotten easier. A new baby would complicate our lives significantly. I always pictured myself with a daughter and it seemed shocking to me that I would never have one. Again, *never* seemed like such a final word. Was my lost relationship with my mother the only quality female familial relationship I would ever have? Was I destined to sit at baseball and basketball games my entire life and miss out on ballet and piano recitals? The unfairness of it all seemed intolerable.

On a positive note, I had two close friends who each had two boys as well and within a couple years of trying for their third child, had conceived girls. They were all so happy. Strangely, before their third pregnancies, my friends and I had never talked about our "all-boys club" or whether they wanted a daughter as much as I did. I was delighted for them and bought wonderful "girly" gifts for their daughters, but inside, I couldn't contain my jealousy. It made me want my own daughter even more. I started to feel more positive about my chances. Could I possibly be that lucky if we tried again? My husband seemed to pick up on my thoughts.

"You want to talk about this baby issue again now, don't you?" he said.

"Yes," I began, realizing that we hadn't discussed having a third child for a very long time. "I always thought that after two boys, our chances of conceiving a girl were low, based on the scientific studies, but look at our friends. It could happen for us too."

Aside from these lucky friends, we also knew some couples who had had a third boy. To me, that seemed distressful, but was the possibility of getting my girl worth the risk of having a third boy? That was the big question and neither of us had the answer.

"We should try again, because I don't sense you will ever let this issue go," Jon said with a smile. "Let's start researching ways to make sure it's a girl. Gender selection is getting more popular and you know how much I like science."

I laughed nervously and my heart beat faster. I was shocked and delighted that he had conceded to have a third child. I had been thinking for so long that he would never agree based on our last conversation and it felt like a big weight had been lifted from my shoulders. In many ways, that conversation changed everything for me. I began looking at life and our future differently. I gained a positive outlook for the first time in many years, but the bad news was that my focus (and concern) shifted to the big issue: What if we didn't get a girl?

WORKING WITH SCIENCE

I grew up with one brother. My husband, Jon, has no siblings, a fact that he hated as a kid and still complains about. A family of five definitely seemed large to both of us. Jon expressed the fear of being outnumbered by the children and whether we could handle that. "When you give up that one-to-one ratio," we heard from our friends who are parents of three kids, "it can be overwhelming."

We had little extended family support. My husband's father and small extended family lived on the opposite coast. Visits from them were wonderful but brief and limited to summertime due to their aversion to Seattle's notorious wet weather. We wouldn't be getting much support from them.

About three years after my mother died, my father remarried a wonderful woman named Maryellen, who instantly cared for all of us like we had always been family. She had a son named Eric from a previous marriage who was almost an adult by the time she met and married my father. I was grateful that she loved my boys like a true grandmother and they in turn loved her. She enjoyed having the boys over to the house, planning treasure hunts for them, and taking them for rides in their golf cart.

When my boys were young, my father and stepmother spent six months every winter in Southern California, mostly golfing, and when they lived in Seattle, they spent most of their time on the golf course. We couldn't expect them to be more available to help us out than they were. It meant we had to manage the kids on our own, and more important, on *my* own when Jon traveled. Another child would definitely make life more difficult.

It would extend the years that we would need babysitters, more years with car seats, and another round of preschool.

Did we really want to complicate our lives further by starting over again? There were so many questions and no answers. We thought this was the most difficult decision we would have to make, but little did we know that this issue would become the least of our problems.

Although we weren't really sure we wanted three kids, I was certain that I wanted a daughter. However, the probability was great that we would have another boy if we tried on our own. We started researching the science available to pick the sex of our next baby, as Jon had suggested years ago. On the Internet, we researched the newest sex-selection methods, fertility doctors' opinions on sex selection, clinic locations, and success rates. We read articles, called several clinics for information, and even flew to California to meet with a doctor about "sperm spinning."

Given that we had two sons in quick succession, we both assumed I was very fertile and were optimistic about becoming pregnant if we decided to use scientific methods to sway the odds. Based on what we found out about the mediocre results of getting the gender we wanted using the spinning process (only a 60 percent chance), we looked in a different direction.

By chance, we saw a story on *NBC Nightly News* about a clinic in Virginia that had a procedure for "laser sperm sorting." The process was called MicroSort and was developed by the Department of Agriculture for use with livestock, although a clinic in Virginia was adapting it for human sex selection. This method had the highest success rate of producing a baby of the desired sex. People weren't using the method as much as the spinning method because it was only available in Virginia and the cost was substantially higher. We decided to try it.

After we spoke by phone with a nurse at the Virginia clinic, she sent us information about the procedures and protocols. Although there were many details involved with this relatively new process, it looked similar to any other insemination process, with the exception of what they did with the sperm sample before insemination. Timing and travel would be the most difficult issues. We would need a local doctor to get the process started, so we asked our regular doctors to recommend a fertility specialist in Seattle and made an appointment. There was a long wait just to meet him—the first of many such long waits.

As we sat in the reception area waiting for Dr. Seth Cresner, I felt optimistic about our new adventure. The office was clean and recently remodeled, with newly released magazines and books on infertility. In the course of our research, we had read widely about the fertility problems facing many childless couples. The fertility business was definitely thriving. The other three couples sitting in the room looked like they were ready for the firing squad compared to our happy-go-lucky expressions. Perhaps because we had two children already, we felt confident that we would be successful in getting pregnant a third time. I was so excited to be on the road to having a daughter that I was just feeling happy to be there. In hindsight, we were just far too naïve about the whole process to feel apprehensive.

One of the nurses finally called us. She led us to a small room with a fantastic view of Seattle's downtown area and the waterfront. A clear view of the Olympic Mountains greeted us as we waited for the doctor. When Dr. Cresner finally knocked on the door after another ten-minute wait, we were delighted to see a kind-looking man in a white coat who wore his reading glasses on the tip of his nose. He shook our hands and asked what he could do for us. While jotting down some notes, he listened intently as Jon explained the Virginia process we had recently learned about and why it was important to us to have a girl.

"We want to try this technique and the clinic in Virginia said it would collaborate with you. It's not how they typically work on these cases because most of their clients live near Virginia," Jon said.

Dr. Cresner's smile turned into a more serious look. "Jon, I have heard of MicroSort and am familiar with the science behind its work, but I haven't had any patients who have requested my help with the actual process," he began. While taking his reading glasses off, he said, "I have to tell you both that I'm not altogether in favor of sex selection in fertility cases."

The smile fell from my face and I began to feel anxious. "If it makes you feel any better," Jon said, "we haven't had any problems getting pregnant. Both pregnancies were relatively easy and without complications so we are only dealing with one issue, not two. Hopefully, it will only require one cycle. The fact is we have two boys and we want a girl, and only a girl. We need MicroSort's help to make sure we get one and would appreciate your help."

"I think this kind of thinking will lead to other selective problems," said Dr. Cresner, "but let's agree to disagree in principle for now and move on. Family balancing affects many couples, so I'm sure your request to do this won't be the last I will come across."

Dr. Cresner was a nice man who had helped hundreds of infertile couples have children. Our case was different and we understood his moral reservations. It didn't change our ultimate goal, nor did we like him any less.

Naturally, he was compelled to tell us the risks, the chances of success, and the detailed steps we would need to take before, during, and after this type of insemination. Dr. Cresner informed us that this pregnancy would be harder than the last two. Even if we were successful in conceiving a child, staying pregnant would be more difficult. He told us we would need to be even more vigilant about prenatal care this time—as if that was possible. He clearly didn't know me very well.

In addition, he told us that working through the clinic in Virginia would require extra planning, given the sensitive timing issues involved with the insemination process. We would need to spend several days there when the time came. I immediately started thinking about finding someone to stay with our two young sons.

Finally, and most upsetting to me, was the doctor's comment that it had been several years since my last pregnancy and the implication that I wasn't getting any younger. I was almost thirty-eight and my optimism started to fade just a bit. The entire process seemed daunting given all the factors working against us, but we decided to go through with it anyway. I knew Jon was ready; he loves science.

Dr. Cresner handed us a pile of paperwork and said, "You need to talk about it after reading all of this information before you commit. If, after you have read through everything and thought about what we discussed today, you still want to do this, I will call the doctor in Virginia to discuss your case and how our offices can coordinate."

"Thank you, Doctor," I said enthusiastically as we both got up to shake his hand. I think he actually welcomed the new fertility method, as a scientist, and I didn't want him to think we were hesitant. We left his office with many forms to fill out and documents to read, but feeling a little less optimistic than when we came in. I felt like we were about to climb a mountain, with no experience and no ropes.

We read everything we could about MicroSort, in addition to what the doctor gave us, and called Dr. Cresner the next day. We filled out all the paperwork and decided to give it a try. We didn't tell anyone about this, including our children, to protect them (and ourselves) from disappointment should we be unsuccessful. We would need some good excuses for sudden trips to the East Coast.

The first phase of the process required me to take pills to generate a larger number of eggs at ovulation. The hope was that this would raise our chances of success with my husband's girl-producing sperm. The insemination would occur after the clinic washed, stained, and then sorted the sperm sample with the laser technique. This process raised the odds of becoming pregnant with a girl to about 95 percent. At the same time the odds of getting a girl went up, the odds of becoming pregnant at all were significantly below normal. Because the MicroSort process decreases the usual sperm volume by about half, the success rate is not nearly as high as a normal insemination. But we felt we had a good fertility history on our side and remained optimistic despite the odds.

Once everything was organized and we paid the fees to all parties involved, I began to take the fertility medication Clomid. The trips to Virginia had to be timed perfectly with my cycle, so I drove to Dr. Cresner's office in Seattle many times at dawn to have an ultrasound, which allowed him to monitor the maturity of my eggs.

I remember sitting in the doctor's office one dark morning as my family slept at home, wondering if we were doing the right thing. I looked at the other women in the room, who looked much younger than I did and who I assumed had no children waiting at home. I thought about how sad it would feel to have to go through all this without the confidence we had. We had never suffered a miscarriage or received a phone call because "the fertility cycle didn't work." We had several friends who had gone through many cycles of disappointment before becoming pregnant. Infertility was a curse and sitting in the waiting room was depressing.

Equally concerning was the fact that everything about this process would take time and energy away from our boys. Was I being too selfish? Was this all going to have a negative effect on my boys? The doubts started to overwhelm me. I decided that I was too tired at the moment for questions like that and would take it one step at a time. If the time and emotional demands became too intense for our family, we could always back out (unless I was already pregnant, I thought optimistically).

The process I had to go through personally wasn't easy either. No one likes to get up early in the morning, brave the traffic when you're still half asleep, find parking, sit under the fluorescent lights of a waiting room filled with strangers, have your feet put in stirrups, and have some nurse stick a cold probe inside you, while looking at a screen to report on your "egg progress" several times a week. There was nothing happy or easy about infertility. However, like all the other women in that office, I *chose* to go through these steps to get what I wanted.

On the last of several early morning trips to the office, the technician told me that an "average" number of almost-mature eggs appeared on the ultrasound screen. "We were hoping for more, but this should be plenty if everything works out with Virginia's process," the nurse said. I wished her tone was more cheerful, but I rationalized that she was probably thinking I was too old for this procedure. The nurse called the Virginia clinic to let the staff know we were on our way. She wished me luck and sent me home to pack.

Because the MicroSort process required several days in Virginia, plus a day to get there and another to get home, we had to make up reasons we needed to be in Virginia for our family and our friends. Fortunately, Jon's family lived on the East Coast, which provided a believable reason for the trips.

Six weeks after our first meeting with Dr. Cresner, we kissed our boys good-bye, leaving schedules and notes for our nanny Jennifer, and flew to Virginia. We stayed in a nice hotel in Tysons Corner surrounded by several large office buildings, a shopping mall, and a movie theater.

The trip to Virginia definitely felt like a business trip. This was not a lavish vacation designed for romantic baby making. We dismally walked down the long hotel hallways, got in and out of elevators, and slept in a strange bed all to make a baby. We were nervous, not relaxed. I was suddenly shocked we got pregnant with the boys without even thinking about it. I had never really appreciated that before.

Just as had been the case with my dawn office visits in Seattle, I had an early appointment at the clinic in Fairfax, Virginia, to monitor my ovulation the following day. Since the boys were not with us, Jon joined me for the early drive from our hotel to the clinic. As we sat in the waiting room, which was much smaller and less professional looking than the office in Seattle, we took a few pictures, documenting our journey, and looked through the big scrapbooks on the coffee table. The books had letters and photos from parents who had three girls and wanted a boy, or the families who had all boys and, like me, really wanted that girl. It was encouraging to look through them. The clinic had been doing the process for a couple of years by the time we got there and many "family-balancing" babies had been conceived there. The letters were touching and I was excited that we were so close to my dream.

According to the detailed protocol, it was Jon's turn to take an early morning drive to the clinic the day before I was supposed to ovulate. The clinic specialists sorted his sperm using dye and a laser. We anxiously spent the remainder of the day in Washington, D.C., walking around the national monuments and touring the museums with Jon's cousin Ina. She lived in North Carolina and was the only family member who knew what we were going through. She was very comforting and we were both grateful that she had made the trip to be with us.

When the call came on Jon's cell phone, I was excited and nervous all at the same time. Jon answered and immediately looked concerned.

"Medications?" he repeated. "Yes, well, I've been taking Tagamet daily for my stomach for years . . . really? That's very upsetting. I had no idea about the side effects that came with the prescription. Just a minute."

He put his hand over the phone and told me what happened. "They asked me what medication I had been taking because my sperm count was abnormally low. I'm so sorry. They said if we decided not to go through with it, they would not blame us."

"Not go through with it? After all we've already been through?" I exclaimed, trying to stay calm. "Do they know where we live?"

"I'm sorry, it's all my fault," Jon said apologetically. He clearly felt awful. "I should have asked my doctor about the medications or read about the side effects. You've gone through so much already. I'll leave it up to you."

"Oh, we're going," I insisted. "If they're ready, let's go."

We drove to the clinic immediately and went through with the insemination. When the technician brought the sorted sperm into the procedure room where we were waiting, the syringe was in a box with pink ribbon tied around it. We laughed nervously at their levity in the face of a procedure we took very seriously. The insemination was fast and painless. The technicians gave us little hope of a successful pregnancy given all the factors working against us, but wished us luck as they gave us some quick instructions and left us alone. We tried to maintain our optimism but it was looking bleak.

I stayed on the clinic bed for about twenty minutes after the insemination as directed, and then we left the clinic, praying that we would be going home the next day with our baby girl growing in my belly.

Unfortunately, we soon received confirmation that the process didn't work. I got my period two weeks after we returned home. We hadn't thought to worry about Jon's sperm count, but starting with a low count further reduced our odds.

Jon's doctor told him that the reduced sperm count side effect of Tagamet was undocumented, so it was truly not anyone's fault. We decided to try the process again after the medication was out of Jon's body. Although it was a stroke of bad luck, we had gotten used to fighting back and trying to make our own good luck in response.

We made our second trip to Virginia several months later after Jon had his sperm count tested in Seattle. That time, the injection of sperm caused me extreme pain and immediate cramping. It seemed almost as painful as childbirth but without any pain relief. Even the doctor at the clinic couldn't explain why my body reacted that way. No one else at their clinic had experienced anything like that before. However, it was a fairly new procedure and they still had a lot of testing to do. For the second time, we returned home less than optimistic and it was difficult to admit that most likely, all that work with the Seattle clinic, travel, and time away from the boys was probably for nothing. When I took the pregnancy test the following month, we were not surprised that it hadn't worked (again). Every scientific process has its risks, but we decided the process was not for us. Still, we remained determined to keep trying for our girl through other methods.

The next cycle, we tried combining two different scientific methods. Jon stopped in Virginia on his way to New York for a business trip and left a sperm sample with MicroSort. They sorted, froze, and shipped the processed sperm to Seattle to be used with in vitro fertilization (IVF), a complicated and invasive process requiring daily injections of expensive drugs we had to mix at home and even more visits to the clinic. The doctor would then remove my mature eggs and add the sperm. After fertilization in the laboratory, the embryos would be implanted in my uterus. An added element to IVF was that we had to make a critical decision about how many fertilized eggs or embryos (potential children) to deposit in my uterus. We could have ended up with five more children, rather than just one, if they all survived.

The thought of multiple births was daunting, but after what we had already been through, we decided to try IVF. After two weeks of self-injections and more egg-monitoring ultrasounds, the physicians removed my mature eggs. After much deliberation, Jon and I decided to have the doctor implant three embryos. The day just happened to be Halloween, and one of the nurses was even wearing a scary mask. Jon took pictures so our child would remember the day she was conceived and after we finished laughing, we started praying.

I had to give myself more injections in the two weeks following the procedure to keep my body from rejecting the embryos. Sadly, we were unsuccessful again. Frustrated but still optimistic, we implanted the last of the embryos with the next cycle the following month. The doctor was hesitant to send us down that emotional path again, but we insisted since it felt like the last attempt we could make. Clearly, I wasn't as fertile as I had been five years ago and it wasn't going to get any easier to get pregnant as the months progressed. I suddenly really understood the pain and frustration of infertility.

As I walked out of the doctors' office for the last time after hearing the bad news, past the women in the waiting room with hope in their eyes and hearts, I thanked God that I had two beautiful boys at home. I was more grateful for them than ever before. How could I have dealt with this disappointment had this scientific roller coaster been the only way to have a child? Here I was feeling sorry for myself because I didn't have a daughter when there were women in that office who couldn't have *any* children. I vowed to be much more understanding with the couples I knew going through fertility struggles and to stop feeling sorry for myself.

We gave up on science. I was glad that we had tried it instead of wondering years later whether it might have worked. The experience also opened my eyes to how excruciatingly painful infertility treatments can be, both physically and emotionally. The procedures seemed too burdensome for us to keep trying, and with my fertility seemingly dropping every month as I got older, we began to think that our fate had been sealed. We were clearly supposed to have boys in our family and we (I) began to look for ways to be satisfied without a daughter. We had many good things in our life: a loving marriage, a beautiful home, and two wonderful boys.

On the bright side, Jon understood my needs more than ever, after seeing all I would go through to get a daughter. "You never would have known the result if we hadn't tried," he said. "At least now you will never look back and wonder why you didn't try harder to get your girl."

"You are right, Jon. I know you're not used to confronting a problem you can't solve and I'm sure you're frustrated at not being able to give me what I want," I said, smiling and grabbing his hand. "I love you for giving it all you had on my behalf."

We had just started to move on with our life, putting this all behind us, when I got pregnant. We had given up on pregnancy after the trouble with the scientific methods and we weren't using birth control. I suddenly felt like I was in an elevator of emotion. I was excited about the pregnancy one minute and then down about the likelihood of it being another boy. Jon and I just started to talk about how amazing that was and feeling like it was real when I started spotting at six weeks. We consulted the Internet and then our doctor, thinking this might be normal at my age.

As fate would have it, when we went for the first ultrasound, the doctor confirmed that there was no heartbeat. The pregnancy ended with a miscarriage only six weeks in. It wasn't enough time to have gotten really excited or really worried, depending on how we looked at it, so we deemed it a fluke and got back on track with our life.

When another spontaneous pregnancy happened a year later, with the same result, we decided to use birth control again. It was too risky and too emotionally painful to endure another miscarriage. The pregnancies ended too soon to know if either baby was a girl, but I have always wondered.

In 2001, when we felt "finished" feeling sad that we would never have a third child, we decided to add a dog to our family. Jon and I did our usual research, trying to understand which breeds worked well with children, and then located a breeder about an hour from our house. We piled the kids in the car to go pick up our new family member. As luck would have it, the only puppy left at the breeder when we arrived was a male who was just too cute to pass up. We added another member to the "blue team," as we referred to the boys in our family, during spring break from school. The boys, big and small, and I loved our new yellow Labrador retriever, Jasper, but the "pink team" was definitely still understaffed.

CONSIDERING OUR OPTIONS

Spending sleepless nights with the new puppy refreshed my memories of the frequent, round-the-clock needs of a newborn. I began questioning becoming parents of a newborn baby again at our age. Sleep deprivation created even crankier moments for us than it had six and a half years earlier when Micah was born. Thank goodness Jasper quickly acclimated to a reasonable sleep schedule.

Jon and I agreed that we were happy with our new puppy and two beautiful, now very conversational, boys. We never said we were "glad" that we didn't have a third child. It just seemed clear to us that we were supposed to parent only boys. We finally got the message and decided together that this was *it*. We were done trying for a girl and would be happy with what God had given us.

But was I *really* done? I may have stopped talking about it, but I never stopped thinking about it.

Family life was easier for me when the boys were in school full-time and I started reviewing my options on how to keep busy during the rainy season in Seattle when I couldn't get out and golf. I spent more time volunteering for charities but I still seemed to have lots of spare time. There were definitely days when I still lamented not having a girl. I didn't have anyone to talk to about it and the frustration grated on me. It was especially bittersweet when my close, pregnant friend (and mother of two boys) announced that she just received confirmation through amniocentesis that she was having a girl. This was the third good friend of mine whose third baby was a girl after having two boys, without the use of science.

Every time I saw cute little girls at the mall, at birthday parties, or in my boys' classes, I wondered why those mothers had been "blessed" with a girl and what I had done wrong. I loved my boys, but it just wasn't enough for me, no matter how I tried to reconcile not having a girl. I was more than willing to give up sleep and free time for a daughter, but what else could I do to make my dream come true?

I kept asking myself, "Is God punishing me by taking my mother away and not giving me a daughter? Did God make a conscious decision to give me healthy boys, a loving husband, a beautiful house, wonderful vacations, but no girl? And how can I ever tell anyone how I feel and expect that they will understand the emptiness I feel? What is wrong with me?" This had been going on for years by then and I needed help to get over it, but didn't know where to turn.

I knew there were unhappy childless women. There were women my age that couldn't find the right man, let alone have children. There were women working and struggling to make ends meet, and here I was wondering how I would productively spend my days when the boys were in school. Logically, it made no sense to be depressed, but emotionally, I couldn't get over it. Jon and I had agreed we would be happy with what we had. I knew this was much easier for Jon to do than me; he had moved on. I was stuck, but all I could say out loud was, "All right, we're happy. I'll keep reminding myself."

ꟷ

September 11, 2001 had a dramatic impact on many Americans. It was a tragic day. Most Americans felt sick about the loss of life and the sense of vulnerability, as well as the loss of many freedoms. That day severely affected our nation and I doubt it will ever be forgotten. I felt devastated and emotional about that day, but for me personally, that day also spurred an amazing revelation for which I will be forever grateful.

We were standing in our synagogue about a week after that fateful day that took so many American lives, talking to some friends about the horrific events. There were still many questions about what was happening in New York City, as well as the other terrorist targets. One person we knew casually, who was standing in a group with us, mentioned that he heard there were many children in New York City who had been orphaned by the fall of the World Trade Center buildings. That statement stopped me in my tracks.

I was stunned by my reaction to that news. I was devastated for those children but I also realized at that moment that I might be willing to raise someone else's child. It had never occurred to me before. I knew there were many happily adopted children whose parents appeared to love and care for them as much as natural parents, but it had never occurred to us to try adoption. I had heard about how hard it is to adopt an American child and most people I knew or had heard about had adopted from China or Russia instead. I had just assumed the adoption process was too arduous and time-consuming. But I had never researched American adoption myself.

I understood that adoption meant raising a child that might not look like my own children and that my boys might feel awkward about their sibling. I wondered if, after all was said and done, the adopted child would really feel like part of our family. Somehow, none of those concerns seemed important enough to keep me from considering adoption as a solution to my problem.

When this conversation after 9/11 came up, I thought raising a child who was born to Americans who had worked in the World Trade Center might appeal to me. I felt instantly connected to those people and wanted to honor their sacrifice by raising one of their children.

Jon saw the wheels turning in my head. Clearly, he knew what I was thinking. At the end of the day, I said, "Jon, please call your friends in New York to see what they know."

After discussing the idea over the next couple of days, I was surprised that my husband was as interested in the potential of adoption as much as I was, or at least he acted that way. Perhaps he wanted an excuse to talk to the New York friends he hadn't seen for a while or to make sure they had survived that horrible day. Maybe he was once again trying to get me what I really wanted. Whatever his reason was, my spirits were lifted when he agreed to make the contacts.

He called a friend in Manhattan who was managing some of our investments and who happened to be struggling with infertility herself. The problem was everywhere. Coincidentally, she and her husband, Brett, had also considered adoption.

"Hi, Serena, how are you?" Jon said.

"I'm fine, but we're still a little shook up around here," she said. "Brett had an awful time getting home from Wall Street that day after the attack. He witnessed the destruction firsthand and was in shock. We live on the upper east side of Manhattan and he walked over a hundred blocks because everything shut down."

"I'm so sorry you both had to deal with that," Jon said. "It must have been crazy for everyone who lived there. I can't imagine what it was like. I hope the city can recover from this."

"Me too. You know I'm finally pregnant," she said.

"Congratulations, Serena," Jon said enthusiastically. "Patty will be so happy for you when she hears. You and Brett had a long battle. Hey, on a related subject, we heard that there were children orphaned by the attack on the World Trade Center. Have you heard anything about that?"

"No, I'm pretty sure that's not the case, Jon," Serena said. "I live in the same building with an executive who managed one of the large financial firms in the World Trade Center. His firm was completely destroyed. His account of the devastation to his employees' families was upsetting, but he didn't mention any orphans. All the children of the deceased employees had family to raise them. I haven't heard anything about other firms though, but if there were orphans, I would hope that the kids would be given to relatives rather than strangers."

"You're probably right, Serena, and you've been really helpful. Thank you," Jon said, sounding a little disappointed. "I hope you and your husband are okay. Congratulations again. I'll talk to you soon."

"You can't be disappointed that those poor kids don't need new homes," Jon said to me after he hung up the phone.

"I'm absolutely not disappointed," I said. "Children should live with their families, especially if they lost their parents. I just want to make sure that we know what's really happening there. Who else can you call to see what they know?"

Jon called one of his former lawyers, who had a successful family practice in New York.

After hanging up, Jon said, "He confirmed that there are no orphans needing homes in NYC, but he *did* say that if we are looking to adopt, he knows a great adoption lawyer in Orange County, California. At least he's on the same coast and in the same time zone as us. He also has a partner who works on surrogacy cases if we want to investigate that option."

Although we were relieved for all of those children who sadly lost their parents in New York, we were a little disappointed for ourselves. It would have felt good to help those devastated families while also answering our prayers. But most surprising to me was Jon's subsequent comment: "Maybe we *should* really talk about adopting a baby girl."

"Or maybe even an older child?" I said excitedly, keeping our age in mind. We both felt that adoption might be a good solution, but where should we start? We knew nothing about it.

We called the number Jon's New York lawyer had given us and asked for Roland Blankston, the lawyer at the firm that specialized in adoption. We used Jon's lawyer's name hoping to get a quick callback and it worked. He called within the hour, which was good given my budding excitement about this new project.

"You know," he said after our introduction, "now that you have given me your recent history, you might want to consider surrogacy as well as adoption." This was an idea we certainly hadn't considered. He continued, "The advantages are significant if you want a child with your own genes. There are, of course, disadvantages to this process as well. I suggest that you talk to my partner and rule this option out first. Then we can move on with the adoption issues if necessary."

Roland referred us to his partner who specialized in surrogacy cases. After a brief phone call, we all agreed that we should meet in person. These were critical decisions for us and we wanted to look the experts in the face when they talked about the options, including costs and legal issues.

We initially considered a trip to California to meet with both lawyers, but since the boys were in school, we didn't want to leave them again unless it was vitally important. We set up a video conference call at the local Kinko's, as Jon suggested, for the following week.

"This worked great the last time I had a meeting with people on the East Coast. It should be even easier with California," Jon said, referring to the time zones.

The video conferencing technology was not great back then and movements were delayed by three seconds or so. It was like watching people doing a slow-motion robot dance without the music. I couldn't really see their facial expressions unless they were laughing, but they definitely knew their business.

Roland's partner, Bart Duncroft, discussed the surrogacy procedure in detail and how the surrogate is chosen. The initial search for suitable candidates might take months and the screening process even longer. He also emphasized the risk of having multiple children if more than one embryo was implanted in the surrogate, the same dilemma IVF had raised. We also understood the risk of getting nothing if you only implanted one.

My heart sank when Mr. Duncroft described the risk of a child being born with developmental problems because the surrogate wasn't careful about her diet or suffered other health issues when she was pregnant, by choice or not. "You hope to know who these women are well enough to trust them, but in the end, they are doing this for the money and that tends to bring risky people to your door," the lawyer said matter-of-factly. "When you construct the agreement with the surrogate, you just have to help them understand how their actions affect the baby they are carrying."

Any pregnancy, my own or a surrogate's, could have a disappointing result, including a severely disabled baby. I was especially concerned about having a baby who required constant care beyond infancy and the effects that would potentially have on our current quality of life. Our sons' happiness and well-being was important and taking parental concentration away from them would be irresponsible and unfair. At my age, the chances of these problems were higher, so a younger surrogate theoretically reduced the risk. But unless the surrogate lived with us during the pregnancy so that we could watch every move she made, I would be worried sick the entire nine months.

There was also the real possibility of the surrogate giving birth to another boy. We couldn't be 100 percent sure that the pregnancy would be a girl, even using the sex-selection methods we were familiar with, until a test was done at sixteen weeks (or a riskier test at twelve weeks). The child would be ours biologically no matter what the outcome.

The potential legal contracts between the surrogate and us brought up another set of risks and sad scenarios. It all seemed nerve-racking and excessively risky. Jon and I exchanged a look that confirmed what we both knew: surrogacy wasn't for us. We thanked both the attorneys for their time, ended the conference call politely, and started moving emotionally down the adoption path to our daughter. We had made our decision quite easily, in fact, and were ready for the journey.

Roland was one of the most successful adoption lawyers in the state of California, and not just according to him. Over the next week, we did some research and checked references, confirming that he had an excellent reputation. There were also local lawyers who knew about adoption, but from what we had read and heard, the quickest way to adopt was to have a reputable lawyer with adoption experience among young women from lower-income areas. Roland had helped many single mothers find good homes for their babies and his referral rate was high. He received dozens of calls a week.

Roland was clearly the man in California who birth mothers and potential adoptive couples alike came to for help. Adoption statistics led us to believe that California was the place to look for our birth mother. He assured us that he would give us the best chances of finding someone who needed our help and that if we found our birth mother in California, he could handle the entire transaction. He was willing to do everything over the phone, so there was no travel involved, which was great for us.

Because we were in a rush to move forward, Roland suggested that he advertise for us in several other states' classified ads to locate a birth mother sooner. We agreed, as long as our name was kept anonymous. Ads were placed in Alabama, Arkansas, Illinois, Indiana, Kansas, Louisiana, Michigan, Nebraska, Oklahoma, and Utah. We went along with his recommendations, although we really felt the ads should run in every state. Now that we were ready to adopt, we wanted it to happen immediately.

We declined his offer to place an ad in Washington; we didn't want to adopt a baby from our own state because we wanted there to be some geographical separation between our child and the birth mother. We thought that after everything was said and done, it would be better for our family to avoid "chance meetings" with the birth mother. We weren't opposed to having our adopted child meet her birth mother when she was ready, but we wanted to make sure it didn't happen before then.

Our impatience to adopt led Roland to advise us about issues over which he had no control. "I want to warn you that you are considered older parents in the adoption world, which might affect your ability to find a birth mother willing to give you her child," he said. "Many birth mothers think the adoptive couple should be closer to their own age and able to see their kids grow into adults and have kids of their own. At thirty-nine and forty-nine, some people may be hesitant to consider you."

Although this struck me as reasonable, it hit me hard. "Are we crazy to even try to do this then?" I asked him, sounding slightly agitated.

"Absolutely not and don't be discouraged," he responded. "I'm just giving you the worst-case scenario. Most of the couples I work with are over thirty-five and have spent years in infertility treatments. Some birth mothers want experienced parents for their child, but it might take a little longer to find those birth mothers. Besides, this child will keep you young."

"Yes, we understand all about that," Jon said, laughing.

"But that is not the biggest factor in your case," he continued. "I should also warn you that it might take a long time to find a birth mother who knows she is having a girl when she is choosing the adoptive parents," he said.

"How long is *long*?" I said.

"Probably two years," he said. Our jaws dropped in disappointment. "Most mothers choose the adoptive parents early in the pregnancy so they can get help with the associated costs like living expenses, prenatal care, and delivery. At that early phase of the pregnancy, they rarely know the sex of the baby. You only want a girl, right?"

"Without a doubt," Jon said. "Are we the only couple you know who wants to even out their family?"

"Most adoptive couples don't have *any* children and don't care what sex they adopt. Birth mothers want to find those couples so they are sure that the couple won't back out right after the birth. That's the last thing they want to worry about during labor and delivery," he said.

"Let me get this straight," I began, looking directly at Jon. "We will only be chosen by someone who doesn't care that we are older, who's fairly late in her pregnancy, and who definitely knows she is having a baby girl, right?"

"Yes, you are looking for a very rare case, unfortunately," Roland said, "but don't be discouraged."

I nearly hung up the phone without saying good-bye. Instead, I put my hands over my face. Jon laughed nervously and thanked the lawyer for his time.

"Is *anything* easy?" I asked Jon in frustration after he ended the call.

"Yes," Jon said, "the boys were easy."

I worked hard at remaining positive, even in light of this distressing conversation. We agreed that we should get the process started, pay for the advertising and the advance on legal fees, and see what happened. Roland suddenly became an important person in our lives.

We didn't mention anything to our boys, or anyone else, as we began this journey. We didn't want them to get excited (or worried) about another sibling and then be disappointed when nothing happened for a year or two. We didn't want people asking questions and making us more anxious about the time ticking away. On the one hand, two years seemed like *forever*. Living through the waiting time "alone" would become harder and harder in many ways. On the other hand, it felt as though we had turned a corner and were now on the right path, leading us to the place where my dream would come true. Living with the decision to stop trying to have a daughter didn't work for us, especially not for me. I never felt complete, or done, no matter how hard I tried. Adoption was not only an excellent solution to our problem but was also an exciting concept. I was glad that we had investigated and tried other methods to conceive a child. It made adoption the clear choice. I wondered if our daughter was growing in someone's belly at that moment.

MOVING FORWARD

The first step in the adoption process was a home study. Roland told us that the home study was required by law to ensure that adopted children weren't placed in unsuitable homes. Roland felt it was a good idea to get this started right away in case the right birth mother came along soon.

"The home study takes time. You need to set up the all-day interview at your home and the adoption specialist will need to write the detailed placement report, which is quite in-depth," he explained. "You wouldn't want this issue to hold up the process if things happen quickly." He gave us the name of someone in the Seattle area that could help.

We scheduled the study in October, and Cecelia Dokes, an adoption specialist, came to our home in mid-November. Before the interview, she asked us to complete an application for an adoption report, as well as a contract for her services. We were getting very good at filling out paperwork with detailed personal information and signing contracts.

Cecelia had graying, short, curly hair and round glasses, and reminded me of my elementary school piano teacher. She had worked in the adoption business for many years and lived in a small town west of Seattle. Although she was calm and friendly, we were nervous throughout the interview. We wanted to make a good impression. Her written opinion of our home and us would influence the judge who would ultimately make the decision about whether we could legally adopt a child.

Although Cecelia, who asked us to use her first name, was easy to talk to, professional, and knew her business, it was still an odd visit. The interview itself was contrary to how we lived our lives. We had to expose our health and educational history, our home, our children, and our financial situation to a complete stranger. We weren't convinced that we'd ever need the placement report Cecelia would be writing because of the realistic picture Roland had painted for us. We were feeling too old and inflexible about what we were looking for to even find a birth mother who would let us raise her child. However, we persevered and kept a good attitude the entire day.

During her visit, Cecelia toured our home, met with us together, and then interviewed us separately. We each described our extended families, our childhoods, our careers, and our marriage. We discussed our attitudes toward adoption, parenting philosophies, and our roles in both our home and our community. We wanted her to see us as good parents and providers, as well as people who cared about others through volunteerism and philanthropy. She made us feel good about our answers and explanations. Her visit was easy and pleasant, lasting about five hours.

The boys were at school during her visit, but Cecelia did want to meet them briefly before she left. When they got home, we introduced her as a "business friend of Daddy's." I held my breath to see how they would respond to her without my preparing them at all. I was relieved that they used their best manners during the brief encounter. In her final report, Cecelia described the boys as "happy and well-adjusted."

When she left shortly before dinnertime, explaining that she had enough material to start her report but would have more questions later, we were exhausted but more optimistic than before her visit. She didn't seem to think we were too old to adopt and even offered to assist in finding birth mothers in Washington State should we decide to look locally. This was apparently a larger part of her business than the home studies. We still felt strongly that we should adopt a child outside the state for security and peace-of-mind reasons.

Cecelia also gave us a list of documents that she needed from us in order for her to complete her report. The list included copies of our birth certificates, our marriage license, income tax returns for the past two years, Washington State Patrol criminal history information, medical reports, health insurance verification, and four letters of reference.

Only the last item gave us some concern. We needed to find four people, not related to us, who had known both of us as a couple for at least two years. Because we were trying to keep this adoption process a secret from our boys, finding four people whom we could trust not to spread the word might be difficult.

"What about Mrs. O'Malley?" I said.

"The boys' kindergarten teacher?" Jon said.

"She's perfect. She's known us for over two years and knows our kids. Neither of them is in her class anymore and she won't likely see them, so it won't be difficult to keep it to herself," I explained. "Plus, I'm sure this isn't the first time she's been asked to write a letter of recommendation."

"Okay, there's one," Jon agreed. "Who else?" We both thought for a few seconds.

"How about Harvey in San Diego?" Jon said. Harvey was Jon's good friend from college and was the best man in our wedding. He was Micah's godfather but didn't visit much, so there was little chance of this issue coming up between them. He was also a Hollywood screenwriter and wouldn't have trouble writing something witty about us as a couple.

"Great idea," I said. "How about my friend Liz?" We knew Liz from Microsoft and she had worked with both of us in her position in the public relations department. Although she lived locally, she wasn't connected to most of our family friends and wouldn't normally see the boys on her own. We also knew she was good at keeping secrets since new software releases are always kept under wraps for years before being announced to the public.

"Perfect," Jon agreed, "as long as you can get her to get it done by the deadline. She doesn't have a good reputation in that department." He was right. Liz was late for every lunch we had together and we knew she struggled to get work in on time.

"I will stay on it," I said. "We need one more."

"How about Chris?" Jon said. Chris was our attorney and friend that Jon liked to golf with. He was very good at writing and keeping confidential information.

"Sounds great. Please ask him, as well as Harvey, and I will ask the other two," I said. I was encouraged by our progress and teamwork. Jon was really stepping up to these early challenges and my relief was palpable.

Over the next two days, we called each of these people to see if they would write a letter of recommendation for us and keep our attempt to adopt confidential. When we explained the purpose of the call and why we needed the letters, they were all surprised at our new venture. I couldn't blame them, as I could barely believe it myself. All four agreed without hesitation and three wrote the letters for us quickly. True to form, though, Liz needed more time and prodding than the others; she finally faxed the letter to Cecelia a day after the deadline. We were truly grateful for all of their support.

Now that the placement report was under way, we turned our focus to hastening the outreach process along, rather than relying solely on our lawyer's advertisements. Both of us held college degrees in communications from fine universities and we knew that we needed to broaden our reach to get the word out to prospective birth mothers. We wanted our adopted child to have a close relationship with her brothers, who were already seven and nine years old, so time was important to us. In addition, we were almost forty and fifty years old, respectively, and waiting two years seemed unacceptable. Our feelings, of course, had no effect on the process itself or anyone trying to help us. We were told repeatedly that the chances of the adoption happening anytime soon were low.

Jon and I are many things, but patient is *not* one of them. We were the people who paid extra for "24-hour" photos, long before digital cameras came along. We wanted to be finally settled with our complete family after such a long journey already, but we had no control over that. Jon was far more patient than I was, so as usual, I suffered the most.

Roland placed ads in newspapers around the country the week after we had met. To me, this seemed like a good way to find people who read the morning paper, but what about birth mothers who didn't read the newspaper? While I understood he was the expert in finding birth mothers, I couldn't understand why a teenager or young adult, assuming that was our target audience, would use the newspaper for locating adoptive parents. I barely took the time to read the daily newspaper and we received the paper every morning at our doorstep. Our target audience may not take the effort to purchase a newspaper; I certainly didn't before I was married to the nation's biggest fan of the *New York Times*. There had to be something else that made more sense. I called Roland and asked what else we could do.

He suggested an adoption facilitator in Southern California called A Loving Alternative. "They currently advertise in approximately twenty-five states using the yellow pages and help between twenty and twenty-five adoptive couples at one time, matching approximately three to five adoptive couples with birth parents per month. The average waiting time is about six months for couples without children and nine to twelve months for couples with children," he explained. "I will contract with them on your behalf if you choose to pay their fee."

I agreed to check the agency out and get back to him. "Nine months is much better than two years," I said excitedly to Jon after I explained the idea to him.

"Yes, but I'm sure it's nine months when the couple will take either sex, right?" Jon said, deflating my enthusiasm. "Let's look at their website together."

A Loving Alternative had a great website for both adoptive couples and birth mothers. The site featured pictures of about a dozen couples waiting for a child. If you liked their photo, you could click on it and read the profile that was in the form of a "Dear Birth Mother" letter. You could also request additional profiles that weren't on the site if you filled out a questionnaire. The site also featured photos of about forty couples who had successfully adopted children. This was a very good sign.

We decided to call the phone number listed. The owners, Cindy and Jim Simonson, had started the business after they adopted their daughter five years ago.

"Through our own search for a child to adopt years ago, we found that very few of the adoption attorneys and agencies provide couples with an aggressive outreach program," Cindy said. She had introduced herself as the person who talked to all prospective parents and birth mothers. "We started this business to fill the void and have significantly reduced the time people have to wait to adopt a child."

That was exactly what we were looking for.

"We work with a limited number of couples at a time to give everyone as much of our attention as possible," Cindy said. "I listen to my clients' goals and dreams for adoption and we assist them in fulfilling those dreams by finding birth mothers who fit their criteria."

"Sounds pretty simple," I said. "I always thought the birth mother chooses the couple."

"They definitely do," Cindy said. "Once a birth mother calls on the 800 number, I talk with her in a nonjudgmental way to understand what characteristics she is looking for in an adoptive couple. If she seems serious, I have her fill out a detailed questionnaire so I know more about her. After receiving that document, I evaluate it against the couples I am currently working with. I then send her an average of ten 'Dear Birth Mother' letters written by the couples that fit her requirements and vice versa. She reviews these letters and hopefully selects one of those couples to adopt her baby."

"That's amazing," I said. "Sounds like a complicated process. Do all the birth mothers that you speak to by phone return those questionnaires?"

"No, and that's how we weed some of them out," Cindy said. "If they aren't completely sure what they want to do, the questionnaire will scare them away from adoption. It makes them really think about giving up their child to strangers. If they aren't sure what they want when they meet our couples, it can be overly stressful for all involved. The questionnaire identifies the mothers who are absolutely sure."

"Makes sense," I said. I felt good about her thoughtfulness and responsibility to the couples who were waiting for a child.

"I should also tell you that this is not an adoption agency," Cindy said. "We cannot finalize any adoptions or handle any legal aspects of an adoption. We are merely in business to help locate a birth mother through nationwide advertising and match birth parents with clients, after the prescreening process is complete."

"You would probably run out of time if you handled anything other than what you're already doing," Jon said. "Sounds like you're a busy woman. Besides, it's always smart to leave the legal logistics up to the lawyers."

"I am busy," Cindy said with a chuckle. "We receive about fifty calls from new birth mothers every month, but only about eight to ten of those end up selecting a couple and moving into the adoption process."

"Sounds like a great business, Cindy," I said. "You're bringing people together for such a great purpose."

Cindy was patient, understanding of our situation, and most important, promised that she would be available for consultation before, during, and after the initial matchup. I liked her right away and understood why young, single, pregnant women would feel comfortable working with her.

She listened as I described our family in detail and our fears about adoption. She understood how worried we were about the impact a new baby would have on our boys. She helped us understand the process and possible pitfalls beyond what we already knew. She told us some stories with good endings and some unhappy stories.

She was completely honest with us about the process, agreeing with our lawyer that it may take longer to find a girl. "I can't promise you that I will find someone who knows she is having a girl when she calls me. You may have to decide if you want to take the risk if the birth mother who chooses you doesn't know the sex of her baby. You may want me to wait until I find someone who absolutely knows what she's having before I send out your profile. That takes longer, of course," Cindy said. "You are competing with every couple out there who wants to adopt and most of them don't care about the sex of the baby."

Jon and I looked at each other, wondering how much risk we were willing to take and how long we were willing to wait. We could spend months supporting and getting to know a birth mother until she found out that she was having a boy. Would we be able to walk away at that point?

Cindy continued. "No matter what you decide about the gender issue, if you decide you are going to take the next step with us, it'll cost six thousand dollars for two years of our advertising." I silently moaned about the two-year wait. "Usually we match parents up long before the contract expires," she said.

Two years still felt like a lifetime, but she assured me that over the last five years, the average wait period had been four to six months, which was significantly less than our lawyer had told us. We assumed it would take closer to a year for our birth mother to come along. We wanted the clock to begin ticking right away and asked her to send us a contract, promising to send it in signed with a check right away.

Jon said, "Cindy, we can't imagine having our photo posted on your website for privacy reasons, but do you think doing so would help us find someone sooner?"

"Absolutely not," Cindy said. "Birth mothers don't normally choose a couple from the website without talking to me about the couples who don't choose to 'go public,' plus most of them don't have computers. I will send your profile out to anyone who looks promising and fits your criteria."

After we said good-bye, I took a deep breath and smiled. "This is a good step, Jon. I hope you agree we should do this.

She has the right attitude and seems to really care about the people on both sides of these arrangements."

"I agree," Jon said. "Her advertising concept is simple but probably effective. Plus, it's always better to have more than one team working on your side."

After receiving and signing Cindy's contract, the next step was to fill out another questionnaire about ourselves and the baby we were looking for. The number of questions on the document amazed us. There were questions that raised issues we had never considered. Would we take a baby with developmental problems? Would we take a mixed-race baby? Would we take a baby whose mother took drugs during the pregnancy? Were we open to meeting the birth parents prior to the birth? Were we comfortable sending pictures and updates yearly after the birth and subsequent adoption? What about visitation with birth parents after the adoption?

Clearly, we had a lot to think about. On the one hand, we didn't want to lower our chances of finding a baby by narrowing the field of birth mothers too much. On the other hand, we didn't want to get involved in a risky situation or with someone of questionable character who might back out or a baby we wouldn't end up adopting after birth.

Three questions were particularly hard to answer:

"Are you open to adopting a child that is not an infant and, if so, up to what age?"

We really wanted an infant. Children with a troubled or unhappy past seemed much more difficult to raise, as we had heard firsthand from foster parents we knew. A child joining our family as an infant would grow up with our nurturing, our rules, and our attention to educational and emotional issues.

"Would you be ready to accept a situation where the baby is due immediately or already at the hospital?"

We were in a hurry to complete our family, which was not getting any younger, so we responded yes to this question, even though we wanted to have time to check out the birth mother. We wanted to do the right thing for our boys, as well as ourselves, and needed to consider the situation in the decisions we made.

"Are you open to a situation where the birth mother consumed alcohol or did drugs while she was pregnant?"

Again, our boys were our first concern, and a child with physical, developmental, or emotional issues would probably take a significant amount of our time to care for properly. This would more than likely take too much time away from our boys. We didn't want them to suffer because we needed a girl.

We thought long and hard about all the questions on the questionnaire and filled it out as best we could. On our second call with Cindy, we told her that our answers on the questionnaire indicated what we thought then, but if a potential birth mother came our way with extenuating circumstances, we might change our minds. Cindy understood and told us what else we needed to do.

"The next step is to write a profile of yourselves as a couple in the form of a letter to the birth mother," Cindy said. "It's important that the letter accurately portrays who you are as people, as parents, and as a family, why you hope to adopt, and what you have to offer a child. Pictures are also an important part of the letter and should give the birth mother a glimpse into your life together."

"Wow, that's a tall order," Jon said looking at me.

"I'll send you some samples so you can get a feel for what we're looking for," Cindy said. "You can also view some of them on our website."

As we read other couples' "Dear Birth Mother" letters, we looked for comments we liked and comments we didn't. Some couples had a condescending tone. Some seemed to be begging or bragging too much. We felt sorry for some of the couples who described their sad infertility stories in their letters.

We wanted our letter to show who we really were and why the child would be happy in our family. We felt that any responsible birth mother would need more information about how the child would be raised, rather than how badly the couple wanted a baby.

We spent many hours working on our letter to convey a profile of our family, our values, our philosophies in parenting, and why we wanted to adopt. It talked about Saturday mornings at home and vacations as a family. It talked about baseball games, both little league and major league, and holidays with extended family. It included pictures of our home, our boys, our dog, and of course, ourselves. Most important, we talked about how we would take care of and love our new baby.

Jon and I both enjoy writing, so although it was relatively easy to start this letter, the editing process took us forever. Our perfectionism took over and we edited and re-edited and, in some cases, argued about the smallest of word choices. We were worried about looking too affluent with our lifestyle description and photographs of our home. We wanted to make sure we explained accurately why it was important for us to "complete" our family. We knew we were older than many of the couples we were competing with, so we used that fact to our advantage and talked about our parental experience and how it made us excellent candidates for another child.

We don't celebrate Christmas and thought the birth mother might want to know how a prospective family celebrates holidays. Jewish holidays are in general much less celebratory than Christian holidays, and we didn't want someone to reject us because of religion, so we left that specific issue out. We would make that clear when we met the birth mother. I said, "We don't want the birth mother to think her child won't have any spiritual upbringing at all. We need to add *something* about our religion and how important it is to us."

We tossed around a few ideas, but they got too complicated or didn't properly communicate what we wanted to say. In the end, we decided that we'd just include: "We will support this child in every way—emotionally, spiritually, and financially." We were both happy with that and we were finally finished with our letter. It read as follows:

Dear Birth Mother,

Choosing parents to raise your child is an extremely difficult decision to make, and we appreciate that you are taking the time to consider us. We want trust and honesty to be the foundation of our adoption. We hope this letter will provide a useful introduction to who we are.

We are Patty and Jon. We have been happily married for ten years and have two wonderful boys, but we would both like to have another child to complete our lives. For many years, we have tried to have another baby, but even with the help of fertility specialists, we have been unsuccessful.

Jon moved to the Seattle area to join a major corporation as vice president. He met Patty there, who was working as an account executive. He now works with a number of local companies as a consultant and investor.

After the birth of our first son, Patty quit her job to spend her time at home. She keeps busy as a volunteer at the boys' schools and helps local civic organizations including the zoo. Most of her time is devoted to taking care of our family. We are both busy during the week but make it a point to be home when the boys come home from school.

We eat dinner together, discussing the day's events, and spend the next hour and a half completing homework, playing catch on the lawn, reading books, or playing an old-fashioned card game like Go Fish.

On a typical Saturday, after a breakfast of French toast, we all go swimming in the indoor pool, including the dog, who is as good a swimmer as our boys and dives in for the ball frequently and hysterically. Saturday afternoon is spent watching our boys play soccer or baseball or going for a family bike or boat ride.

As a family, we enjoy seeing new places. We had a great

trip last year to the East Coast to visit Jon's family and see the birthplaces of our country. To prepare, we helped our boys read history books. We are planning a road trip for next summer to visit six major league ballparks before the boys go to camp. We enjoy being outdoors together, skiing, going for walks, swimming, or playing golf.

We recently moved into a new house and have a beautiful room overlooking Lake Washington that will be a perfect nursery. Our community has the best public schools in the state and a "small town" feel with lots of playfields and parks.

We are committed to being a kind and loving family. We will support this child in every way—emotionally, spiritually, and financially. We will provide a warm and stable home with a mother, a father, and two brothers to love and nurture your child for the rest of our lives.

Thank you for considering us as parents for your baby.

Sincerely,

Patty and Jon

We understood the process Cindy described. A birth mother would call A Loving Alternative and describe the type of couple she wanted for her child. Cindy then matched her with several waiting couples looking for that type of child or, in most cases, any child. She then sent the profiles of ten couples to the birth mother.

It seemed simple enough, but I wondered how any birth mother could make such a big decision from just one letter. Because we had never met Cindy personally, we wondered if she assists a birth mother with additional information about the couples if she wanted to know more. Were we at a disadvantage, being in another state and not having met Cindy in person?

How could she honestly and equitably represent all these couples to birth mothers?

Cindy had assured us that we would get a fair shot with any birth mother that seemed like a good fit for our family. I totally trusted her but the competition with all those childless couples depressed me.

"Why would someone choose a couple that is already blessed with two boys over some young couple who hasn't had any children?" I said to Jon while he was working on his computer. He was only half-listening to me and didn't answer, but I was compelled to get the reassurance (and attention) I needed from him.

I continued, a little louder. "Hmmm, let me think about what I would do if I were in a birth mother's shoes . . ." I said, watching Jon to see if he would look up.

"Are you kidding me?" he said, finally looking up from his work. "You would *never* consider giving up your child and therefore this would never be a decision you would have to make. How could you possibly hope to have any meaningful perspective on such a decision?"

I laughed and agreed to end the discussion. He was right. I could never give up a child, but lucky for us and other waiting couples, there were women who could, under the right circumstances. It was a difficult process for all parties involved, but in the end, the reward was sure to be worth it.

We decided not to send Cindy the final draft of our letter until after we took our winter vacation with the boys in December. We doubted anything would happen over the holidays and it seemed sensible to take a break and then revisit the entire process, as well as the letter again, when we returned.

When the year ended on December 31, we felt more ready to be parents again than ever after relaxing and spending time with our boys. We looked toward the New Year with hopes of a new baby girl to love and cherish.

On January 15, 2002, when we were both happy with our entire letter, which included photos, we printed it out on fancy paper with a pretty ivy border and sent two dozen copies in folders to Cindy in California. It was an exciting moment when we dropped off the package at the post office. "The child we adopt could be growing in someone's belly right now," I said to Jon. "I hope she finds us soon."

MARCH 1

After we submitted our "Dear Birth Mother" letter to A Loving Alternative and Cindy approved it, we entered a notoriously hard part of the adoption process: the waiting. Up to that point, we had done everything under our control to make the process go faster, but as with most things, our impatience alone was not enough to speed up the things we had no control over.

Our home study and everything related to it was complete by the time Cindy received our letter and Cecelia Dokes's placement report was extremely positive. She recommended us highly as adoptive parents. We were relieved to have completed that complicated and anxious process. In her letter accompanying the report, she again offered to help us find a child through the adoption side of her business. Even though it would increase our adoption opportunities and outreach, we were still very sure we didn't want a birth mother who lived in Washington State.

Our California lawyer, Roland Blankston, continued placing newspaper advertising in several states for us and our profile was in the hands of the adoption facilitators, ready to be sent to any birth mother who called looking for a family like ours.

Cindy's business had two phone numbers listed in the yellow pages (still a critical reference tool back in 2002) and on its website: the 800 number for birth mothers to call and the regular business line, for waiting adoptive couples to call. Cindy always answered the 800 number because those calls could be from new birth mothers who might not call a second time or be willing to leave their phone numbers if they were to get an answering machine. I wondered how Cindy ever managed to take a vacation.

Cindy said that most of the birth mothers who used the 800 number were calling with pregnancy updates, decisions on adoptive couples, or requests for emotional or financial support from the adoptive couple via Cindy. The 800 number calls we wanted to hear about were from newly pregnant birth mothers looking to find an adoptive couple. There were fewer of those calls. I had to resist the temptation to call the birth mother line to reach Cindy in person, rather than leave a message on the regular line, as she requested, and wait for a callback.

I knew there were many other people relying on Cindy for help and emotional support, including pregnant birth mothers and other impatient adoptive clients, but the waiting was painful. Every day, I wanted to know how many mothers had called and if any sounded like they were the right fit for us. I knew it was an unrealistic expectation. I tried to limit my calls to Cindy to once a week. Each time I reached her, Cindy reassured me in different ways that as soon as a birth mother called who was carrying a girl and fit the description based on our answers to the questionnaire, she would send our profile out. She wasn't ever willing to give me any specifics about the recent activity on the 800 line.

In early February, on one of our weekly calls, she said a tad impatiently, "Patty, you should expect to have to wait at least eighteen months based on what you want." I groaned even though she was telling me what I already knew. Cindy said, "However, I was thinking of sending your letter to a new birth mother who is willing to take the risk and choose a couple before she knows the sex of the baby."

"Why would she do that if she knows we only want a girl?" I said. "If she chooses us and we find out later she isn't carrying a girl, she'd have to choose some other couple in a hurry."

"Perhaps she wants to consider a wider variety of adoptive couples, not just the ones who will take any baby," Cindy said. "She also might want a mother as experienced as you are.

Couples completing their families are a safe bet for birth mothers. They know those people understand how hard it is to be a parent."

Although that new development could potentially have led us to a baby sooner, it could also have created more apprehension about the emotional trauma the whole process could cause. The situation Cindy spoke about gave us a fifty-fifty chance of getting our girl. However, if we agreed to go through with it and spent months supporting this mother emotionally and financially, we might end up with nothing. We could also lose more time if Cindy didn't send our profile to mothers who might have really been carrying a girl during those months. It was risky. We might get excited about a baby and then, for one reason or another, it wouldn't happen. I was a little relieved when Cindy said she would make the decision on that mother and let me know. I decided her job was more difficult than I originally thought.

I would have liked a daily recap of phone calls from birth mothers around the country. I would have liked the opportunity to reach out to each woman myself and tell my story. I wanted each one to know that I would care deeply for her child. I wanted her to understand the incredible relationship I had with my mother and that I would treasure her daughter. I knew I was being unrealistic about my expectations and that I had to control my impatience. I realized I wouldn't be able to think about much else while that was going on.

I don't know why we hadn't considered adoption earlier. I found that I was more excited about it than anything else we had tried before to have a daughter. It amazed me how different life can look when you are informed and motivated. Given everything that had happened in my life over the last few years, I had become even more convinced that I needed a third child and after some research, adoption seemed to be the right solution for us. The only problem was that I had to remain optimistic and *patient* for a *very* long time. I tried to be patient but only succeeded for the first thirty days. It was only mid-

February and I thought I would go crazy waiting another twelve to seventeen months.

I remember sitting on a chairlift in Colorado, during our midwinter ski trip with the boys, complaining to my husband. "Tell me why someone would choose a couple that already has two kids to raise their child," I asked when we were alone.

"Haven't we already talked about this?" Jon said impatiently.

"But there are so many couples on that website who don't have *any* kids and it seems unfair of us to take a baby from them," I said, ignoring his question. I imagined that any birth mother who was making such a huge decision would approach it impartially.

Jon looked at me as if I was crazy and said, "A woman giving her child up to strangers is going to make a decision based on emotion and how she feels about a couple not based on what's fair to everyone else. Once she talks to you, she's going to understand the minute you get on the phone with her what a great mother you are and how perfect you are for her baby."

I smiled and thought he could be right, but he could also be wrong. I thought about how I would feel if a year went by and we were still waiting. I would never survive. I had barely made it through one month and I was already crawling out of my skin with anticipation.

I pestered Jon even more. "Did our letter say enough? Did we make it persuasive? Was it too overbearing?" He just rolled his big brown eyes at me. "How can you be so calm?" I said. Fortunately for him, we had reached the top of the mountain and he didn't have to answer me.

My head was spinning with anxiety about the whole process and when it would really get started for us. I would have to be *patient*—I hated that word. I relented and decided to stop calling Cindy.

ᔕ

March 1, 2002 arrived in Seattle quietly on a rainy Friday. March 1 was always a special day for me. Not only was it the day Jon and I got engaged, but it was my grandparents' anniversary. I loved my mother's parents from Canada and had fond memories of them. My grandmother Pearl died a few years after my mother died and I was sure she had died of a broken heart after losing her daughter. My grandparents had been married for over sixty years and produced the most amazing woman, my mother, God rest her soul.

March was going to be a busy month for us: Jon and I were flying to New York the following Monday, Jon and Micah were heading to Phoenix with friends for baseball spring training mid-month, followed by a birthday party for Jon the next weekend, and finally a big Passover Seder in our home at the end of the month. I was delighted to be so busy and it also meant I wouldn't spend so much time worrying about birth mothers and phone calls.

I was sitting in my office at home that Friday afternoon, adorned with my first-of-the-month flower bouquet from Jon. I was preparing a schedule for our nanny who would be staying with the boys while we were in New York when the phone rang. It was Roland's secretary. "Good afternoon, Mrs. Lazarus. I'm calling with some interesting news. I want to let you know that a birth mother has chosen you and Jon from the ten profiles the adoption facilitators sent her."

"Are you kidding me?" I said, standing up from my chair, unable to fully digest what she had said. Her tone was so professional and calm, she could have just told me something about my dry cleaning, rather than speaking the exact words I had been anticipating for weeks. "A birth mother chose us?"

"I'm not sure why Cindy at A Loving Alternative didn't call you herself, but apparently Mr. Blankston had left instructions with her to go through him on everything first," she said calmly.

"Is she pregnant with a girl?" I said, trying to stay calm and focusing on the important facts.

"Yes, she says she is."

Although I had been impatiently waiting for this moment for well over a month now, I really didn't expect anything to happen so soon, based on what Cindy and everyone else said. It had only been forty-five days since we sent in our profiles. I didn't even know that Cindy had sent our profile out to someone she knew was having a girl. I assumed this was not the same birth mother that Cindy mentioned a month ago who was willing to take a risk on us.

It made sense that Cindy didn't inform couples when she was sending their profiles. There was no reason to get their hopes up unnecessarily. It just amazed me that she had already found someone that fit our needs and who liked our letter. I was ecstatic.

"Please tell me what you know about her," I pleaded with the woman on the other end of the line who had no idea that this call was what I had prayed for every minute since we started thinking about adoption.

"Her name is Fayth, spelled F-A-Y-T-H," she said, "and she lives in Missouri. She is twenty-one years old and has two little boys. The couple who had said they were going to adopt her baby girl just backed out and she is already in her ninth month."

I swallowed hard and felt my pulse quicken. I quickly emailed my husband while I was still on the phone. My hands were shaking with excitement and it was difficult to talk on the phone and type at the same time. "She has two kids and she's only twenty-one?" I repeated.

"Yes, but we don't have very much information on her yet, so Mr. Blankston doesn't want you to get your hopes up," she said.

Fat chance of that, I thought. My hopes were already sky high. "You must be kidding me," I said. "Now let me understand all of this. Her name is Fayth?"

"Yes," she said.

"Tell me more, please, and I'm sorry, what was your name again?" I said, wanting her to tell me everything right now so I could decide if this news was as good as it appeared.

"My name is Helen and I don't have much more information, other than what I gave you already. The adoption facilitator Cindy Simonson is the one that called me. She wasn't sure if she could call you directly. She has more information than I do if you want to call her," she said and started to give me the phone number.

"I have the number," I interrupted. "I've been talking to her a lot, so I'm surprised she didn't call me herself. I'll call her right away. Is there anything else you need to tell me?" I said.

"No, except that we are still advertising for you in newspapers and won't pull those ads until you tell us to or this particular adoption goes through, okay?" she said. "Good luck with this one."

"Thanks so much, Helen," I said as I hung up. I sat there for a moment to digest what just happened. The room seemed to suddenly change. It was no longer a dreary, rainy day. The room was bright and almost sparkled. A person somewhere in the Midwest chose me to raise her child and I could not stop smiling. I brought up a map of Missouri on my computer while I dialed Cindy's number.

"Yes, isn't this great news?" Cindy said when she heard my voice. "I knew you'd be pleased."

"When did you first talk to her?"

"Fayth, originally from Texas, called me a week ago from West Plains, Missouri, crying about this family from Texas that backed out of the adoption. They told her there were too many lawyers to hire in Missouri. They thought it would just be easy because they were friends of her family, but the interstate adoption rules are significant regardless of who is involved. They couldn't afford all the legal costs to complete the adoption, so they backed out. She found our number in the yellow pages and called me, desperate to find a family to adopt her child."

"Wow, I'm sorry for that family but how lucky for us," I said. I wondered if that was the real reason the family backed out, but it didn't really matter.

"Yes, and she says she's having a girl."

That was music to my ears. Cindy continued to tell me more about Fayth. She was a single mother with two boys, ages one and two, and was living in subsidized housing on welfare, with no car, no job, and no phone. I couldn't imagine her situation and instantly wondered if she chose us based on the picture of our boys and our home. I hoped that someday, I would find out why she picked us. In the meantime, I had to worry about the practical issues. She was due on March 27, two days before my husband's birthday, and she had been very early with both of her boys. I realized that left us with at most three weeks to get ready for a baby amidst a very busy month.

Cindy said, "You need to call her tomorrow morning as a first step and see how you feel about her. You should see how you get along before talking about the baby. It's pretty rare that the first birth mother you talk to turns out to be the right person."

I tried to ignore the possibility that Fayth wasn't going to work out and took her phone number from Cindy. Cindy's tone changed and it felt like she was reading my mind when she said, "Patty, I want to warn you. Although she has spoken with me a few times and sounds serious, we don't have enough information about Fayth yet, so don't get your hopes up." I agreed, crossing my fingers while I thanked her, hung up, and screamed.

I called Jon at work and told him everything I had just heard. He hadn't seen my email yet. He was busy at work and seemed pleased but subdued, like Helen, but I was not going to let him diffuse my excitement. Perhaps he intuitively knew that getting our hopes up was premature. I knew I wouldn't be able to operate that way. I was overly optimistic, even if it wasn't the prudent thing to do.

That evening, when Jon and I spoke about the upcoming phone call, he was still much calmer about it than I was. I knew he was protecting me from potential disappointment, but I wanted him to be as excited as I was.

"I'm sure you're excited, honey, but just like Cindy said, we really need to know more about her," he said. "This woman may not even be pregnant for all we know. Besides, how can we possibly get ready for a baby in three weeks?"

"We'll do what we have to, of course. How many times have we had impossible challenges in our marriage?" I said defiantly.

"Not many," he said, "but this one is difficult for us to control. I don't even know what Missouri laws will require from us. I'm sure that Texas couple backed out for some good reason."

"You always say you can't meet the challenge, but in the end, you always do," I said with conviction. I knew him well and he was always up to a good challenge.

Suddenly, I realized we needed to keep our voices down so the boys didn't start asking questions. Controlling my emotion in front of the boys, especially the night before calling Fayth, was difficult. I never lied to my boys and keeping a secret like this felt like lying. Protecting them was not always easy.

When I calmed down later in the evening, my excitement faded and worry kicked in. First, we had so many plans for the month that I would have to cancel or change if we received a baby soon. Bringing a new baby home was much more important to us than any of our plans, but it would affect our family and friends. If it was going to work out, I would need to know very soon and clear our calendar.

I also realized that given all I had read and heard about other adoption stories the chances of this particular situation being the right one for us were low. We needed to understand so much about Fayth's health and lifestyle, which would take some time. I knew that couples frequently rule out birth mothers due to drug dependencies, health history, or just not feeling right about the person. We were also frequently reminded that birth mothers can and do change their mind before the process gets started and even after the birth.

After heading down so many different paths, I felt like I had just found the mountain I needed to climb. It was progress, but now there was so much to understand about this new person in our lives and the risks involved. We had to figure out how to approach the issues and how to prepare for both the best and the worst results. I decided to be cautiously optimistic and keep my emotions under control, which was not my strong suit. When I dove into something this important, I gave it all I had. This would be a challenge in many ways.

As I tried to sleep, I decided to wait until after the phone call the following morning to draw any conclusions about Fayth or, if it felt right, to cancel our March plans.

THE FIRST CALL

According to Cindy, the Saturday morning plan was for me to call Fayth at 10:00 a.m. Pacific time, which was noon in the Midwest. I was told Fayth had no phone so I was curious what phone number Cindy had given me.

Although the call was not particularly early in the morning, I woke up frequently during the night to make sure I didn't oversleep. I was running at a completely different speed now that someone had picked us to raise her child, and sleep wasn't a priority for me. I couldn't stop worrying. So much hinged on this first phone call. If it went well, we would have so much to do and so many decisions to make before the baby came in less than three weeks. If it didn't go well, I knew I would be disappointed. I couldn't help it. I already had my heart set on this baby.

I wanted to know everything about Fayth as soon as possible. What did she look like? Was she tall or short? Was she educated? Why did she want to give up her child? Why did she pick us over the other couples? Question after question had run through my head since Helen had called the day before.

As the early morning hours slowly ticked by, I tried to keep from getting too excited. This was going to be the first call of many between us, I hoped, and the fact that she was due in just three weeks made it even more exciting. I promised myself the night before to stop getting ahead of myself, but as usual, I couldn't resist. I couldn't think about anything else.

Most mothers have nine months to plan, but by the end of the month, my baby could be here. The guest room that would be turned into the nursery wasn't going to be ready in three weeks. We had no baby furniture or equipment except the adorable bassinet my mother had bought when Jake was born. Even though I had kept some old furniture in storage, Jon said he wasn't about to use the same crib for our daughter that we had used for the boys. "We have to get something girly and feminine," he had told me during one of our previous, short-lived pregnancies.

I wanted to have the room all done when she was born, not months afterward, even though she would sleep in the bassinet initially. I wanted friends and family who came to visit the new baby to understand how important her arrival was to our family. I wanted to show off her room, her furniture, and all the adorable pink clothes. The list of things to buy was getting longer by the minute.

I also thought about all the trips and events we had planned in March and what would have to change to accommodate a sudden trip to Missouri. We had been told that Fayth's first two children were born early. Her second child was born two weeks early. If this pattern continued, she could have the baby in mid-March.

My husband's upcoming trip to spring training in Arizona with Micah was definitely a problem. Micah, who adored baseball, had been looking forward to this trip since last October when baseball season ended. He would be so disappointed if Jon canceled it, especially because we couldn't tell him why until much later.

We had also planned a casual birthday party for Jon the week after the baseball trip with twenty couples in our home. They were all our closest friends. We would either have to tell them all that was happening or lie. The risk of one of them innocently telling their kids, who in turn would tell ours, was high. We decided we would cancel the party and lie to our friends about the reason. Not a good option but it was the only one that seemed viable.

Our plans were to end the month of March with a table full of family and friends for the first night of Passover. My father and stepmother would be coming home from California just for Passover, a very important holiday to our family, so canceling the Seder was not an option. If our baby came late instead of early, how would we explain why we weren't at our own Passover Seder? I didn't want my father getting his hopes up about the adoption almost as much as I didn't want to risk the boys' disappointment. Imagining having to lie to my father put me over an emotional edge, so I decided to end this entire line of thinking until after the phone call with Fayth. I hoped I would have enough information after the conversation to answer my questions and settle my nerves.

Jon agreed to watch the boys while I made the phone call alone, which made me extremely nervous. I wanted him with me, even if he wasn't going to be speaking on the call. What if I messed it up? What if she asked me questions I couldn't answer or answered badly? I felt like the Queen of England was waiting for my call.

At 9:55 a.m., I kissed Jon, locked myself in my office, and watched the clock tick away the last five minutes. I let Jon deal with "Where is Mommy going?" as I left the family room. I decided to use one of my husband's office phone lines, connected to the same phone system as our home, so if Fayth had caller ID and she turned out to be someone we didn't want to stay in touch with, we could effortlessly cancel the phone line and get a new number. After talking about the possible scenarios with Cindy, a little paranoia was definitely in order.

Over the previous few years, we had heard many negative stories, which had initially convinced us adoption wasn't an option for us: Birth mothers changing their minds at the last minute and the adoptive couple going home empty-handed after months of hopeful support. Birth mothers changing their minds years after giving up a baby and annoying the adoptive family. Couples deciding they couldn't handle their adopted child after years of trying to cope with unexpected health or emotional issues. There definitely were risks associated with adoption, but at that moment, it felt good to take the initial steps while still keeping our eyes wide open. I knew we needed to remain anonymous for the safety of our potential new baby and the rest of our family.

As I sat waiting for the big hand to strike the hour, I watched my husband, boys, and the dog across the courtyard playing in the indoor pool. We had a wonderful family and were so happy. We were indeed lucky, but deep down I knew a daughter would make it so much better.

I picked up the phone at 10:00 a.m. At the same time, the sun came out from behind a cloud and bright sunlight streamed into my office. I took it as a good sign. I felt my heart beating like it was outside of my chest. Why was I so nervous? I had been a Microsoft sales executive and negotiated with presidents of huge companies like AT&T. How could a small-town twenty-one-year-old from Missouri make me so anxious?

The phone rang and rang and rang. My heart sank more with every ring. "Please pick up," I whispered into the phone. Cindy had told me that she didn't have enough information about Fayth to trust that this was authentic. She warned me not to get my hopes up. It didn't matter though—my hopes were already sky high. I refused to believe that she wasn't there. Maybe she was just changing a diaper. I called again five minutes later. No answer after eighteen rings. Even worse, there was no answering machine, so I couldn't leave a message.

I called Cindy to double-check the number. Maybe she took it down wrong or I wrote it incorrectly in my excitement. When Cindy called me back, an extremely painful forty-eight minutes later, she confirmed that I had the correct number.

"I'm sorry, Patty. I thought she would be waiting for your call. She said she would when we spoke late yesterday. I'm very surprised she wasn't there," Cindy said. "Maybe she'll call me later today to reschedule."

My heart sank after I hung up. All I could think was that it wasn't going to happen after all. This woman was flaking out already and I hadn't even gotten to talk to her. I was beyond disappointed. I was heartbroken. I walked slowly into the pool room where the rest of my family was sitting in the hot tub. I sat down hard on the chair next to them, looking at the floor. We couldn't talk about the call in front of the boys, but my husband said it was "written all over my face."

"Come join us, Mommy," Jake said enthusiastically. I found it excruciatingly hard to smile. "What's wrong?" he said.

"Oh, the person I was supposed to talk to on the phone wasn't home, and I'm disappointed," I said. "I'll swim with you another time, Jake."

"Who, Mommy? Who isn't home?" Jake said. It was just like him to ask lots of questions.

"Just a lady I wanted to talk to, honey," I said, and tried to change the subject.

"She wasn't home?" Jon said when the boys had gone upstairs to shower. "Is that all it was that upset you like this? Since you were away for such a long time, I thought you talked to her and you hated each other right away."

"It *is* upsetting," I said firmly. "She's probably already changed her mind."

"I disagree," Jon said in a dismissive manner. "I'm sure it's just a mix-up on the timing of the call. That's what happens when you have several people involved in scheduling. She will certainly be home later in the day and you should try again." In a not-so-funny role reversal, Jon was now the optimist and I was the pessimist.

As I walked away from Jon, I realized how invested I already was in this woman and her baby. How could I have let myself get so excited? I knew I should have listened to everyone who told me to stay calm, reasonable, and aloof at first. Instead, I went into the other room, closed the door, and let my emotions take over.

After a painfully depressing day, Cindy called at 5:00 p.m. I had to give my husband credit for being optimistic. There was a good reason why the call hadn't happened earlier. Cindy explained that she had tried the number several times herself, which turned out to be Fayth's neighbor's phone. They lived in the same duplex.

"Fayth's neighbor, Doris, apologized for not being there all day to take your call, as she knew about the arrangement," Cindy said. "Fayth doesn't have a phone and had to ask Doris to use her phone at the appointed time."

"Did you ask her why she doesn't have an answering machine?" I said.

"I'm sure she would have one if she could afford it," Cindy said. "Doris works all day at Wal-Mart, so she couldn't be there to take your call at ten o'clock."

"But where was Fayth?"

"You'll be relieved to know there's a very good reason why she wasn't there," Cindy said in a serious tone. "There was an accident last night. Fayth and her boys had to be driven to one of the larger towns in Missouri shortly after talking to me about the adoption. Apparently, her one-year-old son fell backward in his high chair through a plate-glass window in the kitchen."

"Oh my gosh," I gasped, putting my hand over my mouth. I imagined how a little toddler might put his feet on the edge of the kitchen table while seated in a high chair and then push off, launching the top-heavy chair backward toward the floor. He must have been sitting in front of a big window. "How terrible for them. Why did they have to drive so far for a doctor?"

"They saw a doctor at the hospital right in West Plains as soon as the ambulance arrived, but the hospital doesn't have a CT scanner, so Fayth's boyfriend, who was visiting for the weekend, took them all to the hospital in St. Louis for the test," Cindy explained. "It's about a hundred miles away, so they will be gone until midday on Monday. At least there's a good excuse for her absence today. She was being a good mother."

"Hooray!" I said and caught myself realizing how self-centered I was being. "I hope the little boy will be okay." I regretted my initial reaction to the seriousness of the accident, but I couldn't help myself. I was delighted that not only had she not changed her mind about the adoption but that she also showed signs of being a good, concerned mother even before I spoke to her. I explained my overreaction to Cindy, and she laughed.

"No need to apologize to me, Patty. I understand completely. We will all keep our fingers crossed for the little boy. In the meantime, you should really try to stay unemotional about this opportunity. It may not be what you want," Cindy said. "So what time should I tell her neighbor to expect your call on Monday?"

I thought about our plans for Monday and started worrying again. "We have plans to travel to New York on Monday morning, so it's a bit risky to schedule it for that day, but I don't want to wait any longer. We should set up a call for 5:00 p.m. Eastern time if Fayth will be back home by then."

"Okay, I'll call Doris so she can tell Fayth the new plan," Cindy said. "Safe travels." I thanked Cindy for her help, and she wished me luck getting through the weekend. I needed all the luck I could get to tolerate the next two days. She was right: I needed to think about something else, but how?

On the one hand, I could remain positive for the rest of the weekend and risk the huge disappointment (again) on Monday afternoon. On the other hand, I could try to remain calm for the rest of the weekend and not think about the many unanswered questions that kept popping into my head. Either choice was not going to be easy. I knew it was going to be a long forty-eight hours.

Perhaps it was fate, or coincidence, or the fact that I couldn't think about anything else but the pending phone call, but something amazing happened at a party we attended that Saturday night. Something that would probably have upset me if I hadn't received the call about Fayth on Friday.

While at a party hosted by some Microsoft friends, Jon and I talked to an old friend who mentioned that she had a boy and a girl. When I said, "It must be nice to have a little girl," she went into this extended harangue about how wonderful it was to have a girl. She talked about the ballet lessons, the adorable shoes and clothes, the fun manicures together, and on and on. She was well aware that we had two boys, which I had mentioned early in our conversation. She wasn't aware that most women who have only boys, at least the ones I knew, don't necessarily want to hear about how great it is to have a girl.

On any other day, her words would have been like poison given my yearning for a girl, and I would have tried to get away from her as quickly as possible. That evening, however, I actually welcomed everything she said and felt hopeful that I would get to enjoy all those things soon. Jon was smiling at me while this was all going on. He seemed to know that he no longer needed to protect me from conversations like this. We were on our way to completing our family.

We arrived at our hotel in New York just in the nick of time Monday afternoon after an extremely stressful trip. Our flight left Seattle late due to a mechanical problem. When I saw the United Airlines mechanic walk into the cockpit in Seattle, I regretted scheduling the call with Fayth so close to our arrival time. I knew mechanical problems can potentially take hours and even cancel flights, and I was worried that bad luck was following us that morning. When the flight attendant closed the door and we pushed back from the gate, I relaxed a little, until the plane sat on the tarmac for what seemed like hours. With every passing minute, the delays made me more and more anxious.

I sat in my seat nervously thinking about missing our second chance to talk to Fayth. If I didn't call her at 5:00 p.m., would she think I forgot all about it, like I initially thought she had forgotten on Saturday morning? If I was stuck on the plane, I wouldn't be able to reach her. What if this changed her mind about us because we appeared unreliable? I berated myself for not scheduling the call later in the evening.

My thoughts then focused in another crazy direction. What if Fayth chose us after we had this phone call, and while we were still trying to find out all we needed to about her, she gave birth to the baby before we could get to her? It could happen because she gave birth to her second boy two weeks early. We were only three weeks from her due date. This was her *third* pregnancy and the third child usually comes earlier than the second. What if the miscommunications and delays so far were a sign that this opportunity wasn't meant to be? Should we give up on Fayth? Cindy said that some cases were extremely complicated, but with the way things were going over the last three days, I thought my stress level would become intolerable before the week was out.

It was a great relief when we finally took off. The pilot informed us that we had tailwinds and we made up some time on the way to New York. I tried to relax on the flight and stop worrying about Fayth. "There's nothing you can do right now," Jon said, "so relax and watch a movie or something." He dug into his stack of unread *New Yorker* magazines and relaxed. I tried to emulate him, but it wasn't easy. Fayth was all I could think about.

The luggage took seemingly forever to come when we finally landed at JFK International Airport shortly after 3:00 p.m. Eastern time. I was grateful that we had two full hours to get to our hotel, but my patience was running out. I kept checking my wristwatch while we waited, and waited, for our luggage. Several flights had arrived at the same time and the baggage claim area was packed with people. "I told you we should have just brought carry-on luggage," Jon said. I rolled my eyes and tried not to panic.

The next challenge came after we loaded our luggage into the town car and then sat in traffic. The driver was aggressive, weaving through the cars lined up bumper to bumper, three lanes across. I usually enjoyed that ride into the city from the airport, looking at the views of Manhattan between buildings and watching for the Empire State Building. I hadn't yet seen the New York skyline without the twin towers in person. But that was far from my mind. All I could watch was the traffic that was keeping us from getting to the hotel. New York City drivers are always impressive, honking with every spurt of impatience.

They are so different from Seattle drivers, who rarely seem in a rush to get anywhere.

We checked into our hotel only twenty minutes before five o'clock and I was exhausted from all the stress. I could have called Fayth from the car if I had to, but I was afraid of losing the signal in the middle of the call, which always seems to happen on important calls. And the call wouldn't have been easy if there was constant honking in the background.

I flopped down on the king-sized bed in our hotel room after we arrived and waited the remaining ten minutes before the call. The room was quiet and serene compared to everything we had been through to get there. I could barely hear the honking from the busy street forty-eight floors below. I closed my eyes, thinking about how this call might go and praying for the best. I wondered if Fayth would still be upset about her son's accident or if she would even be home from the trip to St. Louis. I dreaded the idea that I might have gone through a stressful travel day for nothing.

We decided that I would talk to her first and if she felt comfortable, we would let Jon talk to her alone or use the speakerphone so we could both join in. I felt just like the previous Saturday morning. My heart pounded as I moved toward the desk, sat down, and dialed the Missouri phone number.

The phone rang several times while I waited. Finally, a woman with a raspy, just-finished-my-cigarette voice answered. I assumed it was Fayth's neighbor that Cindy spoke to named Doris. She was abrupt and seemed impatient about having to receive a call for Fayth that she was obviously expecting. In my nicest voice, I asked to speak to Fayth. "Just a minute, I'll have to go next door to get her."

She clanked the receiver down hard on a table and then I heard a squeaky screen door open then slam shut. I heard knocking and yelling through a door that must have been just a few feet away from Doris's door. Though the phone receiver was still in Doris's house, I could clearly hear what was happening next door.

"Fayth, the phone is for you," Doris yelled. I heard some barely audible children's voices from inside Fayth's home. I heard the screen door open and Fayth's voice seemed to be getting closer when I heard her say "Thank you" to Doris. After several footsteps, the receiver was picked up.

"Hello?"

Fayth was on the phone, finally. *She does exist,* I thought. I gave Jon, who was sitting on the couch next to me, the thumbs-up sign.

"Hi, Fayth," I began. "I'm Patty, and my husband, Jon, is here with me. We are both delighted to finally get to talk to you."

"Hi y'all," she responded happily. "It's so great to finally get to talk to y'all too."

I instantly loved her accent. "We are so sorry about the accident on Friday night. I hope your baby boy is okay."

"Oh, he's okay now, but it was pretty scary on Friday. Lots of blood," she said. "The stitches are already healin' and he doesn't really even notice his big owie anymore."

"That's a relief. It's a good thing kids are so resilient. We're glad to hear he's okay."

"Thank you," she said.

I moved the conversation forward. "We are so happy to hear that you liked our letter."

"Yep, you seem like a real nice family. I was goin' to give my baby to some people down in Texas where I used to live, but they just couldn't afford all the lawyers. I didn't know there were so many rules with adoption. I'm glad there are nice couples like you who want to adopt babies. I've talked to Cindy a couple times and she says you're super nice. I really liked your letter and pictures. You have two boys too."

Perhaps the picture of our two boys in our letter encouraged Fayth to give her third child the opportunity to still have two older brothers, just with different parents. I got the feeling that fate was on our side. I had questioned whether someone would choose us because we were already parents and here she was possibly choosing us for that very reason. Whatever the reason was, I silently praised us for taking so much time with our letter.

"Yes, we thought it was amazing that your baby could still have two big brothers in our family," I said in a hopeful tone, looking at Jon with a smile. We went on to talk about her two little boys and how hard parenting is. The phone conversation was so different from what I expected. I was expecting Fayth to be immature and skeptical of us. I was expecting to be quizzed on parental issues or personality-revealing questions. I was expecting her to test me to see if I was worthy of her child.

Instead, she was articulate, sweet, and obviously happy to talk to me. She seemed almost grateful for the conversation. It was easy to talk to her and she seemed sure that I should mother her child.

She asked about my opinions on child behavior issues, but not as a test. Rather, she seemed to be asking for advice about her boys, knowing that I also had two boys. I gathered from what she said—as a single, twenty-one-year-old mother with no relatives nearby—that their behavior was challenging. She was clearly exhausted and the pregnancy made it even worse.

"I can't wait for this pregnancy to be over. You know I don't have much time left, right?" she asked as if I didn't know. I chose not to tell her that it was all I had thought about over the last three days.

"Yes, Cindy mentioned that. It's so exciting," I said.

"I chose y'all because your letter touched my heart," Fayth said. "None of the other ten letters I read seemed right for my baby. Cindy really likes y'all too."

As the conversation went on, we got to know each other as women, as mothers, and maybe eventually as friends. I kept hoping to get some background information on her, but she just seemed to want advice. I didn't want her to feel pressured to answer lots of personal questions at this point.

Finally, after about twenty minutes, she told me about her past, including leaving Texas to get away from an abusive boyfriend, who was the father of her boys. She moved to

Missouri, where her sister lived in another nearby town and where the welfare benefits are better than in Texas. She also mentioned her brief relationship with her baby's birth father whom she met at a drug rehabilitation facility. That got my attention.

Both Cindy and Roland had advised us that we might expect to hear from troubled birth mothers who needed to give up their child for various reasons, so I wasn't altogether shocked when Fayth brought this up. I just needed to find out more information from her before we made any decisions. In the lengthy questionnaire from Cindy, we had answered the question about whether we'd take a "drug baby" with a "no," but it wasn't yet clear if that was the case with Fayth. We would have to know if she stayed off drugs during the pregnancy. Our main concern was the baby's health. I was relieved that she was already being very honest with me. My muscles tightened as I listened closely.

"Yes, I went into rehab only three days after movin' to Missouri about a year ago," Fayth said. "I had to give up my children for those four months, so I was real motivated to stay clean. I was lost without my boys. The nurses did random drug tests while I was in rehab and the tests continued after I left in September to make sure I was a fit mother again. I wanted my kids back so I stayed squeaky clean."

I relaxed a little as Fayth assured me several times during the rest of the conversation that she didn't take any drugs during the pregnancy. "Don't worry, I've been to see a great doctor here in town about the baby girl I'm carryin' and I've been takin' good care of myself."

According to Cindy, Fayth had no idea that we *only* wanted a girl and I didn't bring it up with her on the phone. She might have felt differently about us if that were the case. I was certain that she would want to choose a couple that would take her baby regardless of the sex. Unless she had an amniocentesis, she would not know with absolute certainty the sex of the baby. Cindy said that Fayth told her she was having a girl on the first phone call, but we would need her medical records and a discussion with her doctor to prove it, along with understanding more about her.

"That's great to hear, Fayth," I said. "Sounds like you have a healthy baby there. We are just delighted that you're considering giving your child to us. I cannot tell you how much it means to us. Are you sure you're feeling okay about all of this?"

"Oh yeah. I feel great about the adoption plan now. When the Texas family backed out, I didn't know what to do, because I never considered adoption by strangers," she said, "but I looked in the yellow pages under 'adoption services' and called one of the free numbers.

"I liked the name A Loving Alternative—plus Cindy is so nice." Nine months pregnant, before calling Cindy, Fayth was obviously worried that no one was prepared to care for her child. It was astonishing that each of us had such opposite problems.

"Fayth, can I ask you why you are giving up your baby?" I wanted Jon to hear the answer but was afraid to change the nature of the call. It was going so well and I thought she might feel more anxious with two of us on the phone.

"Well, I'm so young and I know what I can handle," Fayth said. "One more baby is just too much for me. Plus, I have a new boyfriend in my life and I want to go back to school. Another baby would not fit in my plans."

"We think you're doing the right thing, Fayth, and not just because you picked us to adopt your child," I said, trying to explain myself in a sincere way. "You seem like a smart, level-headed woman who deserves a chance to do what you want in life."

"Thank y'all so much," Fayth said.

I was content with her story and impressed with her reasons for making this critical choice in her young life. It all made perfect sense to me, so far. I still wanted to know so much more about her. Although the conversation went well and after listening to her, I felt more certain that she would go through with the adoption, I still had many concerns. I had hoped that after the call I'd have all the answers I wanted and would be able to plan our life accordingly, but unfortunately, nothing seemed certain.

I told Fayth that I enjoyed our conversation and let her know our lawyer would be contacting her soon so we could move forward. "I'm so excited about this baby, Fayth. I hope you continue to feel good in your ninth month. We will be talking to you again soon, and both Jon and I look forward to meeting you in person."

We said good-bye and I let out a deep breath. I realized how tense all my muscles had been throughout the thirty-minute call.

"That seemed to go really well," Jon said looking up from his laptop. He never stopped multitasking, but I was positive he had listened to every word.

"Yes, it went amazingly well," I said. "It doesn't sound like she's talking to any other couples or that she wants to know more about us. I think she's made her decision. I need to call Cindy before I get too excited."

Cindy answered right away knowing we would be calling after talking to Fayth. After I told her everything Fayth had said, Cindy cautioned us again about being too optimistic, even though we were the only couple Fayth was considering. She was delighted that we had connected so well on the phone, but she was concerned about the drug issue. "You need to call Roland Blankston, or someone else, for some local legal recommendations," she said. "Someone has to visit Fayth in person to verify that there is a pregnancy."

"I can't believe that someone would call your 800 number, fill out a questionnaire, go through that phone call with me, and several with you, if she wasn't even pregnant," I said. "Are you sure we need to be worried about that?"

"Many women think they can get checks for rent and other expenses from desperate couples before they find out there's no baby," she explained. "It's sad, but we *are* listed in the yellow pages and our phone number is a free call."

Jon and I both knew we should be more skeptical, as Cindy had advised. But it was difficult to do anything but assume everything was fine, even if it might not turn out well. We needed to know who Fayth really was and if her health was as good as she said it was. Before we ended the call, Cindy said, "With Fayth's permission, you need to get someone to get the health records from her doctor and then start some real investigative work."

Since it was still relatively early on the West Coast, Jon made some calls to California and Seattle to figure out how to find a lawyer in West Plains, Missouri. We needed immediate help since we had so much to do and so little time.

"I like Fayth and I liked what she said," I told Jon at dinner that evening. It felt so good to be relaxing over a drink after such a stressful day. "I'm going to believe her and think positively."

Surprisingly, Jon agreed. He had amazing control over his emotions so I was shocked he wasn't more skeptical. "Let's go ahead and think positively. It's risky as Cindy said, but we have a lot of time to change our mind if it doesn't work out."

"A lot of time?" I said, looking at him. "We don't have a lot of time for anything this month. It was already a crazy month and now we're throwing the biggest decision of our lives into the mix. We barely have enough time to eat this dinner." We laughed and tried to discuss other topics, like our plans for the week.

Every topic paled in comparison to our discussion about Fayth. I wondered what she looked like and who the baby's father was. There were so many questions swirling around in my head after talking to her. Throwing caution to the wind, I went to sleep that night thinking I would have my daughter by the end of the month. It felt indescribable. I don't think I would have gotten much sleep that night if I hadn't been exhausted.

Our visit to New York changed course after the phone call with Fayth. I was no longer interested in shopping for clothes for myself while Jon had his business meetings. I was now on a mission to buy furniture for our baby girl. New York had everything and I was so excited about our new impending family member. I was delighted at how much fun it was to look at pink bedding and baby equipment. It was everything I had always thought it would be and would only have been better if my mother had been shopping with me. I felt slightly odd to be shopping for a baby without one in my belly, but after all this time and heartbreak, it was time to start thinking positively.

Ignoring my trepidation, I asked Jon if we dared to start shopping for baby clothing too and he agreed that we should. I was surprised at his eagerness to buy things for a baby we might never meet. We had great fun looking at everything pink and frilly as we walked into several fancy baby stores along Madison Avenue. The weather was perfect and our mood was excellent. We were definitely hooked on the idea of a daughter joining our family. We even started discussing baby names as we walked.

By the end of the trip, we had found some adorable furniture, including a white iron crib with a canopy, but we didn't dare buy anything. We wrote everything down and agreed that when we felt convinced Fayth was going to come through for us, we'd order it all. We also went ahead and bought a darling pink outfit and baby blanket. It felt wonderful to be so optimistic.

As we flew home from New York City, it occurred to me that for the second time in our life together, Jon and I had just had a momentous visit to New York in the month of March. Eleven years earlier, we had returned from New York engaged. This time, we returned home having spoken to the birth mother of our daughter in that same fabulous city. March was an extraordinary month for us and I was eager to find out what more the month had in store for us.

THE LAWYERS

Missouri may be an ideal place to live for people depending on welfare benefits like Fayth, but if you want to adopt a baby from Missouri, you need to follow a complex path and hire lots of lawyers. The administrators at the Missouri Department of Social Services are meticulous about how adoptions are conducted, particularly interstate adoptions. Immediately after speaking with Fayth, we started researching the representation that we would need for the adoption. We were beginning to understand how the Texan family Fayth had originally planned to give her baby to couldn't afford all the legal help required. We needed separate lawyers for ourselves, as well as each of the people involved in the adoption, like Fayth and everyone connected to her.

Given Fayth's imminent due date, we had no choice but to work quickly. I couldn't imagine not being with her when she gave birth to our daughter, so I was willing to do anything to get there on time. I was amazed at how one phone call with Fayth had given us so much hope and such a tremendously long to-do list.

"Lawyers, we need lawyers," Jon sang. We had so much information to acquire before we could consider this adoption a real possibility, but for everything to come together, we needed to act fast, and we needed lots of help. I wondered how we could possibly learn all the Missouri/Washington legal issues while we were also trying to understand whether Fayth and her baby might have health issues. It was extremely overwhelming.

We already had our California adoption attorney, Roland Blankston, on retainer, but because we didn't live in California and the baby wasn't going to be born in California, he wasn't useful anymore. We needed to find attorneys in Missouri as well as in Washington State. Roland recommended someone in Seattle with whom he had worked on several occasions, but he was clueless about attorneys in Missouri.

Through his professional contacts in Seattle, Jon secured a meeting with Eleanor Kenant, one of the leading adoption lawyers in Seattle. She was an adoptive parent herself and had a reputation for being as sharp as a tack. It was another stroke of good luck that she was immediately available to meet with us.

The next day, we stepped off the marble elevator on the thirty-fourth floor of Eleanor's downtown Seattle office building shortly before lunchtime. The office was professionally decorated and the walls were covered with impressive artwork. As we waited in the reception area after informing the woman behind the big, marble reception desk that we had a meeting with Ms. Kenant, I listened to the chime of the telephones and the receptionist's confident voice as she transferred the calls. People dressed in suits walking through the lobby definitely seemed very focused and didn't smile. Clearly most people came to that office with serious problems, but we were there for a happy problem. I felt truly optimistic even though we had so much to do.

After a few minutes, I walked into the empty conference room near the lobby and glanced out the window at the beautiful view of Elliott Bay and the Olympic Mountains. Suddenly, I heard someone call our name and a fifty-something woman approached Jon. Eleanor Kenant had silver hair that matched her gray suit, sky-blue eyes, and a pretty face. She introduced herself as she shook our hands firmly and we followed her down the long hallway to her office and its spectacular view.

As soon as we were seated, Eleanor dove into the issues right away. She described her typical responsibilities in an adoption case and what she charged for her services. She was clearly working on the clock and asked us questions about what had happened so far with this case. I was already emotionally invested in Fayth, but Eleanor wasn't interested in that aspect of our story. She only wanted the facts.

After we brought Eleanor up-to-date on the few details we knew about Fayth and our first phone call, she immediately cautioned us seriously about the risks in an adoption and how it might affect our family. Her eyebrows rose when I mentioned Fayth's drug history.

"We are worried about the drug abuse as well," Jon said, "but she said she was clean throughout the pregnancy and we're not willing to walk away from her yet. We need to get much more information about her."

"You can't trust most people who have been in rehab," Eleanor said. "They can be habitual liars and not even know they are doing it. Even when she seems sincere, you really need to rely exclusively on facts and medical records, if there are any. Leave your emotions out of it."

That was not what I wanted to hear. I hadn't come to her for advice on whether to move ahead, I had come to her for legal advice about how to adopt Fayth's baby. However, Eleanor explained to us that in addition to many successes, including her own adoption, she had been involved in several cases that had gone badly. She didn't hesitate to tell us a series of horror stories. "There was one couple who had spent money on a birth mother's housing, medical care, and their own travel expenses, going back and forth between the birth mother and their own home for six or seven months. When the baby was born, they came home crestfallen and empty-handed because the birth mother changed her mind," she said, her voice flat, "and they didn't get their money, or the time, back."

"Yes, we know a couple who had that happen to them several times," I said. "We had concerns about that scenario with any birth mother, but we feel fortunate that Fayth is so far along already. At least we won't spend months waiting for the birth."

Eleanor continued as if I hadn't spoken. "Then there was the case of the crazy birth mother who hounded the adoptive family for years and years out of guilt or jealousy, we never found out which. You never really understand these birth mothers until it may be too late." I looked Jon in the eye, trying to communicate my exasperation with her attitude.

"Yes, we understand the risks and that's why we're trying to be careful about everything," Jon said. "We know about the good and bad possibilities with adoption, but there are risks with surrogacy as well. Nothing is going to be risk-free. We feel like we have the most control with adoption. It allows us to walk away at birth if necessary."

She didn't acknowledge Jon's comments and proceeded as if she was being paid to scare us away from Fayth. I understood that it was her job to protect us but her method was disturbing. We grew more uncomfortable by the minute as we listened to her warnings.

"I can also tell you about the couple whose adopted baby was developmentally challenged years later due to the birth mother's poor prenatal care. In this case, the couple didn't get enough information before going through with the adoption. I will make sure that doesn't happen to you," she said firmly. "All pregnancies are a risk, even your own. But relying on the goodness of a stranger to take care of herself during pregnancy when she isn't keeping the baby is a much riskier scenario." That time, she looked at us intently for our reactions.

"We're not going to walk away from this until we have all the information we need to make an informed decision," Jon said. "We understand that there are risks and I am extremely worried about all of them. But frankly, we are in a rush to complete our family and this woman, who seems honest, is due soon. It seems appropriate for us to take the opportunity seriously."

Eleanor agreed hesitantly and referred us to Sheila Brocken in Columbia, Missouri, who had an "adoption-only" law practice. She would be representing us in the state of Missouri since we needed lawyers in both states. "I have worked with Sheila before and she's very capable," Eleanor said. She then described the complex interstate adoption process in general and what was going to happen in the next couple of weeks, if we moved quickly.

While we were there, Eleanor's assistant was able to coordinate a conference call with Sheila Brocken the next day and we all cleared our schedules. After signing a contract and paying Eleanor's retainer, we left. I was not excited about having to return the next day.

I would have liked to find another lawyer with more optimism and compassion, but time was of the essence and Jon appreciated her cautious approach. "We need someone who's looking out for us and protecting our interests," he said. "We don't want someone who just agrees with us and tells us what we want to hear."

"She didn't even talk about the upside of adoption," I said. "What about the parents out there who have successfully adopted children and are thrilled? She could have at least mentioned one of those."

"She did. She said she was happy she adopted," Jon said, referring to the brief conversation we'd had about her family photos. "We need someone like her to help us make decisions."

"Well, she didn't seem very happy for herself or for us," I said.

The next day, we sat in Eleanor's office waiting for Sheila Brocken to pick up our call. I had no idea what the next couple of weeks would hold for us. We weren't used to doing something so important without any experience.

We had been in law offices before and they were all pretty much the same, with framed law degrees on the wall and thick law books on the wooden bookshelves. That day, I had more time to look around Eleanor's office and noticed more details than the day before. The carpet, walls, and chairs were covered in dark, drab colors. There were a few contemporary pieces of art sitting on the shelves and a picture of a man in his twenties; she had said yesterday that it was her adopted son. I decided it all reflected her personality quite well and felt a chill in the room as we sat and waited for Sheila's assistant to connect us.

Eleanor's pessimistic view of adoption bothered me the most. She had mentioned how happy she was that she had adopted her son, but because she had seen some couples dealing with so much disappointment, she showed us no enthusiasm. It was all business for her. She might as well have been orchestrating corporate mergers and acquisitions, rather than helping parents adopt children.

When Sheila Brocken picked up the phone in Columbia, Missouri, I snapped to attention. I looked at the speakerphone and hoped Sheila was a positive person who would allow us to be excited and optimistic about Fayth's baby. I listened intently to her calming voice as she started the conversation.

Sheila introduced herself as an attorney and a professor at the University of Missouri. Eleanor introduced us, gave her some background on our situation, and asked if she had time to work on our behalf. She thankfully agreed, especially because it looked like a short-lived case, and discussed her fees briefly. She then asked if we were ready to move forward. Jon nodded at Eleanor and that quickly, Sheila became our third lawyer.

"It sounds like what you need is someone to go visit this little lady in West Plains right away," Sheila said. "It's about a four-hour drive from here, so I'd like to find someone in West Plains who can assist me with the face-to-face issues and work on your behalf. That person would go visit Fayth and have her sign releases so we can get her medical records. With someone there, we can gain some understanding of her background, see the environment she lives in, and look at the health of her family."

We agreed with her plan. Sheila did not know anyone who lived in West Plains, but she did know an attorney who lived nearby. "Let me see if I can reach him right now," she said, putting us on hold.

Our fourth lawyer, Orson Shiller, came from a small town outside West Plains, Missouri, called Thayer. He was the former district attorney in West Plains, so he knew the town well. Sheila knew Orson because his daughter had taken some of her law classes at the University of Missouri.

We wondered if West Plains was so remote that no lawyers lived there. The population was less than 10,000. "I'm sure there are lawyers there," Sheila said, "but we are lucky to find someone with Orson's background who is available to meet with Fayth immediately. While you contact him, I will work on the paperwork and compare Washington State adoption laws with Missouri's. Please give him a call right away." We thanked Sheila for his number and her help. I liked her very much. She may have been thinking some of the same thoughts as Eleanor, but refrained from frightening us with tales of ill-fated adoptions.

After just a few minutes of conversation, Orson Shiller sounded perfect for the job. He understood everything we needed him to do; clearly, he had done this kind of work before. Orson promised to call Fayth and set up a meeting with her as soon as possible. Fayth had told Cindy that she was anxious to start the process as well, since the birth was approaching, and she did not want a second couple to back out. I thought it was a good sign that Fayth was as concerned about us as we were about her. I was hopeful that we were all in the situation together for the right reasons and would stick to our commitments, especially Fayth.

We received constant status reports via email from Orson. My husband called him "Barnaby Jones," the television private detective played by Buddy Ebsen back in the late 1970s. Like Barnaby, Orson had a knack for getting the information we needed in any way he could, and in a small town, apparently anything goes.

Without a phone of her own, Fayth was hard to reach. Wasting no time, Orson stopped by Fayth's house but she wasn't home. He had to rely on her neighbor, Doris, to get a message to her. I wondered where a pregnant woman with two toddlers would go without a car. Orson sweet-talked Doris into letting Fayth use her phone when he called that evening.

He finally talked to Fayth, who had been at the doctor that morning, and set a meeting with her for 4:00 p.m. the following day. Based on instructions from Sheila Brocken, we told Orson what he needed to do during that meeting. I had also asked him to take Fayth's picture. I was, of course, anxious to see what she looked like. Cindy had described her to us briefly over the phone, based on the questionnaire, but it wasn't much of a description and my curiosity was piqued.

I checked my watch at four o'clock Missouri time, wondering what was happening in Fayth's house at that moment. I couldn't wait to hear the details. Did Orson like her as a person? Was she articulate? Did she keep a clean house? What did her children look like? I had so many questions for Orson, and thankfully, he called right after his hour-long meeting with her.

Orson had only good news. Fayth was very sweet, had a large belly, and had dutifully filled out all of the forms about her and her extended family's health history, explained what she knew about the birth father, and discussed why she was giving the baby up. She gave descriptions of her personality, her goals in life, and her hobbies. Most important, she signed the releases authorizing Orson to obtain the medical records we needed.

"She's pretty cute and very nice," Orson said. "She's not huge for being nine months pregnant, but there's definitely a baby bump. Real nice gal. Had a little trouble with the legal terms and the paperwork, but everyone does. She asked me if I'd help her with all the legal business. I explained to her that you would hire a lawyer [our fifth] to represent her in the adoption and he or she would assist her with all of that."

"Great, Orson, and we'll need the name of someone to do that for her when you have time," I said. "I hope you know a lawyer in West Plains who can be there right away when she needs help. Fortunately, it's a short period of time so there's no need for a long-term commitment from someone."

"I know almost everyone in West Plains, Patty," he said. "This is a very small town. I'm sure I can find someone who can take this on."

"Great, thanks. Can you tell me about her little boys?"

"Sure. They were cute but busy little monsters, especially the older one. I think his name was Koltin. He was constantly getting into things and picking on his little brother. She seemed tired after a long day taking care of them, and it was only four o'clock. The little one, Caleb, I think, is just beginning to run. That's when it'll get real interesting for her."

"That's good," I said. "Maybe she won't change her mind about giving up the third child if she's so busy with two."

"Oh, she didn't seem to be hesitating about any of the paperwork I asked her to fill out. At least for now, she seems pretty sure of her decision," Orson said.

It was music to my ears. "That's a relief," I said. "Did the boys appear to be healthy and normal?"

"Oh yes, definitely healthy, happy little boys," Orson said. "Well, I should run and get the paperwork going before the doctor's office closes. I'll send you everything as soon as I get my hands on it."

Orson drove around collecting copies of Fayth's files from her doctor, the rehab facility, and the county department of family services, showing the releases she had signed to each one. "No lawyer in New York or Seattle would do this much legwork himself," Jon said. He was very impressed with Orson.

Orson faxed the health records to us immediately after retrieving them from Fayth's doctor and we made copies to send to our pediatrician to get his opinion on her prenatal care. Orson also sent us the form Fayth filled out giving her complete health history. It was a lot to read and digest, but I got even more excited about her baby as I read it.

In all the paperwork, one detail caught my attention. When I received the first call about Fayth on March 1, the facilitator relayed the brief self-description Fayth had given them. She described herself as five foot four (same as me), Caucasian (same as me), and red hair (not the same as me). I was still very excited about her baby, even though I really couldn't imagine myself with a red-haired baby.

In the months before this adoption process got started, when I was extremely excited to have a daughter, I wondered how I would feel about a child who didn't look like my family or me. I started looking around at the children I saw in parks, malls, and the schools my boys attended, wondering if I would be happy with a daughter who looked like that child over there—or like that child—or like that little girl. You truly never know which birth mother will choose you for her child, and I decided I was going to be happy with just about anyone, as long as it was a girl.

I thought it would be easier for the adopted child if she looked like her adopted family. She would want to look like her brothers so she would fit in. We all had dark brown hair, not red hair. A redhead would be adorable and wonderful, but wasn't my first choice. I wanted people to be surprised when they found out my daughter was adopted, rather than knowing it just by looking at her. I wanted life to be easy for my daughter.

When I read the papers Orson sent, I was delighted to learn that the "red hair" Fayth had described to Cindy was probably her dyed hair color because according to the form she filled out later, her natural hair was dark brown. It seemed a tad superficial of me, but it made me happy anyway. I got even more excited about this wonderful opportunity. My husband had to calm me down after I ran into his office waving the paper in my hand. "Don't get your hopes up yet. It's too soon," he said. "There's a lot more than just hair color we have to worry about here."

"Yeah, yeah, yeah, I know," I said, dissatisfied with his overly practical attitude. I was feeling extremely fragile and grasping at even the smallest positive details. As I walked away reading more about my baby's birth mother, I didn't get very far when I quickly turned around to show Jon some disappointing information in the faxed paperwork.

The next few pages in the packet were the patient records from a Missouri rehabilitation facility. Fayth was addicted to methamphetamines just prior to her third pregnancy. She had mentioned the rehab facility on our first phone call, but seeing the official details on paper was upsetting.

Jon and I read every word on the unfamiliar forms carefully. Fayth obviously had good intentions when she checked herself into the Southeast Missouri Treatment Center facility in May 2001. She temporarily gave up custody of her two boys during her stay in rehab until her discharge in September 2001. The records indicated that she had admitted herself into the program because of "amphetamine dependence resulting from interpersonal, family, and legal problems."

Fayth's second son was only four months old when the state took custody of her boys. Her older son was only a year older. I had trouble imagining the desperation and misery she must have felt when she gave up her boys, but she was clearly thinking about their safety and welfare. I admired her self-sacrifice. According to the notes the rehab facility nurse wrote, Fayth wanted those little boys back as soon as possible. She worked very hard to change her habits, stay on the education and counseling plan, and promised to follow through with the mandatory aftercare upon discharge to prevent a relapse. These steps were all required to get her children back. She was given random drug testing during her stay and after her departure from the facility. The records we received indicated "clean" every week after her release. Her sons were returned to her in the sixth month of her third pregnancy.

Shortly after entering the rehab program, she met a fellow patient named Cyrus Lansfield. That relationship was apparently very brief, as relationships between patients in the facility were discouraged, but nevertheless, she got pregnant for the third time. To my dismay, the report on Fayth didn't add any details about Cyrus, the baby's father. We would need to rely on our private detective "Barnaby Jones" to get more information about him.

After reviewing the faxes we had received, Jon called Orson to talk more about his first meeting with Fayth. Orson indicated that he asked her several times about her drug use during the visit. "She insisted that she had remained clean throughout the current pregnancy," he said. "She said she never used meth again after leaving rehab and wanted to get her life back so she could finally be a good mother to her boys."

Jon and I discussed this, and although we wanted to believe Fayth, we decided to speak to our boys' pediatrician about the risks involved with meth use during pregnancy. Dr. Doug (everyone, including his young patients, called him by his first name) called us right back to let us know he had received Fayth's prenatal health records that we faxed to him, but hadn't yet had a chance to review them.

"Well, Patty and Jon, I'm happy you're thinking about adoption," he said, sounding a bit surprised.

"Thanks, Dr. Doug. Obviously, this all came up very suddenly. We aren't telling the boys about it yet, so if we end up in your office sometime soon, please don't mention it," Jon said.

"No problem. I won't mention it to anyone. Tell me how I can help, besides reviewing the records you sent me."

"It appears that the birth mother is a recovering meth addict," Jon said. "She claims she's stayed clean throughout this pregnancy, but we're wondering what the risks are to the baby if she didn't."

"Well, I'll tell you," Dr. Doug said, taking a deep breath, "there isn't a lot of data right now about the effects of meth on a fetus. Most of the time, meth-addicted mothers aren't honest about their drug use, so there's very little medical data to go on. The only way to really know if she was being honest is to test the baby's first meconium after the birth, which will indicate everything the baby absorbed in the womb, including drugs and alcohol."

"That's not going to be helpful in our current decision-making process," Jon said.

"Yes, unfortunately, by the time the results would be available to you, it will probably be too late to turn back," Dr. Doug said.

I was disappointed in what I was hearing. I worried Jon would view this as too risky and might want to walk away from Fayth. Neither of us wanted to end up in one of the adoption-gone-wrong stories Eleanor had told us about.

"The main thing you should know is that most drug- or alcohol-addicted newborns turn out fine once they get the medical help they need," the doctor said. "Having the meconium tested is wise, because then, if the results are positive, at least you'll know if the baby may eventually need help academically or physically. It's always better to have that information as parents."

"Yes, information is important," Jon said. "Would you please read over all the records and let us know if you think the prenatal data looks okay?"

"Absolutely," Dr. Doug said, "and good luck."

After we thanked him and hung up, we looked at each other with concern. I dreaded the upcoming conversation.

"What are we getting ourselves into?" Jon said. I had trouble responding. I wanted to remain positive but I knew Jon was feeling apprehensive.

"Maybe she's being completely honest with us," I said. "The baby may be just fine."

We decided to read more about Fayth in the medical records from her obstetrician and found the following doctor's notes:

11-14-01: Patient is here today for an obstetrical ultrasound, active movement from the baby. No deformities are noted and good images are established.

12-6-01: Patient intends to sign over custody of this baby to her mother after birth. This is bothering her quite a bit and she really feels the need to return to antidepressant therapy.

This was shocking new information. Fayth had told Cindy, as well as me, that she was originally giving the baby to "a family they knew down in Texas." She didn't refer to her mother at all, who also lived in Texas.

"I wonder if her mother was actually the one who backed out of the adoption, or more accurately, taking legal custody," I said to Jon. This made sense, because we were told that the family backed out due to legal costs, which were mounting quickly for us. It must have been a hard decision for her mother. "Perhaps Fayth didn't want anyone to know her mother was the one who backed out."

Still, I was curious why giving the baby to her mother would bother Fayth enough to ask for antidepressants. That was back in December and "the family" Fayth mentioned didn't back out until February. It occurred to me that maybe Fayth changed her mind about who would raise her child. We continued reading the doctor's notes:

1-17-02: Patient had missed her previous appointment but is here at 29 weeks.

2-14-02: Patient feels well and her baby moves every day. Will come back in 2 weeks.

3-8-02: Patient is finally here for a checkup. We had some problems with no-shows. Patient is a single mother with 2 young children and no family support or any friends in the area. She has no transportation and doesn't have a phone.

She has decided she is going to allow this child to be adopted, which she had not informed me of before. She is working with an adoption agency and already knows the prospective parents. They live in Washington State. She is trying to coordinate transportation through the adoptive agency and find a nanny to take care of her 2 kids when she goes into labor and postpartum. At this point,

```
she doesn't have anyone to care for
them and has to take them everywhere
she goes. I paid for her taxi today
to bring her to the clinic.
```

It occurred to me after reading the doctor's notes that Fayth had indeed made the decision not to give the baby to her mother even after she promised her otherwise. My guess was that her mother never backed out of taking custody at all and the legal costs were not the issue. I wondered what the issue was and why Fayth hadn't told us. Maybe Fayth's mother was the reason she moved out of Texas. I wasn't sure if I would feel comfortable asking Fayth for the truth.

I had enjoyed such a tremendous relationship with my mother and I felt sorry for Fayth. As I read more of the doctor's notes, I felt sure that her relationship with her mother was not a happy one. During our first phone call, I had wondered why Fayth asked me so many questions about sibling rivalry and other parental issues. It was becoming clear that she had no one else, including her mother, she felt comfortable asking.

I would give anything to have my mother back in my life. Fayth clearly had the option of keeping her relationship with her mother close but had chosen not to. I thought Fayth's mother must have been an extremely difficult person to cause Fayth to give her baby to strangers rather than her own mother, but I wasn't going to argue with her decision.

This was clearly a very sad situation. I felt sympathy for Fayth on so many levels. She was doing the right thing by giving up the baby when she knew she couldn't cope with another child. I just felt bad that she had to make an additional drastic decision, keeping the baby away from her own mother. It took courage to recognize her problems, put herself into rehab, and do what she needed to do to get her life back on track. Deciding who should, and who should not, raise her child took even more courage. Fayth was definitely a strong woman.

At that moment, I felt a little sorry for myself. It was *so* difficult not telling anyone about our pending adoption when I was so excited and worried all at the same time. We were intent on keeping this situation from the boys so they weren't disappointed if the adoption didn't work out. It would be enough for us to endure the pain of losing this child if Fayth changed her mind in the end, or if we changed ours. We didn't want the boys to suffer similar disappointment.

We were a week into our journey and I couldn't even tell my good friends. I had so many good, bad, and frightened thoughts about everything I was hearing about Fayth. Each day brought something else to consider or worry about, but we felt we had to keep everything to ourselves to protect our boys. I wished I could have called my mother who would have been a huge support to me. It struck me as ironic that I really needed my mother, who was no longer available to me, while Fayth didn't want anything to do with her mother, who was alive and well enough to take on an infant.

I probably drove Jon crazy, because he was the only one I could talk to besides Cindy, who was too busy comforting pregnant birth mothers to comfort me. I just wanted this healthy child to be born soon and join our family. It was excruciating. I needed to find the patience to make it through the month. It was a good thing that Fayth picked us when she was nine months pregnant. If she had been any less far along, I might have worried myself to death.

The next hurdle was to find the birth father. Orson Shiller had his work cut out for him on this assignment. Fayth was uncertain of his whereabouts, although she told Orson that he might still be working at a truck mechanic shop nearby, which was where he worked before she met him in rehab. The rehabilitation facility could not give out any information about him. We would need to track him down, hire a lawyer to represent him in the adoption case, and get him to sign away his rights to the baby.

Orson knew it was going to take some real detective work to find him and possibly some convincing as well. I told Cindy I couldn't imagine a single father recovering from addiction would want custody of a baby girl and that this should be "the easy part." But Cindy said, "You never know what might happen with these birth fathers, Patty. If his parents know about it, they can encourage him to fight for custody."

"Why would they want a baby?" I said.

"Different reasons," Cindy said. "Some people think they can get money in exchange for the signature, which is entirely illegal, and some people might enjoy having control over someone like you. That's why you hire lawyers to do the dirty work."

I was relieved not to have to meet the birth father and convince him to sign over his rights. Thank goodness for our lawyers, all six of them.

THE DECISION

Orson Shiller, our eyes and ears in West Plains, had done a great job for us so far. In just over a week, he had found out more about Fayth than I could reasonably ask her on the phone, and he communicated his impressions of her in an articulate way. We felt like we were getting to know her. She seemed to trust Orson and told him a lot about herself. He generally liked what he heard and saw in his meetings with her.

According to Orson, Fayth seemed to be a good mother to her boys, Koltin and Caleb. She had a new boyfriend named Jared Jackstone, who had a construction job in St. Louis, Missouri, but visited Fayth each weekend. She was taking better care of herself, now that she was able to get to the doctor's office on a regular basis. If Jared wasn't in town and able to drive her to an appointment, she called a cab and took the boys with her to the doctor, who paid the cab fare. As the potential adoptive parents of the baby, we would now be taking over those cab charges.

We liked hearing that Fayth was making a responsible decision about the baby, and not just because we were the beneficiaries of that decision. She wanted to do the right thing for her children and her future with Jared, and that accountability meant a lot to us. If she cared about her life, she probably had been making responsible decisions ever since she left the rehab facility. She told me on the phone that she could barely manage the two young boys. She wanted to complete her high-school education, find a job, arrange child care, and get her life back on track. A baby would definitely complicate that plan.

Cindy encouraged me to call Fayth more often while we worked through the adoption details. Our phone conversations were friendly and fairly brief compared to our first conversation but a bit awkward. I was afraid to ask about her mother, which might upset her, and I was hesitant to talk about our life and children. Fayth would provide me an update on her health, the latest doctor's comments, and how often the baby kicked. We would typically talk about her boys, and how she was struggling to keep up physically as she grew bigger.

It struck me that there was such a huge difference between how we were each raising our boys. A single mother raising two busy toddlers had to be exhausting, even for a twenty-one-year-old, but being nine months pregnant probably made it absolutely grueling. Even though, like Fayth, Jon and I didn't have our mothers' help, we had each other. We were also able to afford child care so we could work, volunteer, and enjoy social events. We drove the boys to the doctor ourselves and could afford whatever they needed. We had many friends, and we were all raising our children together. We enjoyed being part of a community at school events, holidays, and vacations. In contrast, Fayth was all alone, had no extra money, and certainly couldn't take vacations, either with or without her children. She never got a break. I felt guilty almost every time I spoke to her and realized how much I took for granted in my own life.

"I'm so big and pregnant now, I can barely lift my baby boy out of his high chair," Fayth said during one of our phone conversations. "My back is just killin' me." Yet again, I felt sorry for her.

"I remember those days," I said. "You must be exhausted. Is there anything I can do for you?"

"No, I just need to have this baby soon. Hope y'all are workin' on the papers to get this adoption done because she's comin' out any day now," Fayth said firmly.

"We are working hard on it, Fayth," I said. "There are a lot of details to manage, and we appreciate your patience with Orson and all the paperwork."

"Oh, that's no problem," Fayth said cheerfully. "I just wanna make sure everythin' goes okay. When are y'all plannin' to come out here?"

"We are hoping to talk to your doctor about that soon. We want to get a better idea about timing based on your last visit. Did he tell you he thought you'll deliver early again?"

"He wasn't sure, but I hope so," Fayth said with a little chuckle. "I can't wait to meet y'all."

I wasn't sure if Fayth really wanted to meet us soon or just wanted some help with the last weeks of her pregnancy. She had apparently requested help with expenses such as rent, food, and bus fare through Cindy. We consulted with Cindy and Eleanor on what we should send to Fayth, based on the adoption rules in Missouri.

Considering what an incredible gift Fayth would be giving us, she wasn't asking for much. I was willing to buy her anything she needed, but there were strict laws in Missouri and Washington about what an adoptive couple could pay for. We also had to keep records of everything we gave her for the final hearing. The courts would want to be sure there was no "baby buying" or bribery involved in the process.

Fayth never wavered in any of our conversations on her intent to give us the baby. She was certain about her decision to give up the baby and that we were her choice for the baby's parents. Based on her assurances, we were working hard and hoped that she would not change her mind about either issue. I was amazed at how easy these decisions appeared to be for her. She thought she knew us and had already decided that we were the best choice for her child.

However, for us, there was nothing easy about the timing, location, logistics, legal issues, calendar conflicts, and emotional stress of the situation. Fayth was due on March 27 and had given birth early to both of her boys. A third baby usually comes earlier than the first two and it was almost mid-March when our final decision was still pending. Every time I thought about it, I shivered from excitement and nerves. While we hadn't communicated any hesitation to Fayth, Jon and I had to decide to go forward with this opportunity or wait for another birth mother who did not have a drug history and who had more prenatal care.

We had serious concerns about Fayth, but we had to consider whether another call from a potential birth mother would ever materialize. Another birth mother may not choose us from the profiles Cindy would send her or she might not be having a girl. Jon and I weren't getting any younger and neither were our sons. We wanted our boys to have a close relationship with their new sister and the age gaps between them would already be seven years and almost ten years. Waiting six months or a year for another baby to come our way would create an even larger gap, not to mention prolong my impatience. I felt lucky that we found Fayth, and throwing that opportunity away might eliminate any chance we had of adopting.

The decision to go ahead with this adoption felt like the right decision. We could still walk away after meeting Fayth or seeing the baby if we needed to, but I dreaded that outcome beyond comprehension. It was always the critical advantage of adoption over surrogacy; we could give up the baby if something went wrong. The emotional risk was the most frightening component.

We consulted everyone who was already involved in the complicated evaluation phase. We spoke to Cindy, as well as to all of our lawyers in California, Washington, and Missouri. We consulted several doctors, including Fayth's doctor and our own physicians, with whom we had personal relationships. Many of them had been through similar situations with other clients and patients, so we hoped they could shed some light on our predicament.

Our Seattle lawyer, Eleanor Kenant, was not supportive of this birth mother or going through with this particular adoption. She felt there were too many questions about Fayth's behavior during the pregnancy and, subsequently, about the baby's health. She wanted to see more consistency in Fayth's prenatal visits. "I have seen drug-induced developmental problems in children whose mother was an IV drug user during pregnancy," she said, "and it's not pretty. Why would you want that in your life? You should wait for another opportunity, where there isn't a history of drug use."

We were only a little surprised by her attitude and recommendation. Eleanor seemed negative from the moment we met her. Although IV drug use was not Fayth's particular problem when she entered rehab the year prior, we took Eleanor's advice with all seriousness. Her job was to protect her clients, and she was trying to do that, but I believed Fayth's rehabilitation story. I decided that Eleanor's attitude was too pessimistic and we couldn't walk away based on her opinion. Jon wasn't as sure that her advice was flawed. "A drug addict is a drug addict," he said. "We have no idea if we can trust what she's telling us."

Sheila Brocken, however, was more supportive. As a leading adoption attorney in Missouri, she had been involved in many adoption cases and she based her opinion on the amount of medical information we had. She seemed very realistic about adoption situations and considered our case encouraging. "There are very few adoptions done in this country where you have complete confidence in the birth mother's history," Sheila explained on the phone. "There aren't a lot of college coeds putting their unwanted babies up for adoption. You certainly have enough positive documentation to go ahead with this adoption if you feel good about this woman. The next birth mother may bring riskier issues that worry you just as much or more."

She was right. We weren't likely to find a situation that was perfect and completely free of risk. At least with Fayth, we understood the chances of a good, and bad, outcome up front so that we could move cautiously through the process. Another birth mother may seem like a perfect candidate and then surprise us at the end of the pregnancy somehow. So far, Fayth was being completely honest about her past.

"This is all good news," Sheila said. "I believe that Fayth was off drugs during her pregnancy, and you have drug tests during and after leaving the rehab facility to prove it. You should definitely stay with this birth mother."

We had never met Sheila in person, but we liked her and her honesty. We didn't feel like she was just telling us what we wanted to hear, even though it *was* what I wanted to hear. There were statistically many more adoptions in the state of Missouri than in Washington, so we felt confident about her experience and opinion.

Cindy told me that she had a few more detailed conversations with Fayth and felt good about how she took care of herself when she knew she was pregnant. "She really learned how to take care of herself in rehab and claims she hasn't touched anything since her release in September," Cindy said. "Even though she knew she wasn't keeping the baby, her initial intent was to give the baby to a family member in Texas, so she was careful all the time."

I was pleased by Cindy's comments, but in addition to believing Fayth was healthy, Cindy was realistic. She had seen many adoption scenarios turn out well, but some also turned out poorly. "If you decide to go forward and at the last minute you decide that the baby is not going home with you, I can have another couple there right away who will take the baby, no matter the reason. You should never feel pressured to do something that is not the best choice for your family."

Cindy's statement reassured us immensely. We did not want to go to Missouri, let Fayth believe she had parents for her baby, and then back out after the birth, leaving her no options. "This has happened before and there are couples in my database who will take a baby in any circumstance, so I will take care of everything, if necessary," Cindy said. "It might not be a situation that Fayth would want, but at least she would have an alternative choice."

I dreaded the idea of getting to know Fayth better, gaining her trust, and then walking out on her. I wasn't sure that I was the kind of person who could leave a woman in her current condition, or worse, after she gave birth, and feel good about it. It would bother me forever. The time to make a decision was before we got ourselves deeper into the relationship with Fayth.

In an effort to make a clear but quick decision, we tried to get more information about Fayth's health history from her obstetrician in Missouri. We wanted his perception of her character and how he thought she took care of herself and the baby she was carrying. Dr. Pete Kyler was not used to strangers prying into his patients' records and was not particularly forthcoming about his thoughts on Fayth's health, even though he knew she had signed the permission forms and we already had his clinical records. He was reserved on the phone and very hesitant to answer our questions. He mostly answered with grunts or yes/no responses.

The only new concern that resulted from our call with Fayth's doctor was that Fayth hadn't had an HIV blood test. Our doctors had told us that an HIV baby would potentially have a lot more health problems than a drug-addicted baby. Fayth hadn't refused to take the test but the test wasn't part of the prenatal test regimen, so she would have had to ask for it. I remember mentally adding yet another issue to worry about, but refrained from panicking.

Dr. Kyler was unhappy with the number of prenatal appointments Fayth had missed due to transportation issues. He was concerned that if she did go into labor early, the baby would come quickly, and potentially in her home with no medical supervision. I couldn't imagine that happening. "I like to keep a watchful eye on my patients, and Fayth had made this very difficult for me," he said sternly. "She needs someone to help her with those kids and do what's important for this baby." He clearly was not one of her biggest fans, so we resisted relying on his opinions too much in our decision process.

During his regular checkup, Jon spoke to his own doctor about our dilemma. After Jon mentioned some of the issues we were facing with Fayth, his doctor advised him against going through with the adoption. He said that in addition to the drug question, alcoholism could follow a meth addiction and that was also risky to the baby during pregnancy. We hadn't even thought about or discussed alcoholism with her, or anyone else. There was nothing in her records about it, but it didn't matter to Jon's doctor. "Too risky in my medical opinion," he said to Jon. "As someone who cares about you, this may just screw up your life."

I believed that Jon's doctor made his recommendation because he didn't want Jon more stressed than he already was. He knew our life was already complicated and busy, and a new baby with serious medical issues would make matters worse. I appreciated his concern for Jon's health, but happiness is one of the keys to a healthy life too. A new baby girl would cause additional stress, especially during the adoption phase and possibly in the first couple years, just as with any newborn, but we were both optimistic about the joy she would bring to our lives overall. Jon assured him that we were approaching the situation logically and would consider his opinion.

We spoke again to our boys' pediatrician, who also cautioned us about the risks. He had reviewed the paperwork from Fayth's doctor since our last conversation by phone and saw nothing to indicate that the baby would be unhealthy. "However," he said, "she has had minimal prenatal care, and those few appointments cannot detect all health issues." There was a recurring theme in every conversation we had.

At the end of our conversation, Dr. Doug said, "You might want to consult some drug research experts to find out what a meth addiction can do to a newborn. They would have the latest data." The meth epidemic in the country was spreading and its effects, both intrauterine and in children, were just being recognized.

I agreed and did what research I could on the Internet right away. By the end of the day, we had a conference call scheduled with an expert on meth addiction at the University of California at San Diego. The patient technician listened to our concerns and answered many of our questions. He was quite informative, explaining that there was only a 4 percent chance of birth defects developing from the kind of drug Fayth had taken before she entered rehab in May the prior year. He said, "Even if the birth mother had been on meth during the pregnancy, it doesn't stay in your system more than two or three days, which is safer for the fetus than many other substances."

All the paperwork from the rehab facility, including follow-up exams, stated that there was no trace of drug use. With the records from rehab and the Social Services tests since then, we had a lot of evidence of her lack of drug use. Based on her due date, the baby was conceived on July 5, so logically, Fayth was completely sober by then, having been in rehab for two months. We felt a little better with this information in hand, and thanked the technician for his help. Before the call ended, the technician said, "There is very little documentation to indicate absolute effects on a newborn from meth addiction. If there was an effect at all, it might be on the child's development or the vascular system, but you might not know about it for years."

After all our fact finding and medical opinion gathering, it all came down to either trusting Fayth or not. The medical records and personal information she provided looked reasonable. What she told us, Cindy, and Orson Shiller sounded satisfactory. She insisted that she was conscientious after her release from rehab in September. We agreed that even if she wasn't completely honest, our research experts believed that there was no imminent threat to the baby.

Jon and I looked at each other wondering how we could possibly be talking about adopting Fayth's baby with all the questions still lurking in our minds. Was it a mistake to trust her? Were the risks significant enough to walk away from this child? We had two perfectly healthy boys and a wonderful life. If we did walk, would we regret it forever? What was the right thing to do?

After all the paperwork we had studied, plus Internet research, interviews, phone calls, and conversations we had done in the last week, we needed to make a final decision. We probably wouldn't get any additional, useful information until we personally met Fayth and the baby was born. We were facing fear, uncertainty, and doubt. Should we go ahead? Should we take the risk?

I knew our decision to adopt Fayth's baby, or not, would be an ongoing discussion, even after a decision was made. We could choose to accept the risks and move forward, or walk away and let Cindy find another couple for Fayth. I reminded Jon of the many good things that had happened in March for our family, and especially for me. I would still be unhappy without a daughter and that was the bottom line. I knew I would regret walking away and would always wonder about Fayth's baby, especially if no other birth mother ever picked us. I had a hunch about Fayth and I wanted to follow it. I hoped that in addition to March being a month of past happy occasions for us, this year it would also be our lucky month.

DIVING IN

We decided to focus on adopting this baby. We would go to Missouri with positive attitudes. It was a joyous feeling, but we felt like we made the decision based on few facts and lots of emotion. Jon and I were always a good team when it came to making decisions, but we felt like this one was the biggest and riskiest decision we had ever made. Even if we returned from Missouri empty-handed at the end of the month, we agreed that at that moment, moving forward was the right thing to do. I was overwhelmed, scared, happy, nervous, and excited, all at the same time.

We didn't have time to relax and enjoy the moment, or think about the risk issues anymore. Our baby girl's due date was looming. We didn't have nine months to prepare for this baby, like we had with the boys. We had at most two weeks. There were so many logistics to deal with before this baby arrived, and we needed to get busy.

I was overwhelmed with details and plans. First, we needed to cancel our plans for Jon's birthday party, which, as it turned out, had been scheduled almost on Fayth's due date. We were suddenly scheduled to be in Missouri then. This was not a "big" birthday for Jon, and I had planned a casual party with our closest friends, including pool playing and a sushi dinner. Even though they were our closest friends, we decided we couldn't tell them the truth. We didn't want anyone knowing what was really going on. We were concerned about our boys, no matter what happened in the end, and they took priority over everything else. We had only one dreadful choice: we would have to lie to everyone.

We told our friends that Jon's father, who lived in Philadelphia, had a sudden health issue. He was prone to heart issues in recent years, and many of our friends were aware of it. We told everyone that we needed to go visit him and had to cancel the party since we were unsure about our return date. We both felt terrible about lying and looked forward to explaining ourselves later. The truth was that even though Jon's father was in his late eighties, he was in excellent health. We called him to let him know about his "sudden illness," just in case one of our friends called to see how he was.

Earl Lazarus became the first family member who knew what we were planning. His reaction was low-key and a little hard to read over the phone, but that was Earl. He is a sweet man but we usually have to tell him things a couple of times before he reacts. We assumed it would need to sink in a bit more before he could really respond about what we were doing. He promised to keep it to himself and especially not mention it to the boys should the opportunity come up on one of his weekly calls.

As we had expected, our friends expressed great concern for Earl's health. They asked many questions, especially those who were doctors, and everyone wanted to know how they could help. It was excruciating lying to dear friends offering to help us. The only reassuring fact we held on to was that we were protecting our children, which gave us strength.

I also felt incredibly guilty that I couldn't tell the truth to my own father and stepmother, but like the boys, we wanted to spare them from disappointment. My father and stepmother were in California for the winter that year and unaware that we were traveling.

We decided that if the adoption didn't happen we probably wouldn't tell anyone the real story. If Fayth's baby didn't become ours for one reason or another, after all that we had been through, coming home empty-handed would be painful but if we told our boys, they would probably want us to find another baby to adopt. It was frightening to think about starting this entire process again with another birth mother after waiting a few more months, especially with the added pressure of the boys' expectations. Even though it had only been a couple of weeks, we were completely immersed in the project and it was draining. I decided not to think any negative thoughts and we moved ahead with our travel plans.

After canceling the birthday party, the next big hurdle was the imminent boys' weekend trip to Phoenix. Jon had been planning for months to take Micah to Major League Baseball spring training in Arizona with our lawyer (and friend) Chris and his son. Micah loved baseball (and still does), so we didn't want to cancel the trip and disappoint him. The weekend trip was at least ten days before Fayth's due date, if she didn't go into early labor. Unfortunately, all we could think about was what we would do if she went into labor early. I would be in Seattle and Jon would be in Arizona with Micah. This was all very complicated and stressful.

As we considered what to do about the Phoenix trip, Sheila Brocken called us to make sure that we completed another important task before the end of that week. She was calling about a legal requirement in Missouri that could hold up the adoption process. The state of Missouri required an FBI report stating that we didn't have a criminal record. Every adoptive parent was required to send the FBI a fingerprint card. We thought this was unnecessary for such a law-abiding couple, but we agreed to take care of it, thinking it was a minor issue.

Jon looked online to find out what exactly was required. We needed to have each finger individually stamped onto FBI screening cards at a police station or City Hall. Those cards were then sent to the FBI, where it would take a *minimum of three weeks* to finalize the processing. According to Sheila, we couldn't leave the state of Missouri with our baby if this process wasn't complete. In fact, the judge probably would not even let us into his courtroom to finalize the adoption unless the clearance was done.

"Three weeks?" I said to Jon in a panic. "We don't have three weeks. We barely had three weeks when the first call came in."

"I'm sure I can find someone to get this expedited," Jon said calmly. "It won't be a problem. Stay calm. We know lots of civil and criminal lawyers in Seattle who must know someone at the FBI. Let's get the fingerprinting done today so we can get the ball rolling."

We found information about requesting an FBI Identification Record/Criminal Background Check on the FBI website with a mailing address in Virginia, but no phone number to call. We tried the police station near us but they only fingerprint civilians two afternoons a week, so we headed downtown.

As we waited our turn in a small office in the Municipal Building in Seattle, Jon was optimistic about this administrative detail. He expected it to take a few minutes at the Seattle office and as long as he found someone at the FBI office to expedite our case, the authorities in Missouri would receive our cleared status in plenty of time. At first glance, it didn't seem to be a complicated or stressful part of our adoption process.

Unfortunately, that was not how it turned out. After stamping each finger, the woman behind the counter in the Seattle office who routinely handled these forms for people applying for certain kinds of jobs said, "It will be a minimum of three weeks to be cleared through the FBI after today's fingerprinting process. I will be sending these in the mail tomorrow." These clearance reports were obviously a low-priority task for the FBI. Adoptions were secondary to fighting crime.

"Yes, we understand, but we're going to send the cards in ourselves," Jon said.

"You are?" she said, surprised.

"Yes, this is for an adoption and due to the timing of the baby's birth, we don't have three weeks to wait. So we'll need to get this expedited via FedEx overnight . . . unless you have a way to expedite this for us? We're willing to pay the extra costs."

"No, sir, I don't," she said, handing us the fingerprint cards. "Good luck." Her manner was abrupt, almost as if she was offended. This appeared to be the first time anyone had taken part of her job away by submitting the cards themselves, but we didn't have the time to wait for the US Postal Service to deliver our documents all the way across the country. She showed no compassion for our situation and made no attempt to help us out. As we left the office, shrugging our shoulders, Jon made a call on his cell phone.

Naturally, this new development made us a little nervous. We had to get this administrative challenge completed quickly and just using FedEx overnight, without someone at the FBI to receive the package, was useless. We needed someone who understood the timing issues to walk these cards through the clearance process as soon as they received them from us.

Jon searched the Internet for other references to these background checks. The only phone number he found for the Virginia office was on the FBI website for Hawaii. He called but there was no answer. He kept calling throughout the day, and the next, but there was no answer, time and time again.

Between calls to the FBI, Jon called various lawyers he knew who were partners in big law firms, lawyers in smaller firms, and anyone else who he thought might be able to pull strings with the FBI. It was painfully disappointing to hear him leave messages for lawyers who were away from their offices. Their assistants all claimed they were either in court, meetings, or all-day depositions, and "could not be disturbed."

Even after the attorneys returned our calls, none of them could help us. They either didn't know anyone or called and failed to find the right person to expedite our case. One of our friends contacted the US Attorney in Seattle but he couldn't help with the bureaucracy at the FBI. I wondered if we should have left it up to the cranky woman in the Seattle fingerprinting office to send the cards through the normal channels. We had wasted two days in an already lengthy process.

I was irritated that Jon had cost us even more time thinking he could beat the system. "This is a government issue, Jon," I said. "You can't beat the FBI system when they aren't interested in making anything happen quickly. We're going to have to wait it out, just like everyone else."

That was when I started to panic. I wondered why Sheila hadn't told us about the fingerprinting right away. We didn't have three weeks. The baby could have been born within one week. Did the courts really expect us to stay in Missouri until well into April? Being away from our boys for a month was simply not possible.

We had to make a decision about the Phoenix baseball trip regardless of the FBI mess. I couldn't bear the thought of Jon and me being apart. The main reason was purely emotional. I needed Jon more than usual during this stressful time, and being left home alone to worry without anyone to talk to was out of the question. There were so many issues to tackle and phone conversations wouldn't suffice.

The other reason was logistical. Missouri was much closer to Arizona than Washington. Based on her history, the odds were that Fayth would go into labor earlier than her due date. We might have to rush to West Plains straight from Phoenix that weekend, and we would need to take all of the baby equipment with us. However, sitting in Missouri for an extra week waiting for the birth was hard to consider with our boys home in Seattle. If the doctor changed his mind about the earlier due date, and we had an extra week, flying home from Phoenix made more sense. It was all so complicated, and the planning (and packing) for all the different scenarios made me crazy.

Two days before Jon and Micah were scheduled to leave for Phoenix, we received Fayth's doctor report on her latest visit over the fax machine from Orson. It read:

```
3-14-02:    Near-term pregnancy, likely to go
            into labor at any time. Because this
            baby is so low lying, I can actually
            see the baby's head through the
            cervical opening of 3cm. Considering
            transportation difficulties with this
            patient, if she hasn't delivered by
```

```
Wednesday, March 20, we will plan to
deliver that day.
```

I screamed when I read it. He could see the head! He said "likely to go into labor at any time"! I couldn't believe it was all happening that fast. I wanted to board a plane to West Plains immediately, but knew that was completely unrealistic. I had to be practical. It was only Wednesday and she might not give birth until the following Wednesday.

The baby was definitely coming a week earlier than originally expected, putting even more pressure on us to get ready for a newborn, get our FBI report completed, and get to West Plains soon. We still didn't know if labor was imminent or a few days away. We were in no rush to get to Missouri if the baby was waiting another week, but getting to West Plains would be neither easy nor quick if Fayth's water suddenly broke.

Either way, I was afraid to stay home, so we changed the plan for the baseball trip with only a day to go. We would travel to Phoenix together, the four baseball fans and me.

As we prepared for the trip, I said, "Micah, I will be coming on the trip to Phoenix with you and Dad now. Dad and I are going straight from Phoenix to visit Papa Bear," cringing as I lied to my son about his grandfather. "You will fly home with Chris and Will to Seattle after the game on Saturday, and Jennifer [our nanny] will take care of you and Jake."

"But Mom, we don't have tickets for you to see the games," Micah said, showing sincere concern for my feelings.

"No need to worry, sweetheart. I will stay at the hotel and relax in the sun while you go watch the Mariners," I told him while smiling at his adorable face.

We agreed to hide all the baby equipment in garbage bags so Micah didn't ask any questions when we got onto the airplane. Answering his inevitable question "Why do you need a baby stroller for your visit with Papa Bear?" would be difficult, to say the least.

We had to tell Chris the truth about our trip just in case we were called in the middle of the night to fly to Missouri. He had known about our secret project since writing a letter of recommendation for us in November. He was thrilled that we were making progress and happy to help by flying the boys home without us. Our nanny Jennifer, who would be staying home with our son Jake, was also entrusted with our secret.

Our plan was to fly into Phoenix on Thursday afternoon. The boys would see about three baseball games while I stayed at the hotel and tried to relax in the sunshine. On Saturday evening, after the last baseball game, Chris would fly home with the two boys. Jon and I would continue our adventure to West Plains after one more night in Phoenix, depending, of course, on Fayth . . . and the baby.

I was relieved that I had done some shopping for the trip to Missouri before Fayth's due date moved up. Having even some of it taken care of was a load off my mind, even though there was so much more to do. I had shopped for bottles, diapers, and other necessities, and even indulged myself by shopping for baby clothes. This was probably the most memorable and awkward of my experiences prior to the actual adoption. There I was, standing in Nordstrom's newborn baby girl department shopping for my child, with no baby in my belly. Other people were shopping nearby, but they were either pregnant or probably buying a gift. I felt I was in a different category altogether.

It was so strange picking out clothes for my potential child, who was currently in someone else's belly in another state. It felt beyond awkward, but I had yearned for this opportunity for so long. I pushed myself to get over the odd feelings and just enjoy it. I assured myself that I would feel better and better as life unfolded that month.

We had kept Micah's infant car seat, so we only needed to buy a new stroller and other layette items. We picked out a new convertible stroller so the baby could lie down initially and then move to a sitting position as she got older.

As I packed for the heat in Phoenix, as well as the trip to Missouri (number of days and weather unknown), Cindy called. Fayth had just called her worried that she had been unable to locate a nanny or babysitter to take care of Koltin and Caleb when she went to the hospital to give birth. It would be at least a couple of days.

"Did she call any nanny agencies in her town?" I asked Cindy. "We are happy to pay for it."

"Fayth said there aren't any agencies in West Plains. She asked around her doctor's office, but they didn't have any recommendations. She's unable to come up with any other ideas, except for one. She asked if we could fly her mother out from Texas to take care of the boys," Cindy said. "Are you and Jon willing to pay for that?"

I asked her to hold on and explained the situation to Jon, who rolled his eyes. "Isn't this the mother who was supposedly taking custody of the baby, and then bagged out, or not?" he said in a whisper. I nodded. "Sounds like an interesting woman for us to meet. Maybe we'll get the real story from her in person."

When I told Cindy we would be happy to pay for the airplane ticket, she said, "Oh good. I suggested that we buy her a bus ticket, but apparently, she is unwilling to take a bus, even though it's only a four-hour trip. She will only come if she flies."

I wondered how any mother could be so unreasonable with her daughter when she was asking for her help. She clearly knew that Fayth couldn't pay for a bus ticket, let alone a plane ticket. I assumed she didn't know about us yet. My mother would have jumped at the chance to take care of her grandkids, regardless of the cost or mode of transportation. I was starting to understand this woman before ever meeting her.

Cindy was delighted that we had agreed to alleviate some of the stress on Fayth. She needed someone she could rely on. She thought her mother was the best choice and worth the additional expense. We booked her a flight and purchased a ticket with as much anonymity as possible.

While we were busy with the arrangements for Fayth's mother, as well as finalizing our plans in Phoenix and West Plains, Jon was persistent with the FBI problem. He tried the only phone number he had found several times an hour, all the way up to the day we were leaving for Phoenix. I really regretted that I hadn't insisted on letting the woman at City Hall take care of it. At least we would have saved some of the time he spent making calls, and the cards would have been at the FBI by then, instead of still sitting in our home. He was about to give up, admitting he was wrong, and sealing our fate to a three-and-a-half-week process, when someone miraculously answered the phone.

After he recovered from the shock, Jon explained our predicament as sweetly as he could amidst his frustration. The young woman was surprisingly glad to help us. She told Jon exactly where to send the fingerprint cards overnight, said to address them "Attention Angela," and promised to get the clearance report to our lawyer in Missouri before the end of the following week. When he asked for her last name, she said, "There is only one Angela!"

He hung up, stood up, and yelled "YES!" When he came to tell me the good news, we both breathed a sigh of relief. "Another hurdle conquered by confidence and perseverance," Jon said with a smirk as he put the cards into the FedEx envelope.

"And just a little stress," I said with a grin. "You're just a lucky guy. If you ever need to try something like that again, I'll have to leave town while you work your miracle." I found it fitting that her name was Angela. She was truly our angel.

When we arrived in Phoenix that afternoon, we had with us a bassinet, stroller, infant car seat, and small suitcase full of baby clothes and other necessities. It was odd hauling all this baby equipment around when there was no baby with us. It hadn't really sunk in that this adoption was really going to happen. We had so many issues to deal with, people to meet, hurdles to jump, and mountains to climb before this baby was going to be ours. I was grateful but tense.

It all happened so much quicker than anyone told us was possible. We had received the call just two weeks earlier. I was amazed that this could really be happening. Phoenix seemed like the first real step in the process of meeting our daughter, and it was exciting and scary all at the same time. We were excited to meet our daughter, but scared that Fayth would want to keep her when we finally got to do just that.

"Can you believe we are already on our way to pick up our daughter?" I said to Jon. "It only took forty-five days and now we're going to have a baby less than a week from now." He shook his head and smiled as if he knew all along that this would happen for us.

THE STOP IN PHOENIX

Phoenix was beautiful in March. Not too hot to sit in the sun by the pool or go to a baseball game. As I lay by the pool alone reading my book with headphones inserted and iPod in hand, no one would have ever guessed I was beside myself with anxiety. I'm sure I looked like any other sunbather enjoying the sunshine and fresh air. In reality, my adrenaline was pumping so hard I felt like I could have run all the way to Missouri.

In some ways, being at a resort, resting by the pool, was just the right medicine. I had very little to do all day while the boys were at the baseball game, and I was free to relax and read my book in peace. It was a picture-perfect day with no one bothering me because they were either hungry or too hot. The day was not stress-free, however, and the idle time made the waiting and worrying about Fayth more painful. I sat there in the chaise lounge, listening to kids yelling at each other in the pool and reading and rereading the same paragraph of my romance novel without paying attention to the words. The light reading just couldn't hold my attention enough to distract me entirely from the anxiety.

I was amidst a rapidly moving life-changing experience that yet moved slowly enough for me to analyze every step along the way. I thought about all the work we had done and decisions we had made since the phone call on March 1. It had only been two weeks and we had made good progress to get to that point. Jon and I made a good team. I also thought about Fayth and questions kept popping up in my head. Was her water breaking at that moment? Would she get to the phone at Doris's house in time? Was she still willing to give her baby up now that she was so close to the birth? What if she decided she wanted to keep her daughter? What if she didn't like us when she met us in person? What if she went into labor before her mother arrived from Texas to care for the boys?

My anxiety level grew with each minute and as each concern arose in my mind. Among the other issues, we had to figure out how to get Fayth to take a blood test before the baby came, but getting her to the doctor might be tricky. We didn't want to offend her with our concerns about HIV, but the issue was important to us. I thought about different ways to ask her to submit to the test, so she wouldn't think we were worried about her history of drug use or anything else.

On one hand, Fayth said she hadn't been an IV drug user, so the chances of HIV were lower. However, she admitted that she got pregnant during a "very brief relationship," and we wondered how many of those relationships she'd had. Her former lifestyle was not safe, for her or the baby. When I really thought about it rationally, I couldn't explain why we were willing to take our chances with this woman. She was a stranger taking care of our baby for nine months. I could only pray that she cared about that child half as much as I did.

I was startled out of my thoughts when my cell phone rang. When I saw Cindy's number come up, my heart stopped. "Don't worry, Patty, Fayth isn't in labor yet," Cindy said before I could say hello, as if she could read my mind. "But we do have an issue. Fayth's mother has arrived safely in Missouri, but now she needs to get from the Springfield airport to West Plains. As you'll recall, we had arranged for her to take a bus and again, she isn't willing to take the bus. It's 111 miles away."

"What other choice is there?" I said, starting to think about how to solve the problem.

"Amazingly, Fayth's mother told her to get your credit card number so she could go rent a car," Cindy said, laughing, even though she was serious.

"She must be crazy if she thinks she's getting our credit card number," I said. "Let me call Jon and I will call you right back."

Jon laughed when I called him at the baseball game and told him the story. We knew we had to be flexible when it came to Fayth, but this was beyond ridiculous. First and foremost, we didn't want Fayth or her mother to have our personal information. In addition, we would never take on the risk involved in having a complete stranger driving a rental car under our name. We knew there must be another way to West Plains. Jon called Orson Shiller to see what, if anything, he could arrange immediately.

I resisted the urge to panic again. I was already concerned that Fayth might go into labor with no one available to care for her boys. We were cutting it close with her mother's arrival only four days prior to the scheduled delivery day, especially with Fayth's history and latest doctor report. I couldn't believe the problem this woman had with buses. I vowed to ask her when I met her in West Plains. In the meantime, she was stuck in Springfield until we could figure something out.

Fifteen minutes later, Jon called to tell me we were in luck, again. Orson came through to solve the transportation problem. Coincidentally, Orson's mother lived in Springfield, so he knew several people he could ask to drive Fayth's mother to West Plains. Thirty minutes later, Orson had it all arranged. He paid the doorman working at Orson's mother's apartment building to drive the two-hour trip to West Plains with Fayth's mother. He was almost done with his shift and was headed to the airport shortly. It was perfect.

Crisis averted, I called Cindy right away and she promised to communicate the arrangement to Fayth. I wondered how Fayth was feeling physically and emotionally. I was beginning to see for myself how difficult her mother was and hoped the stress of the impending visit wouldn't hasten her labor. I wanted Fayth to go into labor early so we could get home to our boys sooner, but I also wanted us to be there for the birth. I couldn't imagine missing the birth of our daughter, even if Fayth didn't want me to be in the delivery room. Being there at the hospital and holding her shortly after her birth meant a lot to me.

Cindy called me back to let me know Fayth was relieved about the news. "You should really call her yourself, Patty," Cindy said. "She's feeling worried about the birth and having a friend right now would help her."

"I completely understand," I said with a little sarcasm as I thought about Fayth's mother.

"You need to stay in touch with her and build that trust," Cindy said. "She needs to know that you are there for her."

"I'm just worried about saying the wrong thing or upsetting her every time I talk to her."

"Don't worry. Just be yourself and it will be fine," she said. "She really enjoys talking with you."

I called Fayth a few minutes later. Doris was there to pick up the phone. She was much friendlier this time and knew exactly who I was. She had to tell me that Fayth was huge and "ready to pop that baby out." I chuckled with her, and then she said she would go get Fayth. A couple of minutes went by filled with door slamming, footsteps, and some conversation. Then Fayth picked up the phone.

She thanked me for flying her mother out and wondered when we would arrive in West Plains ourselves. "You know this baby is goin' to come before Wednesday. She's not goin' to wait to be induced by that doctor. I want you in the room with me when she's delivered. You need to be the first one to hold her."

I choked back the emotion. Her comments were so unexpected and thoughtful. She was wonderful. She was so young yet had such a mature way of looking at the situation. How did she know I would want to be there? I hadn't figured out how to ask her if I could be in the delivery room, but now I had been invited. I was a complete stranger and she wanted me with her for that very personal experience. I was touched and found it difficult to find the appropriate words.

"Thank you so much, Fayth. That would mean so much to me. I would be honored to sit with you during labor," I said, moving to a new subject before my emotions could overwhelm me. "I apologize that we cannot be there until Sunday afternoon due to the promise we made to our son here in Phoenix." I didn't tell her that we also wanted a night alone in Phoenix before coming to West Plains. If she went into labor, we would definitely come right away. If not, Jon wanted to spend as little time in West Plains as possible.

She agreed that it was important not to disappoint him. "Does your son know about the baby comin' soon?"

"No, we don't want the boys to be disappointed if something happens," I said, regretting it immediately and silently thinking I would tell Cindy "I told you so" after the call.

"What could possibly happen?" She sounded alarmed. "This is y'all's baby."

I couldn't tell her that we would have to walk away if the baby wasn't healthy or turned out to be a boy. I panicked but managed to say, "Oh, I don't know. The lawyers tell us to be cautious. We are thrilled about the baby and cannot wait to see you." To change the subject, I said, "By the way, you sound terrific. Are you feeling just as good as last week?"

"I'm feelin' real good but real big. I didn't get this far with either of my boys, so this is the biggest I've ever been," she said enthusiastically, "and she's kickin' like crazy."

"I'm so excited to hear that, Fayth."

"Hey, I was wonderin' what y'all are goin' to name the baby. I was hopin' you'd name her after my grandmother Hilda. What d'ya think?"

Jon and I already had a long list of names we were considering and I couldn't quite imagine throwing yet another into the mix. But all the same, I was touched that Fayth felt comfortable enough with me to make the suggestion; to ask that some part of her family history be passed along with the daughter that she had the courage to part with, the daughter I had been dreaming about all these years.

I quickly pondered my answer. "I really do like that name, Fayth, and Jon and I will certainly add it to our list of top name choices." I was grateful when she changed the subject.

"Will y'all be comin' to see us when you arrive tomorrow afternoon?"

"Yes, of course," I said. "We'll check into the hotel and then come see you and the boys."

"What airport are y'all flyin' into?"

I sensed another lie was unavoidable. Because there was no commercial airport in West Plains, we were chartering a Lear jet to the small airstrip there. I wasn't about to tell Fayth that. Cindy had warned us about Fayth's financial hardship and suggested some sensitivity regarding our financial information whenever possible. It saddened me to think that her boys would probably never get to see their favorite baseball team in person, like Micah was at that moment. Since they didn't have a phone, I doubted they even had a television.

"I'm not sure, Fayth. Jon is handling all the travel arrangements, and he's not here now. Don't trouble yourself with all those details. You have enough to worry about," I said.

"Oh, I'm not worried. I know y'all are comin'."

"I really can't wait to meet you and the boys, Fayth. Enjoy your visit with your mother tonight, and we'll see you tomorrow," I said to end the conversation. I couldn't lie to her anymore, and I worried about lying to her face, if that became necessary over the next few days.

We hung up and I breathed a sigh of relief. It was not an easy phone call; none of them was. There were so many things I couldn't tell her about us, including our last name, where we lived, and especially that we would not take a baby boy home with us. Every phone call was risky and difficult because I had to watch every word I said. I assumed that the visit in West Plains would be much worse.

When Chris and the boys left Phoenix for Seattle on Saturday evening, Jon and I checked out of the kid-friendly Tomahawk Hotel located close to the ballpark. The boys had loved their baseball experience and Micah could not stop talking about the autographed baseballs and other paraphernalia he was going home with. We enjoyed how happy he was and smiled at him with love. It made everything we were doing to protect him and Jake worthwhile, including the dishonesty. We pretended that everything was normal during the trip, except that we were worried about Earl. Micah understood that he was flying home with Chris and Will, while we continued on to "Philadelphia."

"Mom, when will you be coming home from visiting Papa Bear?" Micah said.

"Micah, we're not sure how long we'll be gone. We'll be sure to call you every day though, okay?" I felt guilty on so many levels. Micah seemed fine with that answer and we hugged him good-bye.

"Thanks for the trip, Dad," Micah said as he ran off to be with Will. Chris gave us a reassuring nod and wished us luck as he walked away to join them.

Everything was going well and according to our plan, but it didn't feel good. Jon and I looked at each other as if to say, "How could we lie to him like that?" Neither of us could actually speak the words. I knew that the boys would understand once they heard the real story and I hoped they would forgive us.

On Saturday night, the night before we flew to West Plains, we stayed at an upscale hotel in Scottsdale: The Royal Palms. We needed a night of pampering to ourselves, and this was the right hotel for that.

The hotel was luxuriously quaint with beautiful flowering ivy on the buildings and trellises. The drive into the property was lined with perfectly matched boxwood hedges. The pool area was small, quiet, and equipped with comfortable chaise lounge chairs that looked more like beds than outdoor furniture. Our suite smelled of lavender and appeared to have been recently redecorated. The bed linens were dark green and gold, and the same colors adorned the floral curtains.

Dinner that night was relaxed. We sat in the outdoor terrace restaurant, with gas heaters surrounding our table. We talked about our upcoming adventure over a nice bottle of French wine. It was the first time we had been alone since our New York trip and we were happy to know so much more about Fayth.

"Do you feel like you are living in someone else's life?" I said to Jon. "We've been dealing with so many weird issues and problems in the last two weeks; things that I've never thought about."

"Yes, but in some ways, it's a good challenge for us," Jon said. "It makes you appreciate your life that much more, doesn't it?"

"Oh yes, indeed," I said. "No doubt about that. But you've been handling every weird issue perfectly as soon as it comes up. How?"

"Let's just say that twenty years of living in New York helps you face lots of realities you never have to deal with in Seattle," he said with a smug look. "New York is a *real* city with *real city people* living in it."

"Okay, I get it. You're a city boy and I'm just a country bumpkin from the sticks out West," I said. "I think it's because you watch too much TV, Mr. Law and Order."

He laughed. We toasted our future daughter, sipped from our wineglasses, and finished our dinner.

That night in our hotel room, Jon finally grasped what was *really* happening in our lives. We had been so wrapped up in settling logistics, hiring lawyers, and dealing with sudden calendar and travel issues that we hadn't discussed the big picture in depth. We didn't get that nine-month period to let it all sink in like most couples. We were four days away—maybe less—from having our third child.

When we started the adoption process, our expectations had been set for a long wait. The likelihood of meeting a birth mother who accepted us as the parents for her baby seemed far off. And yet here we were, only two months later, about to fly to

Missouri to meet our new daughter. That night, we took the time to talk about everything we were feeling. We assessed our relationship, our courage, and our realistic view of our family's future.

We were about to take a risky step and the pressure really hit Jon hard that night, especially after we settled our nerves and went to sleep. Jon woke me up at two in the morning. It was finally his turn to have an anxiety attack.

Jon jumped out of bed as if he suddenly discovered bugs in it and said, "If we had no children at all right now, the risk would definitely be worth taking. But we have to think about the effect on our boys' lives should something be wrong with this child down the road. This whole idea is crazy."

I was suddenly wide awake and felt sick to my stomach. I couldn't believe what I was hearing. After all that we had been through over the last couple of weeks, I thought this would be the easy part—we were finally about to get our prize. Jon's doubts were real, and they could have been the deal killer.

"Jon, you know there are no guarantees," I said as calmly as possible. "We could have problems with a biological child if I were pregnant right now. We are actually getting better odds with a younger birth mother."

"Sure, you never know, but at least with your biological child, you know how you took care of yourself during the pregnancy and you know your family, your spouse, and your genes." Jon stood at the foot of the bed, gesturing. "What if this child needs extra medical care down the road or is developmentally challenged?"

"Then we'll take care of all of that," I said. "There hasn't been anything we haven't been able to handle in our marriage, right?"

"Sure, but we haven't ever done anything this risky," Jon said pessimistically. "What are we doing to our perfect lives? We have no idea what this woman really did during her pregnancy. Even if she did take care of herself, is she being honest about her family history?"

"Jon, I don't have a great family health history if you want to talk about that," I said. I was thinking of my cousin's children who were burdened with autism, my uncle who died of colon cancer, my father with heart issues, and of course, my dear mother. "Anything can happen to anyone these days, regardless of family history."

"I know, I know," he said.

"Tomorrow will explain a lot," I said, trying to soothe him. "We'll get to meet and talk to Fayth, find out what she is really like, and meet her boys. Right now, we have very little information, and it's hard to get a gut feeling about who she is over the phone or through a lawyer. Please calm down, and let's talk about our options."

Jon brought up all the "what-ifs" that Eleanor had cautioned us about and rehashed the risks that we had read about. Jon questioned whether we would know when the baby was born if we should walk away. He was worried we wouldn't recognize that we had made a mistake until it was too late.

"Jon, I can't wait two years for another child to come along. I'm already over forty, and our boys will be even older than their sister if we wait. Who knows what the risks could be with the next birth mother? It could be worse than what we have now, only months or years down the road," I said. "This is our daughter. I can feel it, and she will be perfect."

I asked Jon to think about all the people who have no background information about babies adopted from Russia or China. We had much more information, and meeting the birth mother would make all the difference.

"Please think about all the wonderful things this child can do for our family," I said. "The boys will get a sister, and you know how lucky my brother was to have me."

"Right," Jon said with a chuckle, sitting back down on the bed.

"Seriously, think about what Sheila Brocken has told us," I said. "This is a good scenario compared to many of the adoptions she has worked on. She said it doesn't get better than this. There are always going to be questions before the birth. We can't wait until we find a situation where everything is completely clear ahead of time. That would never happen, even if the baby was growing in my belly."

"I understand," Jon said. "You're right. This situation is actually better than if it were our natural child. Fayth is twenty years younger and pregnancy is always riskier with older mothers."

"Right," I said, moving closer to him. "She has two healthy boys to prove that she knows how to take care of herself during pregnancy. You'll get to see that for yourself tomorrow. Now, let's get some sleep."

Jon was calmer after our conversation, though I doubted that the discussion was finished. We agreed that we would take it step-by-step and assess the situation as unemotionally as possible to make sure we are doing the right thing. We kissed and I went to sleep, certain that I had a smile on my face.

OUR ADVENTURE BEGINS

As the pilots announced our final approach to the tiny airstrip in West Plains, I looked out the window, taking in the patchwork farmland that stretched for miles in every direction. It was striking and so different from any of the other regions of the United States I had been to. We often flew into desert towns, like Palm Desert or Phoenix, or big cities, like New York, or the mountains for ski trips in Aspen or Vail. I hadn't spent any time in the middle of the country and I had a feeling that this would be a new experience for us in many ways.

We landed at the West Plains Airport, which consisted of one runway, a red Phillips 66 sign above one building that looked ancient, and another building that might have been a hangar. As we got closer, however, it became clear that it was a mechanical workshop full of loose airplane parts.

The pilots were chuckling as they came out of the cockpit to open the airplane door for us. "Well, this looks like a fun place to visit," one of them said. "Are you sure you want us to leave you here?"

We laughed nervously as we stepped off the plane and stood on the gravel tarmac. We waited a few minutes but no one was in sight. It was like a picture taken out of an old, black-and-white horror film. The weather was cool and dark clouds loomed overhead.

Jon mumbled, "What are we doing here?"

The pilot shook his head and said, "I'll start unloading the luggage."

The pilots were unloading our stroller, car seat, bassinet, and luggage as a black vehicle drove up to the door of the airplane.

The pilots looked at us for our reaction. The driver and the car both looked like they were fresh off the set of *Mayberry R.F.D.* or *The Beverly Hillbillies*. I thought it was Andy Griffith himself getting out of the black 1970 Cadillac Eldorado.

"I thought you ordered us a large vehicle from the rental company, honey," I said to Jon quietly. "It doesn't even have four doors, and we have a car seat to use, as well as all this baby equipment and luggage."

"I did ask for a large vehicle," Jon said. "Apparently this is all they have."

"Yes, ma'am, this is our top-of-the-line rental car with leather seats and air conditionin', " "Andy" boasted. "I detailed it myself this mornin'. There'll be plenty of room for your luggage—just look at this trunk."

It suddenly became clear to us that "Andy" was not only the West Plains rental car representative but also the gas station attendant and air traffic controller for the West Plains Airport. That was probably why it had taken some time for him to get from the "control tower" (I use that term loosely) to the rental car.

He seemed proud of the Eldorado and clearly thought we should be impressed with it. He gave us some directions to the main highway and a city map. We thanked him and the pilots and drove off to find our hotel, shaking our heads.

Though the car had an interesting odor and the seats were well worn, it drove just fine. It was completely full, however, and the trunk just barely closed over our luggage. Most of the baby equipment we had brought with us was stacked up on the back seat. It looked like we had just come from someone's garage sale. We found our way easily to the main highway into town.

"The whole town couldn't possibly be just like that airport, could it?" Jon said. I just smiled.

As we drove down the streets of West Plains, we agreed that the town was perfectly named. Like the farmland I saw from the air, the town consisted of flat terrain with simple roads and intersections, and small country homes with picket fences. The map "Andy" had given us was useful to visualize the town as a whole, but there was really only one highway leading from the airport to our hotel, making it simple to find. We decided to try to find Fayth's home before checking into the hotel so we could be prepared for our visit later that afternoon.

Once we turned off the main highway, we found that there was more to West Plains than we originally thought. We saw several small fast-food restaurants, a Laundromat, several two-story office buildings, and in the center of the town, the courthouse. Like many others in the town, the courthouse was old, but it stood taller than all the other buildings, giving it a lofty presence, and had character. I anticipated the day we would be in that building as the judge made our adoption official. And yet we had so much to do before that day would come.

We followed our map to Fayth's address, driving slowly through the neighborhood and looking around. What we saw surprised me. I had envisioned her home many times as we spoke on the phone, but seeing it in person was shocking. It was worse than I had expected. This was obviously an extremely low-income area, with several drab-looking, one-level buildings that all looked the same. Each building had two front doors, two addresses, one driveway, and one front porch. The only differences between each building were the blinds or drapes inconsistently adorning the windows. Some had cars parked in front or laundry hanging on the clothesline out back. Although there was little landscaping, the neighborhood was clean and some kids were outside playing.

We drove slowly past each building, looking at the house numbers. I smiled when I saw the front doors covered by screen doors, which I had heard slamming over the phone several times. Fayth's house had no car in front, but there were several toys outside on the brown lawn.

"Wow," Jon said with a grim tone. I was glad that we had looked around before the meeting and had some time to get over the shock of Fayth's surroundings.

"Let's come back later, after we unpack and have a chance to set up a time to meet with Fayth and her family," I said.

The town seemed to be in a completely different world than Seattle. I was used to seeing green hills or snowcapped mountains in almost every view or a body of water nearby. Clearly, I wasn't used to the Midwest at all, much less the Midwest at the end of winter, but West Plains seemed extraordinarily bleak. There were hardly any trees, and maybe because it was March, there was barely any green at all. It was a stark contrast to where we had just come from. Even Phoenix had lots of green. I assumed West Plains would appear less gloomy on a sunny day.

On the way to the hotel, it started to rain, adding to our dismal mood. The hotel offerings were limited in West Plains, but we chose the nicest available—a Best Western. It was about ten minutes from Fayth's house and had an indoor pool.

We had reserved a "suite," which turned out to be the same as a regular-sized room, but with a high ceiling because of where it was on the top floor. We decided instead to take two adjoining regular rooms. Doing so gave us a place for all the baby equipment so we could actually use the Eldorado's back seat to take Fayth to the doctor, or anywhere else necessary during our stay.

The matching bedspreads and draperies looked like they had been installed the same year our rental car was made, and the carpet felt like sandpaper under our feet. The desk and other bedroom furniture looked like wood, until we got close and realized it was actually plastic. The room had an air-freshener odor, so we opened the window. The hotel maid probably had tried to get rid of a smoker's smell after the previous guest checked out. The room was not comfortable, let alone luxurious, in any way and we prayed that this would be a quick visit. We focused on the comment in Fayth's medical report that read "likely to go into labor at any time."

As Jon started unpacking, he said, "Hey look, the yellow pages for West Plains. Let's see if the ad for A Loving Alternative that Fayth saw is in here."

And there it was, listed under "Adoption" but for some reason, it was listed as "Alternative of Love Adoption Facilitator" with Cindy's 800 number. Cindy had told us that she called her company "A Loving Alternative" so it would be the first number listed in the yellow pages, which would guarantee her more calls from birth mothers.

"Look at that," Jon said, "it's not even the first service listed. I wonder why Fayth chose the second instead of the first facilitator. It's called Act of Love Adoptions and also has a toll-free number."

"Another sign of our good luck," I said.

Jon ripped the page out of the phone book to keep as a memento. "You should call Fayth and schedule our visit," he said. "She'll be anxious to hear from you."

Cindy had been our main source of contact with Fayth while we traveled in Arizona. Fayth could call Cindy if she needed to reach us, then Cindy would call us. I wanted to give Fayth the hotel phone number in case anything happened unexpectedly overnight. I think she knew it was me when she picked up at Doris's house after several rings.

"Hey, welcome to West Plains! So glad y'all are here now," Fayth said. "When are y'all comin' over?"

"Thank you, Fayth. It's nice to be here! We'll be there in a couple of hours, and we can't wait to meet you," I said. "How are you feeling today?"

"Okay, but *really* big," Fayth said. "She keeps kickin' me hard now. I think she's ready to come out. My mother is here now, so you'll get to meet her too when you come." Fayth sounded upbeat and happy, like it was Christmas Eve.

We hung up and started getting ready for the visit. I had gone to a toy store in Phoenix to get something for Fayth's two boys, so we didn't arrive empty-handed. I couldn't believe how nervous I was. I felt like I was about to have an important job interview, which was probably easier than what we were doing.

Fayth had never made me feel like she was evaluating me as a mother or reconsidering her decision to choose us as adoptive parents of her baby. She was clearly happy to have found a couple she felt could raise her baby adequately. Still, I was nervous. I didn't want to say the wrong thing or offend her. We also were under instructions from our lawyers and Cindy to be extra careful about how much information we gave her. We wanted to stay as anonymous as possible and hadn't even given her our last name. Eleanor Kenant had warned us that if Fayth knew our name, she'd be able to find us (and her daughter) years later. I wanted my daughter to make the choice to meet her birth mother when and if she was ready, rather than have her birth mother emerge at the wrong time. It was better to be anonymous, but that meant having to watch our words about who we were and exactly where we lived.

We made a plan to eat lunch with Orson Shiller, who was expecting our call. We gave Orson a call and told him where to meet us, based on a recommendation from the hotel front desk.

When we arrived at the Happy Burger Inn, a man wearing a red plaid vest and a big green button, which read "Happy St. Patrick's Day!" greeted us as we walked in and directed us to the counter to place our order. At the "Order here" sign Jon asked for a cheeseburger cooked "rare," the way he liked it. The plump gentleman in the red plaid vest behind the counter replied very seriously, "Sir, we don't serve burgers rare here. We have medium, medium well, and well-done. No pink allowed."

We looked at each other and chuckled. Clearly, the Happy Burger Inn had rules and we were going to have to follow them. Jon gritted his teeth and agreed on medium, with a Diet Coke. I ordered a salad, which seemed like a safe bet. As we looked for a place to sit, I could tell the visit was already challenging for Jon by the look on his face. We sat down to wait for our number to be called, laughing nervously about how different West Plains was from Seattle. This was definitely a new world to us.

Orson Shiller found us easily and sat down at our table. "Hi, Orson Shiller," he said holding out his hand to Jon.

"How did you know it was us?" I said, waiting to shake his hand.

"You look different from everyone in here, believe it or not," he said. "I get used to figuring people out in my line of work."

We both shook hands and thanked him for his hard work over the last two weeks. Orson was an interesting-looking guy. It looked like he was doing everything he could to keep his youthful look. He was physically fit for a fifty-something and wore a toupee.

"I live a few counties away from here," he said, "in a town called Thayer. I used to be the district attorney here in West Plains. Lots of interesting people here in West Plains, that's for sure."

We offered to buy him lunch but he declined. Orson gave us an update on his last meeting with Fayth, his effort to locate the birth father, and what we still needed to accomplish before the adoption could be finalized.

"Getting things done in this town is much easier in person than on the telephone," he said. "I went by the truck mechanic shop Fayth had mentioned and learned that yes, Cyrus Lansfield, the birth father, had worked there recently. He is currently in jail for stealing a truck."

"Perfect," Jon and I said at the same time, looking at each other.

"So now we are looking at adopting a child whose mother is a recovering drug user and whose father is in jail?" Jon said, rolling his eyes and sitting back against the back of the booth, arms crossed. "This just keeps getting better."

"I went to visit him yesterday and he's quite a guy," Orson said. "Better hope your new daughter doesn't look like him."

"Why?" I said urgently, hoping that Orson had taken a picture.

"He's not a pretty guy," Orson said, not elaborating. "The good news is that he has no intention of claiming his rights to Fayth's baby. The bad news is that he wants me to help him out of his current legal troubles in exchange for his signature on the custody release form. I don't think he can afford a decent lawyer and he viewed me as his ticket out since I want something from him."

"That's not going to happen," Jon said. "I have enough work for you with this adoption and you legally can't represent both of us."

"I understand that. I can find someone to represent him for the adoption, as well as his legal problems. That's not difficult. We do, however, have another issue with him that we need to address," Orson said. "This adoption process is going to take some time, at least a business week. In West Plains, they move you to a prison much farther away, or set you free, right after your initial hearing. Cyrus's hearing is coming up on Tuesday, which is only two days away. This is going to make it much harder to locate him when we need him to sign the papers, regardless of the outcome."

"That's not good," I said. "Can he sign the papers before the baby is born?"

"I'll work on it, but I doubt it," Orson said. "I have a few other ideas too."

It made me sick that the birth father would use his unborn baby as a bargaining chip to get himself out of jail. I shook my head, wondering what else could be thrown at us before the week was out. I got up to get our food at the counter when our number was called, taking a brief break from the drama.

"Now, are you ready for the next problem?" Orson said as I sat down again with our lunch.

I tensed and listened carefully. Orson explained that he had been unable to coax Fayth into having the HIV blood test that we had requested. We had asked him to work on that during the previous week's visit since it appeared that Fayth was beginning to trust him.

"She claims it's not necessary," Orson said. "She's just plain unwilling to discuss the possibility that she has HIV."

This was bad news and I was losing my appetite. It was extremely important to know without question that she was HIV negative before the baby was born. We understood that it was a sensitive issue to discuss with a former drug addict, and we didn't want to offend her. We were hoping Orson could get her to do the blood test so our relationship with her would not be affected.

"So, we need her to agree to the blood test and we may have to threaten to walk away if she continues to decline the test," I said. I wasn't sure I would do that, but it was something to consider in the negotiations.

Jon looked at me and nodded without a word. We finished the discussion of other Fayth-related topics over our lunch. Orson told us he had met a few pregnant, single mothers before and he was quite impressed with Fayth in general. She seemed sincere, levelheaded, and honest. This was a good sign, given that we generally liked Orson and trusted his opinion. We thanked Orson again for his assistance on such short notice and we all walked out of the restaurant together.

"Before heading to Fayth's house, I think we need to stop at the Wal-Mart and buy you a temporary wedding ring," Jon said, pointing to the shopping center across the street.

"What?" I said, thinking I had heard him wrong. "Why?"

"When you got up to grab our lunch, Orson mentioned to me that your diamond ring might shock most people we meet in this town. I don't think you want to go to Fayth's house wearing that."

"Oh, okay. I guess you're right," I said, looking at my hand. I needed to wear a ring indicating that we were married, but it had to be something that didn't scream *wealthy*. I agreed and we walked across the street, after grabbing raincoats from the trunk.

The Wal-Mart store was new and gigantic. People were busy pushing carts full of Easter items, housewares, clothing, and groceries. The smell of pizza and popcorn was overwhelming as we walked past the food court.

We found the jewelry department right away and looked in the glass cases. To my surprise, there was an entire case of wedding rings, each for $8.88. I expected to spend more than that, but these seemed just fine. We picked one out with the help of a lady behind the counter wearing a little green clover pin on her collar. She handed the ring to me and gave me a weird look as I removed my ring, handing it to Jon. I tried the ring on for size. It was perfect: a thin, gold band with some "diamonds" on top. It was the quickest and cheapest jewelry purchase we had ever made. Jon said, "That's the first St. Patrick's Day gift I've ever bought you."

We laughed at the fact that our lunch was more expensive than the wedding ring and walked, hand in hand, back to our car. I put my real ring in my pocket for safekeeping and slipped my new wedding ring on my finger, admiring it. "This is a good choice for today, Jon, but don't get any ideas about where to do your future jewelry shopping," I said with a chuckle.

We drove up the lane to Fayth's house for the second time that day and turned into the driveway. We parked our Cadillac Eldorado and got out. I drew in a big breath. I felt nervous and wanted to make a good first impression, even though we had spoken on the phone. I was also excited to meet her and see what my daughter might look like, since the pictures of Fayth I had seen weren't the best quality.

As we walked toward the front door, I looked briefly at Doris's side of the house to see if she was looking out at us. They shared the front porch and probably everything else in their lives. I didn't see Doris but made a mental note to meet and thank her for acting as Fayth's personal secretary. We knocked on Fayth's screen door and I squeezed Jon's hand.

ST. PATRICK'S DAY VISIT

The door of the duplex slowly opened, and a blond boy, about as tall as my thigh, peered out at us with big blue eyes. We smiled down at him and looked up as the door opened wider. There she was.

Fayth looked just like the picture we had seen from Orson. She had blue eyes, light skin, and a cute nose. Her straight hair fell just below her shoulder and was dark red at the bottom, dark brown at the top. Clearly, she hadn't had her hair colored red for quite some time, which I took as a good sign. She was about my height and, as Orson had said, she was not huge for being nine months pregnant.

She gave us a warm smile and said "Hi" with a cute southern accent. "Welcome to our home!" She stepped aside to let us enter.

We hugged a little awkwardly. I introduced her to Jon, who was standing behind me, holding two large presents. They also hugged, but it looked uncomfortable, given that Jon's hands were full and Fayth's stomach was in the way. We all seemed to be trying to make a good impression right off the bat.

I said, "It's so great to finally meet you, Fayth. You look great! And who's this handsome boy?"

"This is Koltin, my oldest. He's two. And over there," she said, pointing across the room, "is Caleb. He just turned one in January."

"Hey guys," Jon and I said almost at the same time. Koltin couldn't keep his eyes off the brightly wrapped boxes in Jon's hands.

The front door of the house opened into the main living space. It was chilly in the room, which had hardwood floors, white walls, and well-worn window blinds. The living room featured a small couch, reading light, coffee table, an antique-looking easy chair, and a kitchen table.

Caleb was a carbon copy of his big brother, but smaller. He sat in his high chair, which had obviously been moved to the safer side of the table, away from the picture window he had tipped his high chair into a couple weeks ago. I noticed no signs of stitches or bandages.

"We brought you guys some presents, if your mom says it's okay," I said, looking at Fayth for permission.

"Yeah!!!" yelled Koltin who ran over and grabbed both packages from Jon's hands. He shook them both, put the bigger one on Caleb's high chair tray, and went to work on the smaller one. Fayth stopped him calmly and told him to make sure he was opening the right present and to say "Thank you" before tearing it open.

Koltin did as he was instructed, without looking up at us, and seemed annoyed at the delay. I told him he had guessed correctly which gift was for him and Fayth gave him the go-ahead to open it. I assumed he must have heard the little bell on Caleb's toy when he shook them.

Fayth explained that her boys rarely had visitors and had not received very many presents in their short lives. There were some toys in the living room, which was about the size of one of our kids' bedrooms, but not enough to keep two busy toddlers going for very long. Fayth lifted Caleb out of his high chair and let him open his present on the floor next to his brother. He looked over at Koltin and got all the information he needed about what to do with that brightly colored wrapping paper. He started ripping it up as quickly as his little hands could work.

The kitchen had room for only one person in the aisle at a time, especially a pregnant person. We did not see the bedrooms. It wasn't a bad place for $90 a month, but it was small for three people, two of whom were growing fast and one (toddler) who was running most of the time. It was cozy and very clean. Through the big window next to the table, I could see that the backyard looked similar to the front yard but no toys. There was a freshly washed load of laundry hanging on the clothesline.

"This is a lovely home, Fayth," I said as the boys played with their new toys on the floor.

"Thank y'all for makin' the trip here," Fayth said. "I know it's a long ways away from Washington."

The front door opened and a woman who looked a bit older than me walked in. She had straight, long, light-brown hair, green eyes, pale, wrinkled skin, and an unlit cigarette hanging from her mouth.

"Hey Mom," Fayth said, turning to introduce her. "This is my mother from Texas. Her name is Rhonda. Mom, this is Patty and Jon." Jon tried to shake her hand, but she wasn't interested. She was quite a character from moment one.

She said "Hello" in a raspy voice and sat down on the easy chair. She was definitely not interested in a hug or even a smile. Everyone in the room seemed to get a negative vibe from her, but I tried to keep a smile on my face and my focus on Fayth.

We asked lots of mundane questions and tried to listen to Fayth's answers above the noise the boys were making. Rhonda lost interest after about five minutes and walked into one of the bedrooms. The boys followed her.

We took that opportunity to ask Fayth all about the most recent doctor visit, hoping to find a good time to bring up some of the sensitive issues that still hovered over us. She was upbeat about her health and especially about the baby's health.

"She's still kickin' like crazy," Fayth said, holding her belly. "Maybe she'll kick while y'all are here, and you can feel it."

"I would love that," I said enthusiastically. "We can't wait to meet her."

Fayth asked about our two boys at home, just as we overheard Rhonda barking a command at Koltin from one of the bedrooms. There was a loud crash and she swore about something. We giggled nervously and looked at Fayth, who got up awkwardly from the couch, holding her belly. She said, "Shall we step outside? I'm sure everything is fine back there," referring to the commotion in the back bedroom.

The temperature outside was almost the same as the temperature inside, and it had stopped raining. As we strolled out onto the lawn, Fayth looked at our rental car in the driveway and referred to it as "shiny and expensive." I instantly felt relieved about wearing my new Wal-Mart wedding ring.

"We can definitely take you for a ride while we're here," Jon said.

"Great," Fayth said. "I want to take the boys to get some groceries tomorrow, if that's okay?"

"No problem, Fayth. Let's chat tomorrow morning about timing as we have a couple of appointments tomorrow," I said.

"Okay, that's fine. Thanks so much for stoppin' by and for bringin' the sweet toys for the boys. I'm sure y'all need to rest after your long trip out here." We hugged Fayth and wished her a good evening.

As Fayth was walking back into the house, Rhonda walked up to the car from the other side of the house. She reeked of tobacco as she got closer. She took the opportunity to talk to us before we made it into the car.

"You know I wanted this baby," she said with a slight drawl. "This is my grandbaby, and I should get to keep her. I don't know why Fayth changed her mind and chose you instead of me. That baby should be comin' back to Texas with me."

I was taken aback and dumbfounded. She clearly hated the fact that we were in town and standing in front of her daughter's home. At that moment, I knew for sure that the Texas family that had "backed out of the adoption in the ninth month" was Fayth's mother. Maybe there had originally been some misunderstanding about how simple it would be for Rhonda to take over custody, or maybe Fayth and Rhonda had disagreed about what would be best for the baby. After Rhonda's comment, I assumed it was the latter and that Fayth was the one who backed out. I was impressed that Fayth had stood up to such a strong-willed, callous woman.

Having been in the software sales business with Microsoft for nine years, I had dealt with some challenging personalities. I had worked with harsh customers, and some insensitive Microsoft managers, but this was the first confrontation that really stumped me.

I would have expected Rhonda to thank us for flying her out from Texas to visit her daughter and grandsons but clearly, no appreciation was forthcoming. A reasonable person would be grateful that we were offering her granddaughter a good life. She was clearly angry about the whole situation. I was good at conflicts, but I didn't want to make the situation worse than it was or upset Fayth.

Under normal circumstances, I would have had a frank, honest, and curt reply for someone like her, but arguing with her in the front yard was not going to change her mind or attitude. It might have also compromised Fayth's good impression of us. I decided this battle required a delicate, upbeat response and thankfully, Jon left it up to me.

The only thing I said was, "Rhonda, I'm sorry you feel that way. You should know that we are immensely grateful to Fayth for trusting us and giving us this important responsibility. I hope you will eventually understand and appreciate her decision."

My comments seemed to take her by surprise and before Rhonda could rattle off more nastiness at us, Fayth opened the front door and called her into the house to help with something, so we made our getaway. As we drove away, we looked at each other and laughed with relief that it was over.

The adoption had obviously been a source of dispute between Fayth and her mother well before we arrived. I wasn't sure why Fayth would want her mother there after making such a drastic decision about her baby. Clearly, she had no choice regarding who could care for her sons. I hadn't sensed that tension with her mother over the phone but after that altercation, we clearly understood why Fayth left Texas to make her home in Missouri.

"That was just round one," Jon said. "There will be at least three more, I'm sure." We agreed that the next visit would have to be easier than that was. It couldn't be more uncomfortable.

Driving back to the hotel, as we were talking and thinking about Fayth, all I could do was say, "This is so weird. The woman we just met is carrying our child, and we can only hope she will feel like ours when she is born."

"I just hope she has Fayth's disposition, not Rhonda's temper," Jon said quietly.

It seemed like we had stepped into some strange soap opera in a matter of hours. In the morning, we had woken up in Phoenix in a nice hotel, looking forward to our adventure. By the end of the day, we were driving this shabby, old car around this small, peculiar town, and meeting people that we had absolutely nothing in common with, but needed to care deeply about for the next few days.

Under normal circumstances, we would never meet a person like Fayth or visit a town like West Plains. We were figuratively and literally far outside our comfort zone. We had been in places that were much farther away from our home, but in this case, the circumstances made me feel like I was on a different continent.

I knew every adoption journey was different and they all had their challenges. Because we were keeping it a secret, however, we hadn't consulted any adoptive couples before we started the process. I wondered if any of those couples felt as out of place and nervous as I did. Most couples had their parents or friends to commiserate with during the adoption, especially when it was coming down to the wire. Jon and I only had each other and our lawyers. I just wanted to call someone who knew and cared about us and tell them all about Fayth, but I couldn't. We had to be silently strong and have deep faith in each other.

Jon and I talked about our visit with Fayth and her mother and how many times that first day we just wanted to walk away and go home. There we were on a Sunday afternoon, alone in a strange town, away from our family. It started to rain again as we parked at our hotel. I wondered how many days we would have to stay there and got even more depressed. I asked myself, again, if we were making the right decision. I felt entirely responsible for our situation and the burden seemed heavier by the minute.

Fortunately, we were feeling more optimistic about Fayth after meeting her and we had so much to do in West Plains, we knew we'd be busy while we waited for the birth. We were still concerned about the pending FBI reports that we needed before the final adoption documents could be signed. Jon was confident that Angela in Virginia would get them done by midweek. We also had many more lawyers to meet, as well as Fayth's doctor.

We were also still wondering how to get Fayth to the doctor for an HIV blood test. There had been no opportunity to ask her about it at our first meeting, nor did it seem prudent. I wondered if she would be as sensitive about it with us as she had been with Orson. I needed to find a positive way to word the request.

Aside from the blood test results, the biggest of our concerns was the long, painful wait until Wednesday, when the induction was scheduled. Last week Fayth had assured us that she would be in labor early, because she had been so early with the boys. Between her comments and the doctor's written notes, I was convinced we had come to West Plains in the nick of time. But after seeing her that afternoon, I started to wonder. Would we really have to sit in the hotel room for four days, waiting for her call and lying to our kids about where we were? Jon was already starting to annoy me about how early we came to Missouri, and I could tell it would get worse every day.

I had to defend myself. "If we hadn't come out to Missouri right after Phoenix, I would have sat in Seattle worrying that we'd miss the birth because it's a four-hour flight," I said for what seemed like the tenth time. "It's important for me to be in the room when she gives birth. If we waited for the call before coming, I might have missed that opportunity. Third babies often come fast. Besides, the chances seemed high that she would go into labor this weekend. We both read the medical report and agreed that this made the most sense, right?"

"Yeah, yeah," Jon said. "I read it. I still wish we were home."

"But we aren't a couple waiting for our first child. We have children at home who need supervision and that takes scheduling in advance. We can't just suddenly drop everything and run," I said, trying to justify our predicament.

As the afternoon turned to evening in our hotel, I decided that I needed some exercise and told Jon I was going to take advantage of the indoor swimming pool off the lobby. He wasn't interested in joining me.

As I left our room, I noticed the hallway had that "just disinfected" smell, as if they were trying to cover up old cigarette smoke and foul carpet odor. The swimming pool room featured steamed-up windows and floor-to-ceiling industrial beige tiles. I got right in and started my laps. I had the pool to myself. It felt good to wash away some of the stress that had been building since early March and that first phone call. As I swam, I had to remind myself that no matter how hard this all seemed, I would have felt much worse if that call had never come and we didn't have this opportunity.

Later, after a good hot shower, we called our boys. "Your grandfather is feeling better, but we need to stay in Philadelphia for a few more days," Jon lied. At ages seven and nine, our boys were curious, asked more questions, and wanted to speak to their grandfather in person.

Jon said calmly, "That's really nice of you guys, but Papa Bear isn't with us right now. Your mom and I will give him your good health wishes when we see him tomorrow, okay, guys?" I was glad that Jon was willing to lie to them. I couldn't do it anymore.

Feeling guiltier than ever after saying good-bye, we finished unpacking the sweats and other items we packed for this part of the trip. We talked about going to dinner and decided to look for a restaurant. We were sure we weren't going back to the Happy Burger Inn and based on her last suggestion, avoided asking the hotel clerk for a recommendation. The phone directory in our room was no help and we hadn't really seen many choices as we had driven through the pouring rain earlier that day. We drove down one of the main streets and ultimately parked in front of a restaurant over whose front door was a red neon sign that simply read PIZZA. It seemed safe.

With lowered voices, we talked over our pizza about our visit that day and what our boys might say when we brought home their new baby sister. Two rough-looking guys dressed in overalls, with arms covered in large tattoos, approached our table and gave us an unfriendly look. For a moment, I thought they were going to kick us out of what seemed like "their table." We smiled at them and were grateful when they sat down in the booth next to ours without a word. Yet again, I hoped that Fayth would call soon about going into labor so that we could speed up the visit to, and especially our exit from, West Plains.

THE LEGAL BUSINESS

We woke up the next morning to more pouring rain, so we elected not to hunt for breakfast restaurants. The pancake house next door to the hotel looked like a stripped-down Denny's, but it was clean and close.

After glancing at the menu, Jon ordered eggs sunny-side up the way he likes them. The waitress looked sternly at him over her glasses and replied, "We don't serve eggs that way, sir. Would you prefer them over well or scrambled?"

We couldn't believe our ears. Was she kidding? What was with the West Plains food rules? We both laughed, and I said, "Here we go again." The waitress didn't find our inside joke funny and walked away to wait on another table before taking our order.

Over breakfast, we discussed our scheduled meetings for the day. Eleanor Kenant had been unsuccessful in getting Fayth to respond to her letters about the HIV test and some other legal issues. We knew the jargon in Eleanor's letters would be difficult for Fayth to decipher, so we had to be patient and explain the details when we saw her later in the day.

Because we had so many questions about Fayth's health and the status of the pregnancy, we were looking forward to our meeting that day with her doctor, Dr. Kyler. Scheduling the appointment with him had required some begging. Apparently, he was reluctant to meet with prospective adoptive parents, especially if his patient wasn't present at the time. Orson had gotten Fayth to sign a release of medical records so her doctor would be able to discuss her case with us. He relented after several phone calls from Orson and then me, but gave us only fifteen minutes on his schedule. Since Orson had failed to persuade Fayth to get the HIV test, we were hoping that her doctor could help us persuade her. We would have to talk fast.

Suddenly, Jon's cell phone rang. My heart skipped a beat but Jon said, "Hi, Orson," so I knew right away it wasn't Fayth. Jon laughed at me while he listened to Orson and I waited, my fork frozen in my hand. Jon said, "Great work, Orson. I can't wait to tell Patty. Thanks for calling." The call ended and I was relieved Orson was calling with good news.

"You're not going to believe this one," Jon said. "In the manner that only Barnaby Jones could imitate, Orson found himself at a cocktail party last night with the local judge who is presiding over Cyrus Lansfield's auto theft case. Orson used to work with that judge here in West Plains."

"You're kidding me," I said. "Did the judge know who Cyrus Lansfield was?"

"Yes, it's a very small town and this probably isn't Cyrus's first interaction with the law. Orson explained to the judge that Cyrus was the birth father in an adoption case he was working on. Orson asked the judge to continue the case for another week so Cyrus has to remain in town, as opposed to being sent across the state to the penitentiary or set free. This way, it will be much more convenient to get his signature when the baby comes."

"That's amazing. I can't believe a judge can actually do that. I kind of feel sorry for Cyrus though."

"Oh come on, it's not his first offense," Jon said matter-of-factly. "Besides, you're probably doing him a favor by keeping him in the town jail longer along with the mild offenders, rather than with the truly evil crooks in the state penitentiary."

"You're probably right. I can't believe we're even talking about this kind of stuff. Keeping criminals in jail, getting HIV testing—what are we doing here?" I said, sounding like Jon.

"We're getting the deal done, baby," Jon said. "It takes a lot of work and a lot of luck to do something this important. At least we know that after the baby's birth, Cyrus is not going anywhere before the forty-eight-hour waiting period is over."

"Right," I said, trying to take it all in. "The rules for adoption are so precise. It's amazing that a guy like that still has rights to an innocent child when he's not even married to the birth mother. What would we do if he wanted to keep her?"

"Let's not even go there," Jon said. "Let's discuss how amazing Orson is. That was truly a brilliant move."

I agreed and we finished our breakfast just in time to leave for our first appointment, which was with another attorney named Carlos Villagos. After Orson hired Mr. Villagos for us (our sixth lawyer), he set up a meeting to go over the legal proceedings that would follow the birth of our daughter. Mr. Villagos would serve as guardian ad litem or the baby's lawyer. This person had the status of guardian because the "ward" (our baby) was incapable of advocating for her own interests in a court of law.

We drove in the pouring rain to Mr. Villagos's office near the courthouse in the center of town. Parking was easy to find along the curb outside the building, but the channels along the road were full of water from all the rain. I felt like we needed a boat, rather than our big rental car. I certainly needed boots instead of the canvas sneakers I had brought on the trip. I never expected Missouri to be wetter than Seattle.

Carlos Villagos was a pleasant, thirty-something man who had taken on this role several times before with other adoption cases. We sat down on the small leather couch in his office, which overlooked the center of town. Paper-filled manila folders were stacked all over the office and an old Dell computer sat on his desk. This was not a high-tech office by any means, but I did enjoy watching the floating bouncy-ball screen saver as it moved around on his computer screen behind him as he spoke to us.

"I believe Mr. Shiller has scheduled the hearing with the judge for Friday afternoon at 1:00 p.m. We're assuming the child will be born Wednesday morning as planned, is that correct?" he said.

"Yes, but we're hoping the birth will be sooner. If not, the doctor will induce Wednesday morning at 7:30," I said.

"The Friday afternoon time gives us the mandatory forty-eight-hour waiting period after the birth, plus some extra time to gather all the required signatures from the birth parents," Carlos said.

"You understand that you never know how long labor will take, even with an induction, right?" Jon said.

"Yes, I understand and I can adjust the time of the hearing if necessary," he replied, "depending on the judge's schedule, of course. If it doesn't work out on Friday, we'll have to wait until Monday morning for the hearing."

I groaned.

"That would mean that we'd have to stay with the baby in the hospital or hotel here in West Plains for the weekend, right?" Jon said, looking at me as I covered my face in my hands.

"Yes, but let's just hope for a quick labor," Carlos said, reading our pained expressions. "It is her third child, right?"

"Right," I said, "but children can be very stubborn, you know."

We all laughed. "I'm guessing that Mr. Shiller has informed you that each person in this process needs their own lawyer for representation, including the baby," he said in a very official manner.

"Yes, we know," Jon said. "I believe we have paid six lawyers so far since the beginning of all of this. After Orson gave us your name, he suggested another lawyer in town named Reece Brotting, who works nearby, to represent the baby's birth father. His name is Cyrus Lansfield and he is currently in jail somewhere around here."

"In jail, huh?" Carlos said as he made notes on his yellow legal pad. "Interesting."

"So that brings us to seven lawyers," Jon said, holding up seven fingers with a chuckle, "not that I'm counting. I think Orson also hired a lawyer to represent Fayth, the birth mother, as well. His name is Lyndon Pelt. Do you know him?"

"Yes, I do. This town is very small, so I pretty much know all the lawyers in this area," Carlos said, grinning.

Between the lawyers in West Plains, the lawyers in California and Seattle, and Sheila Brocken, who was overseeing everything from Columbia, Missouri, we felt overwhelmed with legal names, locations, and fees. It was a good thing we were keeping track of them in a file. I couldn't help thinking that if something went wrong with the birth, we would have done all of this work and spent all of this time and money for nothing. But it was worth the risk.

Carlos explained in detail the steps needed to get the adoption process completed. Nothing could happen until the baby was born, the moment at which the clock started ticking and the wheels started turning. I couldn't wait.

A forty-eight-hour waiting period after the birth was required before Fayth could sign away her parental rights. Those two days would be the most nerve-racking time for us. I was certain the minutes would tick by like hours. During that time, Fayth could change her mind. Many birth mothers do. I kept wondering how Fayth could see her and hold her, and still give her up.

I felt my stomach tense as I thought about the heartache so many adoptive couples have faced during that waiting period, which varies from state to state. One couple I knew was asked at the last minute to just care for the baby until the birth mother recovered and made her decision (she asked for four weeks). As hard as it was for the couple, they refused even to see the baby unless the birth mother agreed to decide right after the regulation waiting period (seventy-two hours, in that case) and no longer. Forced to care for the child on her own immediately after the birth, the birth mother quickly learned her limitations. Fortunately, she signed the papers after the seventy-two hours. I knew we would also need to be that strong if Fayth asked us for an extension.

We hadn't gotten the feeling that Fayth would change her mind when we met with her or in any of our phone conversations, but we also didn't know her very well. I was sure that many of the disappointed couples we had heard about had been convinced that the birth mothers would keep their promises, and they were probably shocked when that didn't happen. Anything could happen, and we needed to be prepared mentally, emotionally, and legally.

In addition to Fayth's signature, we would also need signatures from the birth father, Cyrus Lansfield, and from Fayth's boyfriend, Jared Jackstone, who lived in St. Louis. Since Jared had no legal right to the baby, that made no sense to us. We asked Carlos to explain why he had to sign.

"Legally, it's always better to make sure that all bases are covered up front, rather than being surprised when something comes up and delays the proceedings," he said. "You never know what the judge may require in court."

"Yes, delays would be extremely unfortunate," Jon said.

"In addition, Mr. Jackstone should sign away any rights to the baby so Fayth can never get the baby back by claiming her current boyfriend is actually the father of the child."

"You mean if she changes her mind down the road," I said.

"Yes, it protects you. Instead of dealing with blood samples and DNA testing, a signature from him now would prevent any of that," he said.

"That's what lawyers are paid for," Jon said, looking at me. "They think of the worst possible scenarios and try to prevent them from happening."

"That's certainly part of our job," Carlos said. "After all the signatures are in place, we will head to the courthouse where a judge will conduct a short hearing to determine if all the documentation is in order and whether you are fit parents. One or both of you will be required to testify."

Fortunately, Orson had instructed us to pack business clothes for that court appearance. I didn't like the idea of testifying in a courtroom, but was willing to jump through any hoop to get my daughter.

"Then she will be yours," Carlos said with a smile. But then he stopped smiling, as if he had forgotten something. "Well, let me be clear—she'll be yours in the state of Missouri. To take her home to Seattle, or even out of the state of Missouri, all the legal paperwork between Missouri and Washington needs to be completed. It's called the Interstate Compact for Placement of Children [ICPC]. That will take at least another two business days after the court hearing. The 1:00 p.m. court time allows us enough time to get the paperwork started before the courthouse closes, so the ICPC should be completed early to midweek next week. Then you can go home with the baby."

For the second time during that meeting, I put my hands over my face. That additional administrative detail meant that if Fayth didn't give birth until Wednesday, we wouldn't be able to legally leave Missouri until at least Tuesday. That meant we wouldn't see our boys for another week. It sounded like forever. I tried to stay positive and hope, again, that Fayth would go into labor much sooner than Wednesday.

I had to remember that nature didn't care what time the courthouse closed on Friday or when we could fly home to our boys. Carlos confirmed that if the hearing happened on Friday afternoon as scheduled, we would still be able to leave West Plains with our new daughter and fly elsewhere in Missouri for the weekend. We could head to a larger city, stay in a real hotel, and enjoy decent restaurants through Monday. We felt a little better about that, even though we would still miss our boys, and hoped that our good luck month of March would get us out of West Plains Friday afternoon or sooner.

Jon's cell phone rang. It was Cindy, telling Jon that he needed to call Fayth right away; she was waiting by Doris's phone for his call. Two clicks on his phone later, Jon said, "Hi Fayth." He shook his head "no" after a few seconds, indicating that she wasn't in labor. I was disappointed, especially given our conversation with Carlos.

Jon said into the phone, "Hold on one second," and put his hand over the phone while he said to me, "She's wondering when we will be coming by. She definitely needs to get to the grocery store soon and hoped we would take her."

"Tell her I'll come pick her up at 1:30 p.m.," I said, assuming that would leave enough time to meet with Fayth's doctor and take Jon back to the hotel to get some work done. He wasn't interested in another afternoon of stress and walking on eggshells with Fayth. I said I was willing to take on the task alone.

We shook hands with Carlos, thanking him for his help and all the information. We said we hoped to see him very soon and went on our way. We left his office and stepped in several puddles on the way to the car. The rain was really coming down.

On our way to Burton Creek Medical Clinic, Jon said that he would work on a spreadsheet to show us exactly when the legal process would be over, depending on the birth and everything that followed it. He said he would also touch base with Eleanor and Sheila on the details we had covered that morning with Carlos, to make sure they were in agreement.

I was relieved that Jon was good at the business issues and that I didn't have to worry about any of them. However, I wasn't so sure that I was very good at handling the emotional issues in return.

THE PANICKING

Jon and I arrived at the Burton Creek Medical Clinic just before our appointment with Fayth's doctor, Pete Kyler. The rain was pouring down in sheets and we were still soaked after walking from the last attorney's office to the car. I really wished I had brought our Gore-Tex jackets from home.

We ran to the door of the medical clinic and walked through the glass doors. It was a stark contrast to the Seattle ob-gyn office, which was located in a high-rise building with new furnishings and a large aquarium. This building was on the end of a one-story strip mall, the beige carpet was well worn, and the chairs had tattered upholstery. The "child-friendly" waiting area was disorganized and gloomy, although I appreciated the fact that they cared about their patients who might need to bring small children with them to their appointments, like Fayth. I wondered if Dr. Kyler was spending his extra money on cab fare for his needy patients instead of on his office.

The nurse that checked us in was confused about why we were there. After she reconfirmed our names twice, she said, "I don't see your name on the schedule. Now, why are you here to see Dr. Kyler?"

"We are the hopeful, adoptive parents of a soon-to-be-born baby of one of his patients," Jon said. "He agreed to meet with us today."

"Oh, which patient?"

"Fayth Wiley," Jon said.

"Oh, there it is. It was scheduled under her name. This is just a meeting and I don't need any medical or insurance information from you, right?" she said.

"Not yet," Jon said, "although some of this adoption business is making me feel pretty sick and I may need a doctor very soon."

The nurse chuckled. "Well, we don't care for many men in *this* particular office, sir."

"No, I imagine not," Jon mumbled as he smiled and walked toward a waiting chair.

After a fifteen-minute wait, we were asked to follow a nurse down the hall to Dr. Kyler's office. We sat in the visitor chairs and giggled at the picture of SpongeBob SquarePants on the wall next to his diplomas. He walked in just as the nurse left us. He was probably in his late fifties and seemed far too serious to have an image of a cartoon character on his wall. "My twelve-year-old granddaughter still likes SpongeBob, and she gave me that to hang on my wall so I'll think about her when I'm working. Obstetricians are on call a lot, and babies never seem to come during office hours, so I've missed quite a few family gatherings," he said. He definitely had a sense of humor.

"Our two boys love SpongeBob too," I said.

"You already have two kids?" Dr. Kyler said.

"Yes, both boys are our biological sons. Now we're here to get our girl," I said enthusiastically.

"You're planning to adopt Fayth Wiley's baby, is that correct?" he said, picking up a file folder from his desk. He brought his reading glasses from the top of his head down to his nose and began flipping pages.

"Yes, we are," Jon said, looking at me with a smile.

"Well now, let me refresh my memory here. Ah, yes, here it is. It looks like we don't absolutely know for sure that this baby is a girl," the doctor said, looking up at me. I sat up straight in my chair and my smile disappeared instantly. "Usually I can do two ultrasounds, one being more detailed than the first, but Fayth missed that second ultrasound appointment recently due to transportation issues. I do believe it's a girl based on the first ultrasound, and I'm rarely wrong, but you never know."

I was sure Jon and I had stunned looks on our faces. I was expecting the doctor to have more conclusive information for us from the second ultrasound. I just figured we didn't receive the results of that test when in fact, she missed her appointment. My mind started racing. All of this effort and emotion could be for nothing. We read the medical documents Orson had sent us, but there was no doubt in our mind about the sex of the baby based on two ultrasounds, the second which was taking place when we were receiving the original medical records. We hadn't even looked for that second test in the records because we were only looking for health problems. Neither of us expected the sex of the baby to become an issue at this point.

I couldn't believe we had been so busy in the two weeks prior to leaving for Phoenix that we didn't even think to double-check that she was having a girl. Could we be going through all this for a third boy? I tried to collect myself and mask my shock, but it was hard to concentrate on what the doctor was saying.

Jon, who seemed much more in control, asked him about Fayth's health. The doctor described her prenatal care, which was not news because we had read all of his comments in the reports. I was hoping he would add more detail. Her care was intermittent given her inability to drive herself to her appointments and subsequently missing a few, and he seemed a little agitated about it. The doctor said he had sent a taxi a couple of times before her appointments and tolerated her two boys while she was examined.

He had other patients like Fayth who needed some extra help with the logistics of trips to the doctor. He obviously cared about her well-being and her baby's health. She had been given all the critical tests and the first ultrasound, as the report stated, so he assumed that the baby would be healthy. He couldn't add anything helpful regarding her diet or vitamin regimen during the pregnancy. He confirmed that she had not had an HIV blood test and that we could bring her in for that any time, without an appointment. He was, however, not willing to ask her to take it.

Because our time with the doctor was limited, Jon moved right into our biggest fear about Fayth's health history. "Are you aware that Fayth was in a drug rehab facility when she met the baby's birth father?" Jon said.

"Yes, I know she had been addicted to meth and had given up custody of her two boys temporarily," he said. "It's still difficult for her to manage those boys, especially in her condition."

"We understand," Jon said. "She told us she was clean when she got pregnant and stayed clean after she left the facility. She told us we should not be concerned about the baby, but of course, we are very concerned. We've done some research, but in your opinion, what are the risks to the baby and what effects might the drugs have if she was using during pregnancy?"

"You really won't know for sure if she used drugs during the pregnancy until the baby is born. You might be able to see physical signs of addiction when the baby comes out or very soon afterward," Dr. Kyler said. It's what we had heard before.

"And what about long-term effects?"

"Drug babies may experience various disabilities as they develop, or they may not. The medical community is still learning about the damage that meth can do," he said. "I wish I could be more specific about the risk factors."

Jon and I looked at each other. Drugs had been our biggest source of worry before we decided to go through with the adoption and we were still worried. The doctor was not helpful.

"So our daughter may not confront any issues, even if Fayth is being dishonest," Jon said. He turned to me. "If we have a problem, we'll get help for her. What else can we do?"

I was pleased with Jon's attitude. He was in this for the long haul. He was meeting this challenge the way he met every challenge. He would solve any problem for his family, using all of the resources he had at his disposal.

I looked at my watch, worried about running out of time with the doctor. The next item on our agenda was Fayth's scheduled induction on Wednesday. Of course, we wanted to move it up. Our goal was to ensure that we didn't miss our

Friday court date. If for some reason the birth took all day on Wednesday, we would miss our Friday hearing and be stuck in Missouri even longer. We knew the baby was ready to come out and Fayth was willing to give birth any day, now that her mother was in town to care for the boys. We also knew this would be a tough sell with the doctor, but it was worth asking.

The doctor originally scheduled the induction on Wednesday because he was going out of town on Thursday. He also wanted to make sure Fayth gave birth in the hospital, not at home without medical care, due to her transportation issues. We were pleased he didn't want to wait until her actual due date a week later, but were disappointed with his reaction to our request.

"I am not willing to push this procedure forward anymore. I would rather let that baby come out when she's good and ready, so Wednesday is the earliest I will induce labor," he said, his tone indicating that he was not willing to bend on this issue. "Now, what else can I do for you?"

"I think that's it, Doctor," Jon said, extending his hand. I shook his hand as well while trying not to show my disappointment. "Thank you for meeting with us." We told the doctor that we would see him at the hospital on Wednesday, or hopefully sooner, and walked out of his office. We had to keep praying that Fayth would go into labor sooner, naturally. We were forced to endure another lesson in patience.

We headed back to our hotel in the dreaded rain. The windshield wipers could not keep up with the rainfall, which was coming down as heavily as the pressure we felt from all we were going through. Not only did we lose the chance to get the induction scheduled sooner but we also may have lost the baby completely. If it was a boy, we would go home empty-handed.

When we got back to our room, the first thing I did was locate the file originally from our lawyer in California, which included everything we had accumulated so far. I started searching Fayth's medical records for the second ultrasound that Cindy had mentioned.

I found only one notation regarding an ultrasound:

```
11-14-01: Patient is here today for an obstet-
          rical ultrasound. This appears to be
          a female child. Patient will be back
          in about 3 weeks.
```

That was good news, but there were no other ultrasounds in the records that confirmed Fayth was carrying a girl. We should have followed up on the second ultrasound. This was supposed to be the fact we could count on regarding Fayth's baby before we assembled an army of lawyers, left our children at home, and stayed in a dreary hotel for almost a week. Suddenly, it was yet another issue to keep me up at night worrying.

Many fellow moms I know believe that when you're pregnant, hormones affect your behaviors and thoughts in unexpected ways and sometimes you say or do stupid things. I remember several occasions during my pregnancies when I lost track of people's names, what I was doing, or where I was going. Although these episodes were only occasional, they were embarrassing, and I blamed them on the pregnancy. After our visit with Dr. Kyler, I wondered if Fayth's pregnancy could possibly be affecting my behavior. How could I have not double-checked the facts on the baby's sex immediately after I first heard from Fayth? What if the baby turned out to be a boy, after all we had been through in the past few weeks? What would we do? What would Fayth do if we didn't take her child?

I felt sick from the additional stress on top of everything else. I picked up the phone and called Cindy's number. She had that calm, pleasant voice that nurses use when you're in labor and screaming for drugs.

"Hi, Patty. I'm so glad to talk to you. How is everything in West Plains?" she said.

"Everything in West Plains is stressful," I said. I gave her my panicked explanation of our revelation at the doctor's office.

She calmly said, "I was told there were two ultrasounds, but you have to know that birth mothers often lie to us to get adoptive couples to take their child. They want us to believe that their baby is very healthy. I'm sure it will be a girl, but if it's not, you do not have to take the baby. My offer still stands to find someone else to take the baby instead."

"I know that, but what about all that we've been through already? And what about Fayth? What would this do to her?"

"I can have another couple in West Plains within twenty-four hours," Cindy said. "There are couples who have been waiting for months and they will be thrilled about a boy. Fayth will be disappointed after getting to know you and feeling good about her decision. But she is aware that it's completely your choice to take the baby or not. I told her things don't always go perfectly for both sides. I'm so sorry that I can't be more helpful at this moment, but accurate information is usually difficult to get in these situations, and you actually have more information than usual. It's a risky business for all concerned."

"I understand," I said, thinking that no one was going to make this any easier or have all the answers for us. After I calmed down a bit, Cindy asked for an update, and I told her about the rest of our visit in West Plains. It felt good to talk to someone other than Jon about everything.

After we hung up, I slumped into the worn-out upholstered chair in our hotel room, putting my hands over my eyes. "I can't believe this. How could we have not asked for more reassuring data, more tests, more anything? We could have paid for another ultrasound or even an amniocentesis, which would have been 100 percent accurate, before we came out here."

Jon said, "You know those tests are only done in high-risk pregnancies and considered unnecessary for young mothers. Dr. Kyler would not have given permission for that test just to satisfy the adoptive parents. Besides, he could barely get her into his office for regular visits before we arrived. Nothing has changed. We're still going to have to wait and pray."

"Should we ask for the testing to be done now?" I said.

"It's too late at this point. We're here. Plus, you don't want Fayth wondering why we are so worried about the sex of the baby. You want her to think we will take whatever comes out."

He was right. The only thing that changed that day was my anxiety level. As I left the hotel to pick up Fayth for grocery shopping, I decided to think positively and move forward. It was the first time I had been in the car alone since we arrived in West Plains. The town seemed even lonelier and more depressing without Jon alongside me. I tried to think about my boys to cheer myself up. I missed them like crazy. It had been five days since I had seen Jake, who hadn't come to Phoenix with us, and it could be another week before we were home again.

I walked in the rain up to Fayth's door and knocked. Fayth opened the door and whispered, "Hello." She slipped out onto the porch immediately, as if she was afraid someone inside the house was going to stop her, and quietly closed the door.

"I don't want to wake the boys because my mother was lookin' forward to restin' while they napped. She's not used to babysittin' and it's wearin' her out," she said.

As she lowered herself gently into the front seat of the car, she asked me to take her to McDonald's for lunch before shopping. As I drove through West Plains, it was hard to see the road through the rain-soaked windshield, especially when I didn't know the roads well.

It felt like I was in an episode of *The Twilight Zone* and the rain made it even more eerie. What was I doing here? Was I living in someone else's life? I wondered if Fayth was feeling as weird about it all or if she was enjoying the distraction from her normal routine. I silently prayed that her water would break when we were together so we could just drive to the hospital and get this all done. The anxiety was starting to get to me, especially now that there was another big question to worry about.

"How are you feeling, Fayth?" I said, pushing my negative thoughts away. "Baby kicking today?"

"Oh yes, she's kickin' all right. The doctor said she's ready to come out but just bein' stubborn and waitin' it out," Fayth said.

"I wish she would move along, because I can barely get through the door now."

"Yes, me too. I can't wait to meet her," I said. "We met with Dr. Kyler this morning."

"That's great," she said. "I really like him. He's so business-like."

"Yes, he is. He really cares about you, which was nice to see. He said you haven't had a blood test yet, because you missed a couple of appointments. Can I take you there tomorrow to do that?"

"Sure. No problem." Her response surprised me after what Orson had told me. I was relieved that she agreed so easily, but then wondered what we would do if the HIV test came out positive. I shoved that thought aside. I couldn't worry about one more thing.

"Great, I'll set that up for you," I said, hoping she would remember agreeing when we got to the doctor's office, and then changed the subject. I wanted to see if Fayth might be having any doubts about the adoption when it was just the two of us. "Your boys are so adorable. They remind me of our boys when they were that age. They were such a challenge but definitely worth the effort. They are a lot easier now. I'm curious why you would want to give away your baby girl when you have two boys. I have two boys and am willing to do *anything* for a girl. Are you really sure you don't want to keep her?"

Fayth seemed like she almost expected that question. She calmly said, "Well, y'all met my mother and y'all are probably not surprised to hear that I've never had a good relationship with her. I just can't imagine that my relationship with a daughter would be any better than the one I had growin' up. So, I only really want to have boys."

I was glad right then that we had flown her mother out from Texas and had a chance to see the entire family picture. If Fayth had told me this before I had met her mother, I might not have believed her.

She continued, "Besides, this baby's daddy isn't in our lives and I want to start my life over with Jared. When I recover from this pregnancy, I'm goin' to go get my GED and then a job; and I just can't do it with an infant around. I know what I can handle. I'm just so glad y'all want to raise her."

"I understand your situation and I am impressed with your goals. Good for you, Fayth. We are so grateful that you have chosen us to raise your baby. Thank you so much for such an amazing gift. I can't even express our gratitude in words," I said, trying to hold back the tears.

I felt so close to her at that moment. She really was our angel. After what we had been through physically and emotionally over trying to have our daughter, I wanted her to know how wonderful she was being. It was a relief to hear her reassuring words and that she sounded as grateful to us as we were to her.

"How do your boys feel about another baby comin' in the house soon?" Fayth said.

I took a deep breath. This was not something I wanted to talk about. I was uncomfortable about lying to the boys about where we were, but telling Fayth we were lying to them would make it much worse. She had asked that question a few days ago on the phone and I was able to give her a vague response and move on. But now that we were in West Plains, she seemed certain that we had told them by now. "We haven't told them yet," I said. "We didn't want them to get their hopes up until a healthy baby is born."

"Oh, she's healthy all right. Kickin' like crazy," she said, as we pulled up to the drive-through window at McDonald's. "I'll have a Big Mac with fries and a vanilla milkshake, and two Happy Meals with nuggets for my boys, please," she said loudly to the speaker box outside my window. Then she looked at me. "What are y'all havin'?"

I declined and drove up to the first window. "So, where do the boys think y'all are right now, if you didn't tell them y'all were in Missouri?" Fayth said.

As I paid for her lunch, I reluctantly explained that we told them we were on a trip to visit Jon's father in Philadelphia, but we were sure they would forgive us when they understood where we really were. She seemed okay with that explanation and thanked me as I handed her the bag of food. I was surprised, and relieved, that she did not pursue the issue any further. I was also glad I had been honest with her.

Our next stop was Wal-Mart to load up on groceries. I was supposed to keep every receipt for the lawyers, even the $12.43 McDonald's receipt. Mr. Villagos had given us strict instructions about what we could and could not pay for.

As we walked through the aisles of Wal-Mart, we noticed the piles of Easter baskets and chocolate bunnies. Easter came early that year and Fayth said, "It'll be so nice that the baby will be here for your Easter celebration."

I took a deep breath as I thought about discussing another potentially sensitive issue with Fayth. Again, I went with the honest answer. "Fayth, we actually don't celebrate Easter. We will celebrate Passover at the end of this month because we are Jewish. It's coming up right after your due date," I said, watching carefully for her reaction.

"Oh that's great," she said enthusiastically. "I'm just glad the baby will have some religion in her life. Y'all know that your letter was the only one I got from Cindy that mentioned religion. That made a big difference for me 'cuz I didn't really grow up with any religion, but I want my babies to have one. That's why I chose y'all as her parents."

My jaw must have dropped to my knees, although Fayth was busy searching for diapers and probably didn't notice. I couldn't believe that the one sentence we added at the end of our "Dear Birth Mother" letter, after a long discussion, made all the difference. We simply wrote: *We will support this child in every way—emotionally, spiritually, and financially.* I was shocked and grateful all at the same time.

I couldn't wait to tell Jon, who would be delighted to finally understand why she chose us. I was so happy that my daughter's biological mother had considered her child's happiness and well-being when making this big decision. I liked Fayth and was even more excited about my daughter, if that was possible. It was the highlight of a mostly grueling day.

Jon and I ended our first full day in rainy West Plains with a phone call home, dinner in a quaint Italian restaurant, and more panicking about timing, blood tests, and a healthy baby girl.

THE WAITING

Tuesday morning in West Plains brought even more rain. Living in Seattle all of my life, I thought I understood rain, but Missouri proved me wrong. I had never seen so much rain come down over such an extended period. There had been constant, torrential rain for hours, and now days, on end. Our adjoining rooms were located on the top floor of the hotel and since the roof was covered in metal, the sound of the rain was constant all night long.

When I looked outside our window, I almost expected Noah's ark to go floating down the street. Puddles were turning into small lakes everywhere. The rain seemed like a metaphor for the anxiety that was threatening to drown us every hour we waited for the birth.

"See, we could have flown out here today instead of two days ago and would have had perfect timing," Jon said as we dressed for another day in West Plains. It was the third time he had brought it up since the day before.

"Come on," I said, starting to feel my anger rising. "We were told she was early with both of her previous pregnancies, and last Thursday, the doctor said she could give birth at any moment. I wasn't going to risk missing it. I had trouble waiting until Sunday to get here, so be happy you haven't been here since last Friday."

Jon rolled his eyes and walked into the other room. We were growing tired of the small hotel rooms, the weather, and the entire situation. We were stuck in West Plains for another rainy, irritating day and had to make the best of it. We hadn't even been there for forty-eight hours, but it seemed like a week. The rain made it all very depressing. I resisted the temptation to call home because that would mean having to lie again. Several friends had called to find out about Jon's dad's health, and instead of calling back, Jon sent emails thanking them for their concern. That morning was one of the occasions I missed my mother the most.

There was nothing to do except listen to the rain and wait. I took another swim in the indoor pool, but we spent most of the morning reading in our room and waiting until it was time to take Fayth to the doctor for the blood test.

Fayth called, via Cindy, late in the morning to ask if we'd be willing to take her to the Laundromat when we went to the doctor so her kids wouldn't run out of clothes when she was in the hospital. We agreed, of course, since she was going to the doctor at our request. It was the least we could do. "Just one more day," we said to each other as we walked out of the hotel.

We picked up Fayth at her home. We helped her carry two large baskets of laundry to the car, in the rain, and drove to the doctor's office. On the way, we talked about how tired of the rain we all were and what tomorrow would bring. Fayth said she was positive that she didn't want to use any pain medication this time and wanted a completely natural birth, except for the Pitocin used to induce labor.

"I admire your bravery, Fayth," I said. "I could never do it." I never understood why women felt compelled to feel the pain of childbirth. I couldn't imagine that it helped them feel closer to the child, but maybe I was wrong. In this case, I wasn't sure why Fayth would want to give birth without pain medication, but it was up to her. I was happy to be talking about the birth "tomorrow" and silently wished the hours away.

The doctor's office visit was quick, and Fayth returned to the car rolling her sleeve down. As she lowered herself into the back seat, she said, "The doctor told me I have to be at the hospital at 7:30 tomorrow mornin'."

"Will you need a ride to the hospital?" Jon said, getting into the front seat after assisting Fayth with the door.

"No thanks. Jared is drivin' here from St. Louis tonight and will take me in the mornin'," she said.

"We're very excited for tomorrow, Fayth. I hope you're still feeling good about everything and the decision you are making about this baby," I said.

"Oh yes. It's definitely what I need to do. I'm not sure I want any more kids after this though. I'm so tired of bein' pregnant after three in a row."

"That's totally understandable, but you make really beautiful children," I said. "If the time is right and you're ready again, you'll make that decision then. It's probably hard to think about right now."

As strange as it may sound, I felt like both a mother mentoring her daughter and a child about to celebrate a birthday, all at the same time. I wanted to do all I could to make Fayth feel more comfortable the day before she gave me the best gift I could ever dream of.

We arrived at the Laundromat. The puddles in the parking lot were huge and deep, and it was still raining. It was difficult to find a good place to step when we got out of the car, especially while carrying baskets full of dirty clothes.

I found it ironic to be doing Fayth's family's laundry when I rarely did my own family's laundry at home. Our nanny did laundry while the boys were at school. It was even stranger to watch Jon helping with her laundry when he'd only stepped into our laundry room to get something out of the extra refrigerator or to feed the dog. I looked at him with a smug smile and he clearly knew what I was thinking.

"Hey, I used to be a bachelor and did all of my own laundry," he said to defend himself. Fayth and I laughed.

This was all beginning to seem like a sitcom, except I hadn't seen the script before acting it all out. The things Fayth talked about while we were waiting for the washer and dryer to cycle through were so foreign to me. We had no idea what life was like without a car, a job, a phone, and a steady income. The money for the coin-operated washer and dryer was a stretch for her and we were happy to help, of course. I worried that I couldn't get a receipt from the machines.

Fayth asked us what we did in Washington State. We hadn't provided her with much personal information, based on the advice from our lawyers. I explained to her that we met when we both worked for the same computer company and that I was currently volunteering for the boys' schools and the local zoo, which was true. We quickly changed the subject and then offered to help fold clothes.

When we dropped Fayth off with the clean, folded laundry late in the afternoon, she thanked us for everything, gave me a hug, and said, "See y'all tomorrow mornin'."

I told her to sleep well and to call us if she needed anything else.

We stepped off the elevator of our hotel and as we were putting the key into the door of our room, we heard the phone ringing inside.

"Hello?" I answered after rushing into the room.

"Patty, it's Cindy," she said in a panicked tone. "You need to call Fayth right back."

"We were just there. What is it?"

"She didn't say, sorry."

I hung up and dialed immediately. Fayth answered Doris's phone on the first ring. "Patty, my mother just told me she's bored and wants to go home. She knows I'm about to give birth, but she's bein' totally crazy."

"Did you remind her of the reason she was flown all the way out here?" I said, wondering how any mother could be that unreasonable.

"Yes, but she doesn't care," Fayth said. "Can you come take me to Wal-Mart again so we can buy her something to keep her busy?"

"I'll be right over," I said and hung up, laughing about this absolutely irrational turn of events as I told Jon.

"She's got to be kidding," Jon said. "If this doesn't make Fayth's water break, nothing will."

"My bet is that nothing will," I said. "I have a feeling that this situation is going to stretch out as far as possible just to torture us. Who would have guessed that her crazy mother would act like a bored child who needs a toy to play with the night before her daughter is giving birth?"

"It is surprising . . ." Jon said.

"I hope that's all it really is because we didn't fly her out here from Texas for a quick weekend visit with her grandchildren," I said. "She has a job to do tomorrow and it's not going to get any easier with Fayth at the hospital overnight or longer. If she takes off unexpectedly, we are in trouble."

"I don't think she'll pay for anything on her own and especially not a ride all the way back to the airport, so don't worry," Jon said sarcastically.

"Unbelievable," I said, shaking my head. "This has been the strangest three days ever. And it just keeps getting crazier. Whoever said adoption was easier than pregnancy doesn't know a thing about it. And we've only been through the easy part of the visit. I'll never make it through tomorrow."

"You *will* make it through this and when that baby arrives, we'll both be happier than ever," Jon said. "I'll stay here and research a place for us to go have a nice dinner when you get back from the errand."

"Any restaurant with a tablecloth would be appreciated at this point," I said with a smile.

I arrived back at Fayth's house within ten minutes and rushed to the door, anticipating being greeted by one of the panicked, emotional women. Luckily for me, Fayth opened the door and already had her purse in the other hand. She calmly walked out the door, holding Koltin's hand. "Let's take him with us and give Rhonda a break for a bit," she whispered. We strapped Koltin into the back seat tightly because we didn't have a car seat for him.

"Cool black car, Mom," Koltin said.

I asked Fayth if she was worried about the lack of a car seat, and she said he would be fine without one. "I'm too old for a car seat, lady," Koltin told me sternly, as only a two-year-old could.

I disagreed with her decision, but it wasn't the time to start teaching her safety rules.

"I can't believe she is makin' all these demands today," Fayth said quietly. "Doesn't she understand how upsettin' this is for me?"

"I don't know her very well, Fayth," I said, feeling like I was walking on eggshells, "but your mother is obviously upset about this baby and the fact that she isn't going to be raising her. She isn't necessarily going to make this easy on you. This is her way of punishing you. She should be showing you that she cares about this child no matter what. I hope it makes you feel even better about your adoption decision. Does it?"

"Absolutely," Fayth said. "I know this is the right thing to do. Look how much more you and Jon care about me, and I just met you two weeks ago over the phone."

Wal-Mart was a scary place to be with a willful, unpredictable two-and-a-half-year-old who didn't get out of the house much. Fayth was in no condition to run after him, so I did. He couldn't make up his mind about which direction was more exciting, so he went everywhere.

First, he ran to the shoe racks, picking up the Power Ranger sneakers. As soon as I got there, he dropped them and ran off again. Next, he darted over to the bikes and scooters. I grabbed his little hand just as he was about to take off down the aisle on a purple monster scooter. Fayth was close behind and tried to give him a stern speech about strangers and how he needed to stay with us. He wasn't interested.

"We need to get somethin' for Grandma, so you need to come with us over to the craft aisle, Koltin," Fayth said. "Then we can go get something small for you and your brother, okay?"

"Okay," Koltin agreed with a stern look, as he crossed his arms over his chest. It was getting easier to understand why she didn't want any more kids. He was a handful, especially for a single mother.

When we arrived in the craft section, I showed Fayth a yarn project similar to the one that I had done when I was pregnant with Micah. She thought her mother would enjoy that.

"She doesn't knit, but this looks easy and fun," she said, picking it up and putting it in the basket. "Okay, Koltin, you can pick somethin' out for $5, but that's it. I will get somethin' for Caleb too."

We returned to Fayth's house around six o'clock. Rhonda seemed pleased with her daughter's choice and the boys immediately got involved with their new toys. I resisted the urge to have a stern chat with Rhonda on Fayth's behalf. It wasn't in my best interest to upset her. Rhonda didn't bother to thank me, but Fayth walked me out the door and said, "Patty, thank you for helpin' me out. I hope y'all still want to be in the room with me when the baby comes tomorrow. It's really important to me that y'all are the first one to hold her."

I swallowed hard. Tears welled up in my eyes. She had mentioned this before, but now, standing here with her the night before she delivered my child, it just meant so much more. I couldn't speak but she understood my reaction.

Fayth took my hand and said, "Thank y'all for helpin' me with my mom, my boys, and this baby. Y'all are the best mom any baby could ask for." I cried aloud as I hugged her tight, and this time, it was a comfortable hug.

As I drove off to the hotel, still crying, I realized how ready I was for a quiet evening with my husband. Every day had been so stressful since we arrived in West Plains. Perhaps it was the rain that didn't let up while we went through the hardest three days of our married life. It was one big, black cloud hanging over us, literally and metaphorically. The rain seemed to magnify the stress, worry, guilt, and exhaustion. I was ready for a change.

Jon told me he had found a French restaurant for us to have dinner at and made sure they had tablecloths. We dressed in our "West Plains finest" and after a call to the boys, we drove to a small strip mall in town.

The restaurant was small but the nicest place we had seen so far. The lighting was low and each table had a small bouquet of carnations in a bud vase, which sat next to a votive candle. The menu was very eclectic and the food was quite good. The chef even cooked Jon's duck medium rare. He was delighted. We toasted to "the last evening before our daughter arrives" and sipped away the worries we had dealt with over the last twenty days. March had been an amazing month and the best part of it was yet to come.

When we got back to the hotel room, the message light was flashing. We looked at each other with eager anticipation. Was it the baby? Cindy had Jon's cell phone number if it had been urgent. He checked to make sure that his phone was on, which it was, and there was no message. Cindy had left us a message in the room to call Fayth, which I did, even though it was late.

Doris answered and told me, "Fayth is in a tizzy again. I'll go get her." It didn't sound like I had woken her, thank goodness. It was only 10:00 p.m. but I thought that might be late in West Plains.

Fayth came to the phone and said, "I didn't want to bother y'all again, Patty, but Jared hasn't gotten here from St. Louis yet, and he left hours ago. I'm worried."

"Does he have his cell phone with him?"

"Yes, but it just keeps ringin' and then goin' to his voice mail and he hasn't called back. Do y'all think he's had an accident?" she said, her voice shaking.

"No, this rain always slows traffic way down," I said calmly. "I'm sure he's fine, but if it would make you feel better, we can call the state patrol and ask if there's a lot of traffic on the highway into West Plains. With all this rain, maybe there was some kind of washout on the road. I'm sure he's just sitting in traffic and doesn't have his phone ringer on or the radio is too loud to hear it."

"Yes, please call them," she said.

"I'll call you back." I hung up.

"Does the drama ever end?" Jon said as he looked up the number on his computer and made the call. According to the state patrol operator, no accidents or traffic problems between West Plains and St. Louis had been reported. "Hmmm, maybe his car broke down?"

"Maybe," I said. "If so, do you think he would just wait for some Good Samaritan to stop on the road and help him if he couldn't fix it himself, rather than calling someone for help?"

Jon nodded in agreement. "Yep, but too bad he doesn't have the sense to let Fayth know where he is."

We called Fayth back at 11:00 p.m. to see if he arrived—still no sign of him. We told her that she should be patient and try to get some rest. We would come get her in the morning if he didn't arrive before 7:00 a.m. to take her to the hospital.

"Okay, but I'm so worried," she said, almost crying. "Good night, and thanks again." We hung up feeling as if we should have done more to help her.

"I hope he hasn't ditched her at this moment in her life," Jon said as he walked into the bathroom to brush his teeth. I hadn't thought of that possibility and dreaded the thought that he might have such horrendous timing. Fayth would be crushed if he never showed up simply because he wasn't interested in her anymore.

We went to bed, hoping that Jared would arrive at Fayth's house before daybreak. We needed our rest that night because we were assuming, and hoping, that we wouldn't get much sleep in the days to come with an infant in the room. We fell asleep, listening to the rain on the roof.

THE BIRTH

Wednesday, March 20, was the first day of spring, and I could see light peeking under the curtains in our room when our alarm went off. When I opened the curtains, I saw that there were still puddles in the parking lot of the hotel and the streets were wet, but sunlight was streaming into our room. The blue sky was crystal clear and there were no signs of rain clouds anywhere. The sunlight gave our room an entirely different atmosphere and gave me a new frame of mind. I knew it would be a great day.

"It finally stopped raining," I said. I felt optimistic as I started packing some things for the hospital.

On the one hand, I was still very nervous. Everything we had been working for since the phone call on March 1 would come together that day, for better or worse. I had the same butterflies in my stomach that I used to get before taking a college exam or making a presentation for work that I wasn't as prepared for. On the other hand, I couldn't wait to meet my daughter, see her face, touch her little hands, count her little toes, and hold her in my arms. I prayed that the day would go exactly as we had hoped.

Finally, we had made it to the day we would make significant progress in our quest to complete our family, not to mention our quest to leave West Plains. On the way to the hospital, I realized that we were so rushed to get into the car that we had forgotten about Jared. "Oh my, did you get a call about picking up Fayth?" I asked Jon.

"I'm assuming he got there, or Cindy would have called the hotel or my cell phone, but let's double-check with Fayth anyway," Jon said. He dialed Doris's number and handed me the phone. I put it on speaker so we could both listen.

"Oh yes, he arrived at about four in the morning," Doris said on the phone. "Apparently, he stopped to sleep in the car for a few hours along the way when he got tired. Too bad he had the whole house worried about him. He should have called her, the creep. I doubt she got any sleep until he finally arrived. They've already left for the hospital."

"Thank you so much, Doris," I said. "You've been terrific through all of this. Fayth is lucky to have you as a neighbor and friend."

"She sure is," she said before hanging up.

We laughed and arrived at Ozarks Medical Center shortly after Fayth checked in, according to the nurse at the admittance desk. The hospital was a big, new brick building and looked more modern than I expected.

"Ms. Wiley is already in the delivery room getting prepped. You can wait in that room right over there," the nurse said, pointing to a small waiting room. It was strange to be having a baby but not be a patient or even family members. Thank goodness Fayth had told the nurse that we were coming.

The nurses seemed to know who we were and obviously had been through this type of situation before. They asked us if we needed anything periodically but were reluctant to keep us posted on Fayth's progress without a lot of effort on our part.

Over the next two hours, we waited and worried. There was no one else in the small waiting room. The chairs were extremely uncomfortable with very little cushioning.

I did some stretching to relieve my stress, but it didn't help much. I kept wondering when Fayth would ask me to join her. I hoped she hadn't forgotten about her invitation to be in the delivery room with her. I would have gone for a walk had I known how long it would be, but was afraid to leave the room except to go to the restroom. I didn't want to miss anything.

Jon kept working on his laptop, as usual, but was staying in tune to my impatience. "They'll tell you when it's time to go in there," he told me. "Don't worry."

He took a couple of pictures of me so we could remember how I looked at my most impatient and worried moment. I could have crawled out of my skin with concern, anxiety, and excitement. I kept bugging the nurses to find out what was going on. "Fayth asked for some private time with Jared, and she will call for you when it's time for the actual birth," the nurse said.

At 9:30 a.m., the nurse told us that they had broken Fayth's water an hour before, but that she wasn't making any progress, so they were starting the Pitocin to move things along. I was certain I would run out of patience. It had already been two hours and I started to wonder if this was going to be an all-day adventure. I had originally thought this baby would come early but it appeared that she was happy where she was and in no hurry.

With all the time on my hands, I did a lot of thinking. I wondered if I would instantly feel love for this child when she was born, as I did when the boys were born. I've met lots of babies who didn't appeal to me. I didn't love taking care of other people's babies when I used to babysit as a teenager. Would I love this child even if she hadn't spent nine months inside of me, kicking and making me hungry? I decided that it was too late to worry about that and moved on to other concerns.

I tried to read my book as I sat in the plastic chair, but instead of concentrating on what I was reading, I listened for any conversation about Fayth's condition in the hallway. I stood up, I sat down. I walked around the maternity ward. I looked out the window. I had a few mindless conversations with the nurses. They were nice, but didn't have (or wouldn't give me) the information I wanted. After another hour, I was fraught with anxiety and couldn't calm down. The minutes ticked by like hours. I wondered how Jon could be so calm.

"You know, Jon," I said, in an effort to get him to talk to me instead of working on the laptop, "March is a great month for our daughter to be born."

"Really?" he said, looking up. "You mean aside from our engagement?"

"Yes, it was the month my grandparents got married back in the 1920s, it would have been my grandmother's birthday tomorrow, and it will be your birthday at the end of the month. Isn't that amazing that all this happened in March? It's my lucky month."

"Yep, it's lucky all right. I was born this month and that was the best thing that ever happened to you," he said smugly.

"Until today," I said. "Today will be the best thing that ever happened to *both* of us."

"I know that as soon as your daughter is born, you are going to forget all about *my* birthday in March, aren't you? It's going to be *her* month from now on, isn't it?" Jon said.

"Oh yeah, you are in big trouble, Mister."

He laughed and continued working on his computer. I kept checking my watch. It was getting closer to the time the baby needed to be born to meet our Friday deadline. The hearing was set for 1:00 p.m., and we needed some time right after the forty-eight-hour period ended to get signatures signed and documents notarized before going to court.

At 11:15, the nurse came to get me. "Fayth is 100 percent effaced and nine centimeters dilated, so you should come in the delivery room now. She's ready to start pushing." She looked at Jon. "Jon, Fayth would like you to stay here or in the hall while Patty comes into the delivery room."

This was no surprise. Fayth had told me she wanted me in the room twice but failed to mention Jon either time, and I didn't ask. I know I wouldn't want a male stranger in the room when I was giving birth, even if he would be the baby's new father.

"No problem," Jon said. I took a deep breath. We walked down the hall to her room together. Jon was squeezing my hand and I felt like I was going to the firing squad. Suddenly everything was so serious and frightening.

I looked at the name written on the whiteboard outside her room and thought about the first time I heard Fayth's name.

The lawyer's secretary had told me her name on the phone on March 1, and I had rolled my eyes and giggled. Because of the unusual spelling, I remember thinking that it sounded like a name some flaky woman made up who probably made up the pregnancy as well. At first, I assumed that this wasn't really an opportunity for us; we'd go through the motions and in a week or so, we would hear that she wasn't really pregnant and just trying to extort money from some unsuspecting, desperate couple.

But there we were. Fayth was giving birth, and from everything we had learned in the last three days, she was going to give us her child. I was so nervous that my hands were sweaty and shaking. I wasn't sure if it was from the excitement of meeting my daughter or nerves from the potential disappointment of it turning out to be a boy or unhealthy.

I hated being in the delivery room without Jon, but having him there wasn't an option. Before walking in, I gave him a last hand squeeze and a smile and said, "See you soon. Stay right here."

"I will be right outside this door," Jon said. Then he whispered in my ear, "Just let me know if it's not what we want and I will make arrangements immediately to get you out of here."

I took another deep breath and walked in. Natural light filled the room, which was clean and pretty, even with all the medical equipment around. I immediately saw Fayth wearing a hospital gown, looking extremely pale in the bed. Jared stood next to her bed, along with two other nurses, and it was a bit awkward meeting him for the first time under these circumstances.

"Good morning," I said quietly to Fayth and Jared. "I'm so excited to be here. Thank you for letting me share this with you."

"You're welcome," Fayth said, trying to smile. "Oh no, here comes another contraction!" she yelled. She grabbed Jared's hand and squeezed hard. I could tell it hurt from the look on his face.

"Breathing is going to be important now that we are close to pushing, Fayth," the nurse said in a calm voice. "You need to focus on your breathing, especially after choosing not to have an epidural."

"I want the epidural now!" Fayth yelled. "It really hurts!"

"I'm sorry, but it's too late," the nurse said. "The doctor is coming in and you'll need to start pushing soon. There's no time to give you an epidural."

"I don't care! I can't stand it. I want this thing out of me!"

When we talked about it a couple of days ago, Fayth seemed convinced that having a natural birth was the right thing to do, but she clearly felt she had made a mistake as she reached the point of pushing. I wondered if her stay at the rehab facility had any effect on her decision. I was momentarily happy about her "no-drug policy."

I finally understood how my husband must have felt when I was giving birth to our boys and screaming in pain. The helplessness was frustrating because I cared about her. I stood there next to Fayth, feeling extremely uncomfortable and wondering how I could help. I remembered that moment very clearly when I gave birth; the realization that this giant thing inside you was coming out of a very small opening, and the pressure was amazingly painful. Bravery (or stupidity) wasn't something I believed in during childbirth and I had opted for pain medication as soon as possible. I never got as far as Fayth was naturally. I opted to have the epidural long before I started pushing.

I did not know, however, what the actual birth felt like because of the epidurals. It is frequently called the "ring of fire" when the baby's head comes through. I knew I didn't want to experience that without medication, and I felt bad for Fayth.

Despite the extreme tension in the room, Dr. Kyler walked in with a big smile, wearing his scrubs. "Good morning, everyone," he said as if we were all there for Sunday brunch. One nurse handed him sterile gloves while the other nurse put Fayth's feet into the stirrups.

"Well, well, well. How are we all this morning?" he said, sounding like he didn't have a care in the world, while we were all in a panic.

"Please let me have some drugs, Doctor!" Fayth shouted.

I felt responsible for all Fayth's pain. Fayth was going through that ordeal for my benefit and I couldn't do anything to help her. The guilt was huge.

"I'm sorry, Fayth, but I need you to start pushing, and there isn't time to wait for the epidural to take effect," Dr. Kyler said. "This baby isn't going to wait any longer. Are you ready?"

"No, get me out of here!" Fayth yelled and started climbing out of bed. Jared and I were caught off guard. Her feet were still in the stirrups and she almost fell off the side of the bed headfirst. Fortunately, we were both standing on that side of the bed.

Is she crazy? I thought. *She's going to fall out of bed, onto the floor, with my baby halfway out of her.*

"Hold on to her!" Jared said, grabbing on to her hip as I pushed her shoulder back onto the bed.

"Calm down now, Fayth," the doctor said calmly. For some reason, I found his demeanor irritating when I was so stressed out. "Take a deep breath. Here comes the contraction. Now start pushing the baby out."

"I can't! It hurts too much!" She tried again to get away from the pain. She was very strong and she did not want to be there.

It might have been interesting for me to see a birth from *next* to the bed for once, but I was too worried about my baby making her way out in all this craziness. I wished I were standing at a vantage point where I could see the head crown, but I was at the head of the bed, holding Fayth's shoulder as firmly as I could without hurting her. This was not what I had expected when she invited me to the birth. I had to use all my weight to keep her in bed. This baby was coming fast and there would be no rest for any of us until she was out.

Somehow, Fayth found the strength to yell at Jared, "I will only do this ONE MORE TIME! Then I am done having babies! Four times is enough!"

We all laughed, appreciating the break in the tension, as Jared said, "Oh, okay, honey."

"Here's the head," the doctor said. I swallowed hard, held my breath, and watched his face for any sign of a problem. Fayth screamed again. I couldn't believe how stressful this was. I wondered what Jon was thinking and hearing outside the room.

"Okay, the head is out. Give me the suction," the doctor said to the nurse. I couldn't see anything because of the sheet over Fayth's knees. Fayth had stopped squirming around and seemed to be calming down. She was clearly exhausted. Although I could have walked to the end of the bed to look at the baby, I was frozen in place.

The baby started crying. A very good sign.

"One more push, Fayth," the doctor said, "there are the shoulders . . . and . . ." The anticipation was killing me. It was probably only a couple of seconds before he spoke again, but it felt like hours.

"You have a daughter!" he said.

My tears exploded as I finally saw my daughter in the doctor's arms. She looked perfect. He cut the umbilical cord and handed her to the nurse. I started sobbing with relief and joy. It was 11:33 a.m.

It occurred to me right away that the doctor didn't say "It's a girl" when the baby was born. Saying "You have a daughter" was meant for me and had so much more meaning. There she was, my daughter. All the stress of the weeks and days before disappeared.

When my boys were born, the doctor put the newborn on my chest immediately after birth. I wondered if Fayth felt bad that she barely got to see her baby before the nurse took her to be washed and weighed.

"Are you okay?" I said to Fayth. I couldn't have felt more grateful.

She nodded, with tears streaming down her face.

"You did so well," I said. "She's beautiful. Can Jon come in to see her?"

Again, she nodded.

I rushed to the door as the nurse pulled the curtain around Fayth's bed. I opened the door and hugged Jon.

"Is she okay?" he said.

"Just look at her," I said, pulling him over to the infant care station in the room. "She's beautiful."

We both walked over to where our daughter lay in a Plexiglas carrier on a blanket. She shivered even though she was under heat lamps. "Why is she shivering?" I asked the nurse.

"I'm not sure. I'm doing some tests, weighing her and taking her temperature. What's her name?"

We looked at each other and said "Sophia Mariel" at the same time. "But we're going to call her 'Sophie,'" I said. Jon and I had been discussing names for the last couple of weeks. I had wanted to name her after my mother whose name was Shirley Merielle. In fact, Sophie now had the same initials that my mother had before she married my father, including the last initial. My mother had always hated the French spelling of her middle name, especially because she went by her middle name most of her life. She referred to it as far too complicated for most teachers and kids. So we spelled it differently, even though it sounded the same. It made me so happy to know that my mother had a true namesake in my daughter.

I wished my mother were alive to meet her and I knew that she would have been thrilled that my dream of a daughter had finally come true. I missed her bringing me a beautiful hydrangea plant to the hospital, like she did when the boys were born. Like the relationship I had enjoyed with my mother and grandmother, Sophie would have completed the perfect trio. I knew I would think about my mother even more as Sophie and I grew closer over the years.

"Hello, Sophie," the nurse said in a soft voice. Another nurse wrote her name on a card for her baby carrier, as well as on three plastic bracelets for security. One was placed on Sophie's ankle and the others were given to Jon and me. They also had Fayth's name on them, as she was still the legal mother. She was already wearing her bracelet.

Jon reminded the nurse that we needed to collect the baby's first stool output so we could test it. The meconium would tell us everything that the baby ingested during development in the womb, and it would indicate if there was any drug abuse during pregnancy.

It was the only thing left to worry about, except for the forty-eight-hour waiting period until Fayth signed the papers. She didn't show any signs of changing her mind, even now that the baby was born.

The nurse working with Sophie looked serious, so I had to ask, "Is she okay?"

"I'm concerned about the shivering. It could be a drug-induced problem," the nurse said.

"You mean like she's addicted and going through withdrawal?" Jon said.

"Maybe, but I doubt it. She's pretty tiny at six pounds and she might just be cold." The nurse unfolded a blanket with baby animals all over it. "Let's wrap her up in the blanket so you can hold her and warm her up."

The nurse who was helping Fayth opened the curtain. Lying in the bed, now very quiet, Fayth looked exhausted.

"Do you want to hold her?" I said.

"Only after y'all do," she said. "Remember, this is y'all's daughter."

Her comment was music to my ears. Fayth had gone through all that pain and was still ready to give up her baby daughter. As I held my daughter for the first time, my tears flowed down my cheeks onto the baby blanket. I couldn't remember ever being so happy. I knew I had felt pure joy when my boys were born, but this event had so much more risk and worry associated with it. It had been many years of torment over the loss of my mother and unsuccessful attempts at having a baby girl. It made that momentous occasion so much more significant and joyful.

At that moment, even if my baby had a drug dependency and required extra care, I was ready for it. She was my daughter and I knew I cared as much about her at that moment as I had cared for my boys when they were born. It didn't matter that she didn't come out of me—she marched into my heart the moment she was born.

I had known as soon as I saw the sun that morning that the day would be spectacular. Our mood was as bright as the day now that Sophie was in our lives. Jon and I took pictures of each other holding Sophie in the delivery room. I wanted one photo with both of us on either side of the bed while Fayth held her. I knew that one day Sophie would want to know what her birth mother looked like, and this was the picture we would show her.

"Are you ready to hold her now?" I asked Fayth, half hoping she would decline.

"Sure," she said with a smile and held out her arms.

I prayed that she wouldn't feel that strong emotion that I felt when I held my baby. If she did, I knew there would be no hope for us. Fayth looked into Sophie's eyes for a moment, agreed to having her photo taken with us, and said, "She's just beautiful. Congratulations."

There was no hesitation as Fayth handed Sophie back to Jon. She probably could have signed the papers right then if the Missouri laws allowed it, but we would have to wait forty-eight long hours.

THE COUNTDOWN

The nurses at Ozarks Medical Center were fabulous. Each nurse who came on duty was better than the one ending her shift. They were warm and welcoming, and somehow showed as much excitement about our new baby as we felt.

They understood the sensitive nature of our situation, as well as the rules of adoption cases like ours. We weren't allowed to take Sophie home yet, as she still legally belonged to Fayth until the adoption papers were signed. They informed us that in most circumstances like ours, we would have had to stay in our hotel at night while the baby spent the two nights in the nursery. But rather than having us drive back and forth from the hotel each night, the nurses showed compassion and allowed us to stay in a room in the maternity ward with Sophie.

We were treated as well as any couple who had just given birth and were overjoyed at their gracious attitude. We kept expressing our appreciation and truly delighted in the fact that we could spend every moment with Sophie. It really helped us bond as a family. As it turned out, the maternity room was large enough for all three of us to comfortably spend the next two days waiting for the forty-eight hours to pass. However, there was only one single bed, along with a large chair that reclined. Jon contemplated sleeping in the recliner chair but in the end, we agreed that I should stay overnight with Sophie, while Jon went back to the hotel. He was reluctant to leave us, as he hadn't left Sophie's side for a minute since her birth, but he knew we all needed our sleep.

All of Fayth's hospital bills were covered by welfare, including Sophie's care, but we didn't fall into the administrative category that enabled the hospital to track our payments, so we were allowed to stay free of charge. It seemed unnecessary and we kept offering to pay, but were declined every time. It was an added bonus.

Our room was adorable. It had baby duck wallpaper, with a pale pink background, a small bathroom, and a wooden rocking chair for feeding the baby. The window had rose-colored curtains and looked out onto the back parking lot of the hospital. Beyond it, we could see the flat landscape of West Plains. The town looked much more attractive with the sun shining.

We were also much happier to be in West Plains after our daughter arrived. I thought about the preceding three days and how tortured we felt by everything that had happened and didn't happen. I knew that Jon regretted spending so much time waiting in West Plains before the birth, but had we not arrived well before Sophie's birth, we wouldn't have spent as much time with Fayth and her family. I liked the idea of knowing as much about Fayth as possible, before we took Sophie to her new home in Seattle. I knew I wouldn't have any opportunities to talk to Fayth after the adoption was complete. I was also pleased that we had the blood test done and had spoken to Fayth's doctor in person.

The nurses came in to care for Sophie when they needed to, but Jon and I fed her, changed her, rocked her, held her, and most important, fell completely in love with her. She was an amazing baby. We never heard a peep and certainly no crying, even when the nurse had to prick her foot for a blood test. The shivering stopped as soon as we moved to our room, just down the hall from where Fayth was recovering in her own room.

"Sophie never cries," I said to the nurse. "Is she okay?"

"She's fine, and she *will* cry, they all do," the nurse said reassuringly. "She's just tired from her journey out into the world. She's only a few hours old. Enjoy it while you can."

I laughed and recalled how much crying Jake and Micah did when they were infants. Perhaps I was forgetting the first couple of days when a newborn was exhausted from the birth and slept a lot. I might have forgotten whether they cried, but I remembered that they were always hungry, even in the first few hours of birth. Sophie didn't seem like she was hungry all the time, but I assumed that would change.

I felt like an exhausted new mother, even though I hadn't given birth. The emotional stress of the last week, and before that, caught up with me. I was grateful for the suspended responsibility in my daily life and napped almost as much as the baby. It had been seven years since Micah's birth, and my memories of all the attention newborns require came flooding back. It felt wonderful just to hold her and watch her. It would have been completely blissful if I didn't have to worry about Fayth signing the papers.

That first afternoon after the birth and into the evening, I kept asking the nurse about Fayth to make sure she was okay. "Do you think she wants to see the baby again? I'm happy to take her down the hall if she wants to see her."

"I think you should wait a few more hours," the nurse said. "She's exhausted and seems a bit depressed. She misses her boys a lot and just wants to go home. She hasn't asked about the baby at all, so I'm not sure she will want to see her again before she leaves tomorrow."

I wasn't sure how I felt about Fayth that evening. I was happy for her that this ordeal was almost over, as she had been wishing, but she had to be feeling some anxiety about giving the baby up forever. I wanted to talk to her but was afraid at what she might say to me. I couldn't resist wondering if her depresssion was about wanting to keep the baby now, as scary as that thought was. I was aware that hormones and emotions can make people do crazy things.

We had the florist in the lobby of the hospital deliver a nice bouquet to Fayth's room. Also, I had previously bought some earrings to give Fayth as a thank-you gift before we left home for Phoenix. I thought about finding the right time to give them to her before she left the hospital the next day. It would also give me the opportunity to see if she had changed her mind. If I didn't get the chance to see her, I worried that I wouldn't sleep at all until the papers were signed on Friday morning.

I walked by her room a couple of times, leaving Sophie with Jon in our room, but the door was always closed. Furthermore, there was no light coming into the hallway from under the door, or around the window shades, even during the daytime. I hope it meant that she was just sleeping a lot, rather than feeling depressed about her situation, as the nurse had suggested.

Jon and I were counting down the hours until we could leave West Plains. Wednesday had been a long day, and we needed to wait until noon on Friday before all the signatures could be completed and notarized on the adoption papers. Sophie was born right on time to get us out of West Plains before the weekend, and we couldn't wait.

In keeping with their amazing hospitality, one of the nurses came in to let us know that as new parents, we were invited to share a romantic dinner in our room that evening. She handed Jon a menu so that we could select what we wanted, including wine. We were delighted, given our familiarity of the restaurant choices outside of the hospital, and made our selections.

Orson called to congratulate us and confirm the plan for the rest of the week. When all the papers were signed around noon on Friday, we would head to court in the town hall at 1:00 p.m. We wouldn't be able to leave the state of Missouri until the ICPC paperwork between Washington State and Missouri was complete, and that would take two business days after the judge signed the papers. We could leave West Plains, however, immediately after the hearing. Jon spent some time making plans for our flight out of town and for our weekend stay in Kansas City.

As we had predicted, the earliest we could fly home with Sophie was Tuesday afternoon. It seemed like ages since we had seen the boys, but in reality, it had been only a week and would be about ten days total when we arrived home. We had been through so much that it seemed much longer. I couldn't wait to see them and hoped they could wait patiently for a few more days. Once we could tell them what was really happening, I was sure they would feel better about being left home for so long. What an adventure this had all been so far.

But the adventure wasn't over; it was really just beginning. Sophie was a breath of fresh air for us. She was so dainty and small. She had big eyes that looked hazel and her skin was very fair. "She has the same coloring as my mother," I said to Jon. "I'm so glad she has her middle name and her initials too."

Jon and I had spent a lot of time choosing a first name for our daughter. We talked about it before we even got the call from Fayth just for fun, then again when we left for Phoenix, and again when we arrived in West Plains. We didn't want to decide prematurely, but we also felt that a final decision on her name showed optimism.

Jon was pickier about names than I imagined most men would be and it made the decision process interesting. We had gone through a similar process with the boys' names—and even the dog's name, so I was ready for it. I loved the idea that she could have the same initials as my mother and proceeded to make a list of S names that I liked from about six baby name books I had bought when I was pregnant with Jake. I also bought a new book of names, which contained newer, trendier names that in some cases seemed ridiculous. Jon and I disagreed about our top choices, but he decided that if we chose his top pick for her first name, he would agree to give her my mother's middle name. We made a deal and thankfully, the name suited her when she was born. I hoped Sophie would love her name.

At 6:00 p.m., Sophie was still napping when our special dinner arrived, complete with a small dining table. We sat together and enjoyed our celebratory steak feast, with Sophie's bassinet just a few feet away. The hospital kitchen even managed to cook Jon's steak to his liking. It was a wonderful end to a perfect day that we had been anticipating for weeks.

Jon told me over dinner that he made plans for us to fly to Kansas City on Friday to spend the weekend with our new daughter at a nice hotel, while we waited for the final interstate legalities to take place. Kansas City had good shopping and excellent restaurants. It would be luxurious by comparison to where we had spent the last four days. We were looking forward to leaving West Plains, even though the weather had improved significantly and the town seemed much friendlier. It was like the sun was shining because Sophie was now with us. March was clearly the best month of the year.

Sophie woke from her nap just as we were finishing dessert. We fed and changed her, and then we both lay down on the bed with her, staring at her tiny hands and beautiful face. She had a little button nose, adorable ears, and her skin felt like silk. She brought so much joy into our lives in just the few hours she had been with us. "Are you happy?" Jon asked me quietly.

"Totally," I said. "I feel better than I have felt in a very long time. I feel like I'm living my dream. Thank you for doing all of this for me, Jon."

"We did all of this together, remember?" Jon said.

"Yes, but you had to hire all the lawyers, get the FBI reports, arrange the flights, the hotels, and our upcoming weekend," I said, tearing up, again. "You've been truly amazing."

"I did all of that for us, for all of us."

We fell asleep with her between us, snuggled together in the single bed. Neither of us slept well because we were afraid of rolling onto the baby. The smart, safe thing would have been to move her to the bassinet, but we were so cozy and loved being close to her. It was worth losing some sleep.

Early the next morning, Jon gently got out of bed, so as not to disturb the baby, and left early to shower at the hotel and bring some clothes for me. It was Thursday morning, and Sophie was almost a whole day old. Thursday was a stress-free day because I was no longer worried about the birth, the health of the baby, or any of the other issues that had filled my mind over the last three weeks. I decided not to worry about Fayth's signature on Friday, and just enjoy the day with my new daughter.

The feeling I had when I awoke was sheer excitement about our life ahead. There had been so many days over the past few years when I woke to dread about my situation. This was a new feeling. I didn't even know how to express it in words. I even felt more love for my boys that morning, which surprised me because it didn't seem possible. They would be so excited to meet their new baby sister. I was convinced she would bring them joy, while teaching them compassion and even a little responsibility. I knew I would be a better mother now that I was happier and completely satisfied. Maybe that was what Jon meant when he said, "I did it for all of us."

Jon returned from the hotel just in time for Sophie's first doctor visit. The pediatrician was arranged by Fayth's doctor, as he didn't recommend we take the pediatrician on call at the hospital. He called a doctor he knew we'd like, named Dr. Rona Tarken. She had come to meet us early Wednesday morning when we were in the waiting room, before Sophie was born, and told us she would make a "house call" to our room to check on her the following day.

Dr. Tarken came into our room while Sophie was napping on Thursday morning. She was a petite woman with dark skin, black hair, and a big smile. She greeted us warmly and asked how we were doing in a hushed tone.

"We couldn't be better," I said. "Sophie is so quiet. She only wakes up to eat and then goes back to sleep as soon as we put on a dry diaper."

"Yes, she's still exhausted, so that is to be expected. So sorry that I'll have to wake her now so I can examine her," Dr. Tarken said. "She's going to be a little mad at me."

"No problem," Jon said. "I miss her when she sleeps so much anyway."

Dr. Tarken gently took off the pink cotton cap Sophie was wearing, and she woke up right away. Sophie put her tiny hand on her face to block the fluorescent light in the room from her eyes. The doctor unwrapped the multicolored baby blanket from around her and took off her tiny hospital T-shirt. Sophie was so thin and tiny, only weighing six pounds. She started to fuss a bit as the doctor listened to her heart with her stethoscope and then put the thermometer under her arm. Sophie started to cry as she started to shiver again.

"Why do you think she was shivering at birth?" I said.

"It could be a number of things," Dr. Tarken said as she looked at the temperature reading. "She's shivering now because she's cold, which is probably what it was after her birth. There doesn't appear to be any kind of substance dependency based on all the other factors. Her APGAR score was nine out of ten yesterday, which is very good. I think she's just fine, and there's nothing to worry about."

We looked up the term APGAR on Jon's computer to refresh our memory. The APGAR score is based on a number of statistics and observations of the baby at birth. A score is given for each sign at one minute and then again at five minutes after the birth. If there are problems with the baby, an additional score is given at ten minutes. A score of seven to ten is considered normal, while a score of four to seven might require resuscitative measures, and a baby with an APGAR of three or below requires immediate resuscitation. The acronym APGAR stands for activity (muscle tone), pulse, grimace (reflexes), appearance (skin tone), and respiration.

"When will we have the results from the meconium test?" Jon asked the doctor.

"Not for at least a week, I'm afraid. Those results will be communicated to Sophie's permanent pediatrician on the paperwork you filled out yesterday, and if you want, we can call you."

"Yes, please," Jon said and gave her his cell phone number.

I remember thinking that the results of that test, or any other test, didn't matter anymore. We were already so in love with Sophie that nothing could change our mind about keeping her. She was ours forever. I hoped that Fayth felt the same way.

The doctor gave Sophie her first set of vaccinations, and took some blood from the bottom of her foot, neither of which made

Sophie happy. Her cry was so sweet and I felt bad letting anything cause her pain. I had forgotten how adorable newborn infants were, even when crying. The new bandage on her tiny foot was so large that it almost reached up to her ankle. The doctor calmly dressed Sophie and cradled her for a moment before handing her to Jon for warming. Then the doctor handed me her business card, saying, "She seems perfect. Congratulations." We thanked her for the visit and as she left, she wished us luck. I was hoping we didn't need any more luck, but we had another day to wait and see.

After the doctor had left, around 11:00 a.m., Jon answered his cell phone while holding Sophie in the rocking chair. She had warmed up again and was content in his arms. "Hey, Orson," he said in a hushed tone. "Wow, great news . . . oh good . . . yes, but we haven't met him yet . . . thanks for calling to let us know. See you tomorrow." Jon ended the call and said, "That was Orson Shiller."

"I guessed that," I said. We were both a little dazed from lack of sleep.

"He said that he called Dr. Kyler's office for the HIV test results from Fayth's blood test and they came back negative."

"That's such great news," I said. "I'm so glad we don't have to put the baby through any additional blood tests. I do feel a little guilty for not having trusted Fayth. What else did he say?"

"He asked if we had met Fayth's attorney, Lyndon Pelt, yet." We had agreed to pay for Fayth's attorney so she was well represented and her rights as the birth mother were clear. "I said no, of course. He wanted me to know that Mr. Pelt would explain the Friday morning procedure for all the signatures to Fayth before she leaves the hospital. Orson and Lyndon will both be there at her house on Friday to witness the signing."

"This is all working out so well," I said. "Friday's court time should work out perfectly once 11:30 a.m. comes, thanks to our daughter's perfect timing. How could we miss with so many lawyers working for us?"

I felt so blessed and happy now that many of the hurdles were behind us. I could see the light at the end of the tunnel and allowed myself to think about life getting back to normal again.

I suddenly really understood how heart wrenching it could be for couples who got this far in the adoption process, only to hear that the birth mother changed her mind. I would completely fall apart if Fayth didn't sign those papers and felt nervous about it all over again. We had put our hearts on the line, and if something were to go wrong at that point, I didn't think I'd be able to recover.

After lunch, the nurse came in to tell me that Fayth would be leaving the hospital later that afternoon and if I wanted to see her, I should go soon. I assumed it would be the last time I would see her. I had written her a thank-you note to go with the earrings I brought to give her. I reread it one more time to Jon:

Dear Fayth,

"Thank you" seems like such an inadequate phrase for the gift you have given us. We hope you will think back on this experience as a positive and rewarding one. You have made us happier than we ever hoped to be.

We pray for your happiness and that you will remember how much we will love and care for your baby. You have two adorable little boys who will always cherish you. They are your source of strength and pride now, and in the future.

We thank you graciously for your trust in us and wish you, and your family, all the best.

Fondly,

Patty and Jon

Jon said, "It sounds just fine and definitely closes the door on our relationship with her. I'm sure she will appreciate the gift, but you'll have to see how the note goes over with her. Good luck." I took a deep breath and walked down the hall to Fayth's room, leaving Sophie with Jon. I assumed Fayth still felt the same way as yesterday and preferred not to see the baby again. The earrings were in a box wrapped in floral paper and the card, with my letter written inside, was on top. I knocked on her door.

"Come in," Jared said from inside the room.

I opened the door and saw Fayth sitting up in bed, still dressed in a hospital gown. She looked pale and worn out. She wasn't smiling. Jared sat in the chair next to her bed, also frowning. I regretted the visit before it even started. The table lamps in the room were on, but all the other lights were off. The drapes were still closed, giving the room a dark, sad atmosphere. It was a stark comparison to the room I had just come from. I couldn't even see the cheery wallpaper in the dim light.

"Hi," I said to Fayth softly, walking in and closing the door again. "Are you okay?"

"I'm okay," she said in a hushed tone. "How's the baby?"

"She's just fine. Sleeping a lot." I laughed nervously. I felt like I was totally invading their privacy.

"Well, they do that. I'm just missin' my boys and can't wait to go home."

"When will they let you go home?" I said, feeling like I never should have come.

"Later today, when they finish their check-off list. My mom is getting' real tired of watchin' the boys, so I need to get home. They're tryin' to speed things up around here. Hey, thanks for the flowers."

"You're welcome. I brought you a little gift to thank you for everything you have done for us. We couldn't be happier, really," I told her while handing her the box and card. "It's nothing compared to the gift you have given us, but I hope you like it."

She looked at the earrings. "They're real nice, thank you." She didn't open the card, and although I was glad at first, it was a bit strange. I figured she would read it after I left the room.

"Do you want to see the baby again before you go?" I said.

"No thanks. I think it's just easier to leave when they say I can," she said without any emotion. "She's your baby now."

"Thank you so much, Fayth. We are so in love with her already. I should leave you two alone. Can I hug you one more time before I go?" I said, hoping to end things on a good note.

"Sure," she said, barely smiling as she held out her arms to me. I bent down and hugged her, feeling overwhelmed with emotion. Then I turned and hugged Jared, who stood up.

"Take good care of her," I said to him as tears started to well up in my eyes.

"I will," he said. I left the room and closed the door.

I stood in the hallway outside her room for a moment as I wiped away my tears. The emotion of saying good-bye to the person who had been so brave and selfless for my benefit was overwhelming. I was relieved when I left the room, but I wondered if there was something else I could have said to Fayth. It felt odd to be so uncomfortable with her, after the three days we had spent together. We had gotten so close and talked about such personal issues. I wondered if she was mad at me for being happy, or had she regretted her decision?

I pondered why Fayth's whole demeanor was suddenly different. She was colder to me than she had ever been. Was it because she no longer needed me? Her baby was in my care and she knew I wouldn't walk away. Or could it be that she would miss our help with her family's needs like driving her to get groceries or helping with laundry? Or was it what I had dreaded the most? Had she changed her mind about keeping the baby and was afraid to tell me in person? Was she waiting until she was safely in her home and had planned to tell the lawyer the bad news when he came for her signature tomorrow?

I knew that if I expressed my concerns to Jon, he would tell me I was overreacting or being paranoid. But he didn't see her face or hear her tone. I put those thoughts behind me and decided not to mention my fears to Jon before heading back to our room. Why worry him?

I was so glad to just be with my husband and daughter right now. I still couldn't believe I had a daughter and that she would be officially ours in less than a day. I prayed that that was still the case. I couldn't wait for the moment when I could just enjoy her without worry. It was going to be a long twenty-four hours.

THE FINAL DAY

I hardly slept for the second night in a row, even though I had the bed and Jon slept in the large reclining chair, still refusing to go to the hotel for a good night's sleep. I was so worried about how the day ahead would turn out. Sophie was safely asleep in her Plexiglas bassinet for almost the entire night.

Friday morning had finally arrived. Sophie awoke briefly for a diaper change and a bottle of formula at 5:00 a.m. but went right back to sleep, as did I, finally. At 9:00 a.m., Jon returned from the hotel. He had snuck out of our hospital room quietly at around 7:00 a.m. to shower and dress for court and to check out of the hotel—for good, I hoped. He had only kept one of our two rooms at the hotel after Sophie was born.

When the nurse poked her head in our room late the day before and said, "Fayth has gone home. Just thought you might want to know," I felt a sense of relief at first. If she had wanted to keep the baby, I figured she would certainly have wanted to see her again. But as I thought more about it, I reminded myself that people operate in different ways, and I am often surprised at how they handle delicate situations.

I didn't know Fayth at all when it came right down to it and her plan could have been very different from mine, if I had been in her place. I was also concerned that Fayth might weaken in her resolve to give the baby up when confronted by her mother, again. I took a deep breath and hoped that the next time I lay down to go to sleep, we would be in Kansas City with our new daughter, free from worries about someone taking her away from us.

It felt good to start taking positive steps toward finalizing the adoption that day. Sheila Brocken was orchestrating the final legal details from Columbia and everything she had done prior to Friday was complete. She had handled hundreds of adoption cases and I felt confident that everything would go smoothly.

Jon had spoken to Eleanor in Seattle and she agreed we were ready. He also spoke to Sophie's pediatrician who called him early to let us know her blood results were back and Sophie was just fine. That was excellent news, but not a surprise. We already knew that she was perfect. I couldn't wait to say "I told you so" to Eleanor; Sophie was as healthy as we had hoped and she was ours.

Orson Shiller planned to go over to Fayth's home at 11:30 a.m. with Lyndon Pelt to get both her and Jared's signature. It would be exactly forty-eight hours after the birth.

Meanwhile, the attorney we met earlier in the week, Carlos Villagos, who acted as the guardian ad litem for Sophie, would meet us in court at 1:00 p.m. So would Reece Brotting, the attorney we hired to represent the birth father, Cyrus Lansfield, who would have already signed the papers from his jail cell.

Fayth didn't have to appear in court, as long as her signature was notarized. At our request, she had signed a document just before leaving the hospital giving us permission to take the baby with us to court. We didn't want to leave her alone in the hospital, even though we would have trusted the nurses to take good care of her while we were gone. Taking her to court with us would also make it easier for us to fly out of town right after the hearing. Jon loaded the car with everything from the hotel room that morning and the pilots would be waiting so we could depart right after the court proceedings.

At 11:45 a.m. we hadn't heard from Orson, and I began to worry. "Isn't it odd that he didn't call us after Fayth signed the papers?" I said to Jon. "It doesn't take more than a minute to sign a piece of paper."

"Yes, he told me he would call." Jon checked his cell phone for a signal. "I'm sure he is just finishing up with her and will call us any minute."

I wondered if Fayth's mother might be giving Orson a hard time, keeping him from leaving right away. Minutes later, Jon's phone rang. I felt relief, until I saw Jon's expression after he answered. "What do you mean, couldn't sign the papers? He what? Left town when?"

I stood up abruptly and started asking questions. "Who are you talking about? Which *he* left town? Did Fayth sign? Say 'just a minute' and tell me what's going on. I can't stand it."

Jon sympathetically put his hand over the phone and said, "Jared didn't know he had to sign the papers. I guess Lyndon Pelt forgot to tell Fayth yesterday when he went over everything with her. Jared left town to go back to St. Louis, and as you already know, he doesn't always keep his cell phone on. Now they can't reach him."

"Oh, is that all?" I said, calming down. "Carlos said we don't really need *his* signature. He isn't even the birth father and we were just being extra cautious about the future because he was with Fayth, right? It's not worth missing our court time. We can just remove him from the case."

"Not anymore," Jon said. "Now that he's mentioned in the legal documents, we need his signature just as much as if he was the birth father. Orson said the judge won't sign off on the adoption until we get it."

"What?" I screamed. Sophie started to cry. I rushed over and picked her up. "Oh my God. What are we going to do? It's a four-hour drive back to St. Louis. When did he leave?"

Jon continued to talk to Orson, who was getting more information from Fayth, and repeated everything back to me. "He apparently left late last night so he could be back in time to go to work today. Orson is going to call the construction site and get him on the phone. Then we can work it all out. Calm down."

I hate that phrase. I don't know anyone who likes to be told to "calm down" but at that particular moment, I was especially irritated. I wasn't going to "calm down" until we were on that runway getting out of that town with our daughter.

"How could Lyndon have not notified Jared that he needed to sign papers with Fayth today?" I said, not expecting an answer. "He hardly had anything else to do to earn his fee."

I wished I had mentioned it to Jared when I saw them at the hospital the day before. But it made more sense for me to stay out of the legal discussions with Fayth and Jared, leaving it up to all the lawyers. I just wished they had taken care of every detail, rather than just most of them. The court time was suddenly at risk of coming and going, leaving us stuck in the hospital in West Plains all weekend, and staying in Missouri longer than we had hoped.

Jon motioned for me to sit down after he ended the call with Orson. He said, "It gets worse."

"What gets worse?" I said as calmly as I could, bracing myself.

"Orson called the construction site where Jared works. Jared called in sick this morning and isn't at work at all," Jon said with a pained expression.

"You *must* be kidding me," I said. "Where is he? Why did he leave Fayth if he was just going to call in sick? What's wrong with that guy?"

"Giving him the benefit of the doubt, Patty, would you want to hang around Fayth's mother all weekend while Fayth recovers from childbirth?" Jon said. "Plus, he's probably exhausted from the commotion surrounding the birth, the hospital stay, and driving back and forth from St. Louis. I can understand not being able to do physical labor after a week like this one. Besides, he didn't know we needed him to sign. He's not hiding from us on purpose."

"I know, but this is so upsetting," I said, not understanding why he was defending Jared. I started to cry from frustration.

Jon handed me a tissue and called Sheila. We needed to contact Jared in a hurry. He wasn't at home or answering his cell phone and no one at the construction site knew where he was.

It was 12:15 p.m., only forty-five minutes until the court time. According to Orson, everything else was all set. I couldn't believe we didn't get Jared's signature when he was in the hospital. He didn't need to sign after forty-eight hours. He could have signed any time. We knew Jared would sign as soon as we found him, so that wasn't the problem.

I suddenly realized that I should have been relieved that Fayth actually signed the papers. All that anxiety that she might change her mind for nothing. She did as she had promised and I couldn't even enjoy that wonderful detail because of this new development.

Jon finished his call with Sheila after explaining the situation to her. "She's going to ask her son-in-law, who's a lawyer in St. Louis, to find him. His name is Calvin Darlton. That's the eighth lawyer on our count of lawyers, for the record." I mustered a half laugh for his effort to cheer me up. "He's going to ask some of the guys Jared works with at the construction site to see where he might be. Let's try to be patient while we get ready to go to court. Why don't you get dressed?" Jon handed me the gray slacks, white blouse, and black sweater that I had packed for the monumental event.

I had been wearing sweat suits or jeans almost every day, and it felt good to wear something different. It also felt good to be getting ready for such a significant occasion. I was so happy Sophie would be with us, wearing the adorable pink outfit we bought her in New York. Thinking back on that trip, we had just a glimmer of hope about Sophie back then. We had come so far.

The head nurse, Candace Rushmont, walked in. She had been in and out of our room at various times during our stay and we had thanked her, again, for arranging our room. She had been through this with other couples before and understood why we wanted to stay with Sophie every minute. She was quite tall, with short brown hair and warm dark eyes. "Good morning," she said, smiling.

"Hi, Candace," Jon and I said at the same time.

"How's our girl this morning?"

"Sophie is the best. We're getting her changed for her big trip to court. She gets to wear her travel outfit," I said happily as I held up the pink designer outfit and matching hat.

"How cute," Candace said with a smile at Sophie and then, looking at us, her expression changed. "I have to talk to you about going to court today. There's a problem with the document that Fayth signed allowing you to take Sophie out of the hospital before the official notice has come from court."

"What problem?" Jon said.

"The hospital can't honor it because the hospital counsel isn't available to review it. Since it's not a court order, she'll have to stay here, with me."

"What?" I said, trying to stay calm. The problems were piling up. "She needs to be with us. We can't leave her here alone."

"She won't be alone. She'll be with me and the other nurses. We won't even put her in the nursery while you're away. She'll stay in her bassinet behind the nurses' station and we'll watch her very closely. I promise she'll be fine," Candace said calmly. "I'll see you just before you leave." She walked out of our room, leaving no time for further discussion.

"Why is everything going wrong today?" I asked Jon, knowing he would scold me for asking a ridiculous question.

"Things could have definitely gone worse," Jon said, clearly referring to Fayth's decision. "Everything will be fine, you'll see."

After all the planning we had done, I had expected everything to go smoothly that day, but each time I turned around, there was another problem. We wouldn't even know if all the signatures would be complete when we went to court, so we could be leaving Sophie for nothing. I hated the idea of being away from her, even for an hour.

Jon told me that he didn't feel like we could argue about the paperwork, especially when Candace had allowed us to stay in the hospital with Sophie for the two days. "It's not her fault, and there's nothing we can do. Let's just go and get this done, and then we'll come back right away to get her. Okay?"

"Okay," I agreed reluctantly, finishing up the last of Sophie's buttons. "And hopefully we'll leave town with her right after that. Any word from Sheila?"

"Not yet," Jon said, grabbing his wallet and car keys. "Let's go."

As we left the maternity floor, Candace stood there holding Sophie, who looked so adorable in her new outfit. I couldn't believe how attached to her I felt already. It had only been two days, and I felt sure I loved her as much as I loved my boys. How could I have ever doubted that I had enough love for a third child?

I felt empty as we left the hospital without Sophie. I hadn't been outside since early Wednesday morning and the fresh air felt good, but I wanted Sophie with me. The weather was still nice, but not like the day Sophie was born. That was the sunniest, and best, day of the week.

We got in the car, which was full of luggage and baby equipment, including the infant car seat that was strapped into the back seat. Jon had installed it that morning to prepare for our departure. I would have to wait a bit longer to see our daughter strapped into it for her trip home, or at least her trip away from West Plains.

We drove to the town hall and parked close to the courthouse entrance. Orson Shiller was waiting outside the courthouse when we arrived. His expression gave me no clues about the status of Jared's signature. We got out and Orson said, "Hello, and I'm sorry."

"Sorry for what?" I said, fearing the worst.

"Sorry for dropping the ball with Jared. It's my fault that we are having this delay," Orson said. "I should have made sure that Lyndon explained it all to him as well."

"But what's happening now?" Jon said. "It's almost 1:00 p.m."

"The judge agreed to give you an extra half hour because he doesn't have another case until two o'clock. That's the good news," Orson said.

"And the bad news?" Jon said.

"Sheila's son-in-law, Calvin, is still trying to find Jared. He found someone at the construction site who suggested where he might be and he's just arriving there now," Orson said.

"Let's cross our fingers," I said.

We walked into the courthouse. The building had a musty smell and the wood moldings looked hundreds of years old. We followed Orson up the wide staircase to the second floor, hearing the loud echo of our footsteps as we climbed. At the top of the stairs was a large hall with several double doors leading to courtrooms.

"That's our room there," Orson said, pointing to Room 4. "Let's sit down here in the hall and wait for news from Sheila." We sat down on a wood bench. "I have all the other paperwork here," he said reaching into his briefcase.

"How was Fayth this morning?" I asked Orson, who had met with her at her home.

"She was pretty tired and more irritable than when I last met with her. She just wanted to sign and then be left alone. I think she's tired of all this paperwork and legal business."

"I can understand that," I said. "I wish she could have been more helpful in finding Jared."

Jon's phone rang, and then Orson's phone rang. They both picked up their calls.

"Yes Sheila?" Jon said. "Uh-huh, good. That's great news. Yes, he's on a call with—"

"My office secretary," Orson whispered to Jon, listening to both conversations. "She's receiving the fax of everything and then she'll make copies. It should only take a few minutes."

"Will the judge accept a faxed copy?" Jon asked Sheila. He listened, and said, "Good. Thanks for twisting his arm. By the way, where did Calvin find Jared? . . . Really? Amazing. Good detective work. Thanks for the extra effort and please thank your son-in-law for us. I'll talk to you when it's all over." He put the phone back into his pocket.

"Sheila said the judge was willing to take a fax for today's proceedings but expects to receive the original document by

FedEx on Monday. Good thing Jared is just the boyfriend. Sheila said if it was the actual birth father, the judge wouldn't accept a fax," Jon said. "I think she really had to talk him into it."

"Thank goodness for Sheila," I said, feeling happier by the moment. "We're going to get out of here today. So where was Jared?"

"He was at an auto repair shop getting his car fixed. It broke down on the way back to St. Louis last night and had to be towed. It took quick detective work on Calvin's part and he really earned his hourly wage, unlike some of these lawyers. No offense, Orson," Jon said, glancing over in his direction. "Calvin had to check out Jared's home, his parents' home, and his favorite bar in town, according to the guys at work, before he found him. He happened to run into someone from the same repair shop, who overheard him asking about Jared at the bar."

"Too bad Jared doesn't leave his cell phone on," I said. "I guess he's not too worried about Fayth's well-being. What if she needed him?"

The front door of the building slammed loudly and then we heard footsteps going quickly up the staircase. A young lady dressed in a maroon suit and worn-out loafers came rushing up to Orson and handed him some papers. "Hi," she said with a southern accent, panting. "I'm Delilah, Orson's assistant." She turned to Orson. "Good thing we have a local office to do all this copying in." She handed him a full file folder. "Mr. Brotting was very accommodating and is on his way over. Is that all you need for now, Orson?"

"Yes, this is it," Orson said, looking at the papers. "Thanks." Turning to us he said, "I'll go and tell the judge we're ready while you both head into the courtroom with Delilah."

I took a deep breath, reminding myself why we were going through all of this. I wondered how Sophie was doing at the hospital. We walked into the courtroom, which was much bigger than I expected. There were many rows of bench seating, made from the same old oak that was in the hallways and large picture windows on two of the walls. The judge's desk was perched on a raised platform. It was huge and daunting, as was the witness stand next to it. Carlos Villagos was sitting there waiting for us, as were two other men I didn't recognize.

Orson joined us right away to make introductions. "You already know Carlos Villagos, correct?" Orson said. We nodded and said hello as we shook hands. "This is Lyndon Pelt, Fayth's attorney, and Reece Brotting, attorney for the birth father." Again, we shook hands. I refrained from giving Lyndon a piece of my mind about the debacle surrounding Jared's disappearance.

"Thanks for letting my assistant use your office," Orson said to Mr. Brotting.

"Thank you all for being here and waiting for us," Jon said. "We didn't expect all the drama this morning."

"We understand and don't worry about it," Mr. Brotting said. "It's all on your nickel anyway."

We chuckled. I was relieved that he was only representing the birth father. We turned around when a door at the front of the room opened and we saw the judge walk into the courtroom. He looked serious in his black robe, with a bailiff in tow.

The judge sat down and smiled at us, which I took as a good sign.

"Shall we begin?" he said. It seemed much more casual than I expected. There were only six of us in the room besides the judge, bailiff, and the court reporter.

Orson stood up. "Yes, Your Honor. As you know, I'm Orson Shiller, attorney for Mr. and Mrs. Lazarus, who are here to legally adopt the baby of Fayth Wiley, represented by Mr. Villagos." Holding up the file, he said, "Here are the documents that the birth mother has signed, as well as her boyfriend and the birth father, represented by Mr. Brotting. Mr. Pelt, at my right, represents Ms. Wiley. Everything should be in order and all signatures have been notarized." He approached the judge's desk and handed him the file.

The judge took some time to look everything over. There was an uncomfortable silence for about two minutes. Orson had told us that the judge would want both of us to get up on the stand to testify and I began to get nervous, hoping I could answer all his questions.

"Okay, could I please have Mrs. Lazarus take the witness stand?" the judge suddenly said. I got up and walked over to where the bailiff stood, near the witness stand.

"Raise your right hand please," he said. I did, remembering my brief stint as a juror twenty years earlier. "Do you swear to tell the whole truth and nothing but the truth, so help you God?"

"I do." I sat down, looking at Jon with a "Why I am doing this instead of you?" look. He smiled at me encouragingly.

The judge asked a few easy questions, like why I wanted to adopt a child and whether I had ever been arrested for child abuse, which seemed silly, given that he was holding the FBI report in the file stating that we were both cleared. After a few more questions, he asked me his final and most memorable question, "Do you know what you're getting yourself into?"

"Oh yes, Judge," I said without hesitation, "we have two boys already and I can't wait to do it all over again."

"Good, then she's yours," he said as he stamped the paperwork with authority. I couldn't believe that was all it took. I was shocked it was over and thrilled beyond words. I looked at Jon across the room and we both let out a big breath, smiling. "Mr. Shiller, I trust that you and your associates will get me the missing original documents next week?"

"Yes, Judge," Orson said.

"Thank you for your patience with all of this today," I said to the judge as I stepped down from the witness chair.

"You're welcome. Bailiff, this case is closed." He rapped his gavel on the big, oak desk and stood up. "Have a nice weekend and good luck," the judge said to us as I was hugging Jon.

"I can't believe he didn't even ask you *one* question," I said to Jon quietly. "Now let's go get our girl."

"Thank you, Orson, Mr. Brotting, Mr. Pelt, and Mr. Villagos," Jon said as we rushed toward the door.

I remembered something and stopped, turned around and said, "Oh wait. Before you leave, Judge, do you mind if we take a photo with you? Sophie may want to see pictures of all the important people involved in her adoption someday."

"Of course," he said as he sat back down at his desk. Jon handed the camera to Orson and stepped up next to the desk with me. We stood on either side of the judge and smiled.

We walked out of the courthouse at 1:55 p.m. and Jon was already calling the pilots. "We're on our way. File that flight plan to Kansas City."

"Do I have everything I need to get the hospital to release her to us now, Orson?" Jon said just before we got to our car.

"I'm working on it. My assistant is making copies of the adoption decree right now and then you can be on your way," he said. "Perhaps you'd like to grab a quick lunch to go in that café?" he said, pointing across the street.

Jon and I ran across the street to grab some sandwiches while we waited for the documents. Jon found a diet orange cream soda he liked so much there that he bought two extra six-packs to bring with us on the airplane. "It's hard to find good diet orange cream soda these days," Jon said. "This is really good."

"You finally found something in West Plains that you like. It's a great day all around," I said as we got into the car after Orson arrived with the file. "Let's just hope we don't have to come all the way back here to buy more, ever."

I don't actually remember the drive back to the hospital. I was deliriously happy and I officially had a daughter. We arrived at the hospital feeling entirely different than we had when we left just two hours earlier. We were not only the parents of two wonderful boys but also the new legal parents of a beautiful baby girl that was waiting for us in the maternity ward. It felt amazing and almost indescribable.

I had spent so many years longing for a little girl, being jealous of other women with little girls, and feeling sorry for myself that I couldn't believe that everything changed with the rap of a judge's gavel. Sophie was our daughter, and nothing could change that now. We had a few more legal hoops to jump through, including the post-adoption visit by Cecelia Dokes to make sure we were treating our daughter well, and finalizing the adoption in a Seattle courtroom three months after her birth. But the important fact remained. Fayth had given up her legal rights to her baby girl and with all the legal power we employed to make sure the paperwork was in order, she would never be able to retrieve those rights.

I would never look back on this adventure as easy, but the stress was worth it. It had been three weeks to the day that I received the phone call from our lawyer's assistant about Fayth. I couldn't believe that it only took one call for us to find a birth mother who not only chose us to raise her daughter but also followed through on her promise. I felt very lucky.

I was so proud of Jon, who got everything completed in the short time frame we had to work with. He was my hero through all of it. He found great lawyers to get the job done in every location we needed, he found someone at the FBI to expedite the fingerprint paperwork, and he arranged all the travel and hotels for us. He wasn't even the person who *really* wanted this baby. He did it all for me—at first. By the looks of it, though, he too had already fallen deeply in love with our daughter.

When we walked off the elevator and into the maternity ward, Jon practically pushed me out of the way to get to her first. I could see that he was just as happy about his new child as I was. Sophie was destined to be "Daddy's little girl."

"Sorry, but I really missed her." He apologized to me after realizing that he was a tad aggressive as we waited for the nurse to bring her back from the nursery. "You have been with her every minute since she was born and I need to catch up from having to go to that darned hotel."

"No problem," I said. "I guess I now know that you're not unhappy about this third child you said would be too much for you."

"Ha ha. Unhappy? I couldn't be happier. Let's get her out of here and show her what life looks like outside of a hospital."

"Here she is," Candace said as she brought Sophie to us, bundled up in the blanket we bought in New York. "She was an angel while you were gone and even just took a little nap."

"She always is," Jon said, taking the baby from her gently.

"Thank you so much, Candace, for everything," I said. "Can we please take a picture of you with her?"

"Of course," she said. We took a few pictures with Candace and the other nurses.

"Before you go," Candace said, "I'll need copies of the legal document allowing you to take her. Also, we prepared a diaper bag full of formula and other baby goodies to take with you on your trip this weekend. Here you go."

Jon handed her the paperwork, which she briefly glanced at. She obviously found what she was looking for and said, "That's all we need. I know it wasn't an easy process for you, but everything should be fine now. She's a lucky little girl. Good luck to you and your family."

"We're the lucky ones," Jon said. "Thanks so much."

WEEKEND BETWEEN TWO WORLDS

As we walked away from the nurses who had helped us care for Sophie for the last two and a half days, I felt a little nervous about caring for her ourselves after so many years without an infant. There weren't any more nurses around to help and we would have to provide constant supervision. Parenting was going to get a lot more difficult and I hadn't really even thought about it over the last three weeks.

We had gotten used to the boys being more self-reliant at seven and nine, and parenting was much easier when they entertained each other, ate by themselves, and changed their own clothes. There was much for me to relearn about infant care. I was a mother for the third time, but most mothers had nine months to prepare themselves, especially with a seven-year break between the second and third children. I had just twenty days and those twenty days were too filled with complicated questions and issues about Fayth to read any books to refresh my memory.

Although I was already reminded over the past two days that infants require constant attention, I was more worried about doing a great job, rather than the sleep loss or extra work an infant would require. I wasn't sure if I was nervous because Fayth trusted me to do a great job now that I was Sophie's mother, or if I placed that burden on myself, like I do about so many other things in my life. One thing was for sure: I looked forward to every minute of it. I knew parenting would be very different with a girl and it was what I had wanted more than anything.

Our arms were full as we carried everything onto the elevator, including Sophie in her infant car seat. I took a deep breath in and out signifying the end of a monumental week. We were finally done with all the stress of West Plains.

It felt awkward leaving West Plains without saying good-bye to Fayth, but she had clearly gotten what she wanted and so had we. It was a good situation all around. She did a good deed for us, and we did a good deed for her. I couldn't imagine doing what she had done, but I didn't live with her circumstances. She knew that having another baby would have put her over the edge. Now she could start a new life with Jared and her little boys. I silently wished her well as we walked out the main entrance of the hospital.

Sophie's third day with us was another beautiful day, and now that she was officially ours, the day seemed even brighter. "This is what outside is like, Sophie," I said. "That's the *sun* shining in your eyes, and the *sky* up there is the color *blue*. You have so much to learn, Miss Sophia Lazarus. We're going to teach you about everything and your two big brothers are going to help. Jon, I almost forgot in all the excitement. When should we call the boys?"

"Let's wait until we're in Kansas City. They'll be home from school and done with all their activities by then. I'll call Jennifer to let her know that we'll be calling so she can get the video camera ready to go. I want her to film their reaction since we can't see it ourselves," Jon said.

"I can't believe we have to tell them that we've been lying to them over the phone. It's also sad that they can't see their new little sister in person for at least four days."

Jon said, "Lying to them was better than telling them the truth if Fayth changed her mind. That would have been a lot harder to explain to them. They will totally understand that we're anxious to bring Sophie home so they can meet her as soon as possible. They are good, understanding boys and we can call them often to tell them about her."

"Yep. We had no real choice before she was born and we have no choice now," I said as I secured Sophie's car seat in the back seat. "They'll be so excited to hear they now have a baby sister. I'm sure they'll forgive us."

We turned off the main highway of West Plains for the last time, at the airport, and drove up to the tarmac in our "black beauty." As I bent down to lift Sophie out of the car seat, I saw her beautiful eyes in the sunlight and realized that her eyes were green, not hazel. They were just exquisite. She was truly the most beautiful baby I had ever seen. I called Jon over to take a look.

I realized at that moment that I had been willing to adopt any baby girl as long as she was healthy. When I looked in her eyes, though, it struck me that we had gotten so much more than just a healthy baby girl. Sophie was beautiful and sweet, too. I felt like the luckiest woman in the world.

The pilots stepped off the airplane with big smiles on their faces. They seemed truly happy for us and had been rooting for us every time Jon called them with updates on our travel schedule.

"She's a beauty," one of the guys exclaimed as he took the car seat up the steps to the plane for me.

"She was definitely worth the wait," the other pilot said. "Congratulations."

We thanked them for their patience and nice comments. As they loaded our luggage onto the plane, I wondered if this was a small sample of the reactions we would get from family and friends now that Sophie was our daughter. People close to us would be shocked but happy once we told them.

We couldn't wait to tell the whole world. It would be a one-hour flight to Kansas City, and then we planned to call my father and stepmother, Jon's father, my brother, and of course, our boys. After we reached them all, Jon would send out an email to everyone we knew with a picture of our new daughter. That email would also include an apology to those friends we had lied to for the prior two weeks. Surely, they would understand our not wanting to risk the boys' disappointment if the adoption didn't work out. In the list of things I had been worried about that month, that was pretty low on the list.

In fact, I was the happiest I had been in years. I was so excited about our future and looked forward to every moment of Sophie's growth and development, just like I had when the boys were infants. The idea of watching her personality develop, her physical appearance change, and her relationships with her brothers grow stronger each day made me satisfyingly optimistic.

I knew the days just ahead would be glorious, too. Our family, friends, and our entire community would welcome Sophie with open arms. I knew many friends would be stopping by the house to meet our new daughter. We would also arrive home just in time for Passover, when our extended family would come to our home to meet Sophie and celebrate. The following night, we were scheduled to attend another Passover celebration with some friends. We had already told them we might be bringing another guest to dinner, one who did not need a seat at the table. We were excited to give them a big surprise.

After we recovered from that holiday celebration, we would throw Sophie a big party called a *brit bat* or Baby Naming Ceremony in the Jewish tradition. Besides celebrating the arrival of the child, the baby girl is formally given a name in English and Hebrew at this event. Most mothers of new daughters wait until they are fully recovered from childbirth to throw a big party, usually two or three months after the birth. However, I wanted the party to occur early in April for our little Sophie. I wanted everyone we cared about to meet Sophie, and I wanted to show them how much she meant to our family. We planned to work on a date for that event over the weekend in Kansas City.

The jet took off for Kansas City without delay. The weather was great and there were no traffic control problems getting out of tiny West Plains. I looked out the window over the town and said, "Thank you, West Plains," as we flew up and over the town center.

"Sophie, you're about to see what a big city is like," Jon said. He took lots of pictures of us on the jet as we flew to Kansas City. It was a quick flight and I noticed a completely different landscape as we approached the airport in Kansas City. It was a relief to see skyscrapers, freeways, and lots of different neighborhoods, rather than just farmland. When we landed, I saw a big black limousine drive up to the airplane.

"What's that, Jon?"

"I hired a driver for the ride to the hotel. You and my daughter deserve nothing but the best," he said with a big smile.

We took more pictures in front of the airplane and limousine, so that someday Sophie would understand a little about what her father had done to celebrate her arrival. After everything was loaded into the limousine, our driver took us to the Fairmont Hotel, giving us a small sightseeing tour along the way.

"I'd be happy to take you to all the sights around the city if you'd like," he offered as he unloaded our luggage in front of the hotel.

"No, thank you," I said. "I think we're ready to relax with our baby daughter this weekend. She's the only sight I need to see."

Our hotel room in Kansas City was beautifully furnished in powder blue and cream with antique French furniture. It had a separate sitting room in addition to the bedroom, with a door between so Sophie could nap in the bassinet we brought with us without being disturbed while we talked on the phone.

The white wicker bassinet had been given to us by my mother and father when I was pregnant with Jake, our firstborn. My mother and I picked it out together and I had used it with both of my boys. I felt great joy the first time I placed Sophie in it, shortly after we arrived in our hotel room. I wished that I could call my mother to tell her about her namesake. I think I missed my mother more than I ever had at that moment—she would have been so happy for us.

After Sophie fell asleep, the first phone call we made was to my father and stepmother. Jon wasn't sure we should call them before the boys, but I said, "My dad would want to be the first person we called. I know that about him." Jon laughed and agreed.

They were still in their home in Palm Desert, California, but would be returning to Seattle on Sunday, before coming to Passover dinner at our home the following Wednesday. They had no idea that we had not returned with Micah from spring training in Phoenix. They would have been curious why we weren't in Seattle when they arrived so the timing was perfect. They were both unbelievably excited to hear from us because we hadn't spoken in a couple of weeks.

"Hi, Dad," I said, trying to contain my excitement. "How is everything in the desert?"

"Great, honey. My golf game is fabulous and the weather is spectacular. It's so nice to hear from you and we are so excited to see you and the kids next week."

"We are too, Dad. It's been so long since November. We miss you both. Hey, is Maryellen around? I'd like her to pick up on the other extension because we have something to tell you both."

"Sure, is anything wrong?" he said before yelling to Maryellen to pick up the phone in the kitchen.

"No, on the contrary. We have really good news for you," I said as Maryellen picked up another phone.

"Hi. I've missed you two. What's up?" she said.

"Well, we are in Kansas City right now."

"You're where?" My dad chuckled the way he does when he's a bit nervous or confused.

"Kansas City, Missouri. You should be congratulated because you have another grandchild!" For the fourth or fifth time in three days, tears started to well up in my eyes.

"What?" My father started to chuckle again, which also happens just before he gets emotional. "Another what?" he repeated.

"You now have a granddaughter and her name is Sophia Mariel," I said, crying. "She's beautiful, and she even has Mom's coloring."

My stepmother surprised me with her enthusiasm as she took over the conversation while my father collected himself. We are both extremely emotional and it doesn't take much to leave us speechless.

"You adopted a baby girl? That's wonderful. When? How long did you know about this?"

"She was born here in Missouri two days ago. We've only known about this for three weeks. It's a long story and I'll be glad to tell you all about it when we see you on Wednesday night," I said, trying to avoid a forty-five-minute conversation.

"I can't believe how excited I am to have a granddaughter!" Maryellen was ecstatic and it made me feel wonderful at the moment I needed it most. "You know it made me so happy to finally have a daughter when I married your father and now, you've given us a granddaughter."

I wasn't sure my father would react as well to the concept of adoption. We had never talked about adoption and I had no idea if he could open his heart to my new daughter, but he surprised me. His acceptance was obvious as soon as he was able to talk. I understood how he felt when he picked the phone up again.

"Patty, I want to tell you how happy I am about this news," he said, sniffling. "This is the best news you could have given us. We are thrilled beyond belief about Sophie, and it makes the upcoming reunion with you at Passover even better."

"I'm so happy to hear that, Dad. We're hoping to have her home on Tuesday afternoon." I explained briefly about the paperwork and staying in the state of Missouri until it was complete. "If it's not complete and we have to stay until Wednesday, you'll have to lead the Seder at our house until we get there, okay?"

"Anything you need, honey," he said. "Have you told the boys yet?"

"No, they are the next call. We wanted you to be the first person we called. I'm going to hang up now. Drive home safely on Sunday and we'll see you on Wednesday night."

"Thanks for calling, honey."

"Oh, and Dad, don't forget to bring us a hydrangea plant." I knew he'd remember what he and my mother had brought to our hospital room when each of the boys were born.

"You got it. Tell Jon I'm happy for you both and for all of us."

After we hung up, I said to Jon, "I loved their reaction." I was delighted that they were so happy about our news. Sophie would enrich our family in so many ways. "Giving good news is so much fun."

"Now I'll call the boys," Jon said, picking up the phone on the desk. "Jennifer should be ready with the movie camera so we can watch their reactions when we get home. I'll press the speaker button to hear both of them when they're ready."

After Jon dialed, I heard him say, "Hello, Jennifer. We're in Kansas City now. . . . She's just great. She's taking a nap after her big travel adventure today. . . . If you can get the boys together, we're ready to talk to them on the speakerphone so they can hear the news at the same time." He pressed the speaker button on our end as well.

After a minute, we heard the boys run into the room, arguing over who sat where and asking Jennifer why she had the movie camera in her hand. We laughed.

Jennifer said, "The boys are in the family room with Jasper and ready to hear your news. Jake is under a blanket because he's still sick today." She had called me the day before to tell me that she had taken Jake to the doctor. He had been diagnosed with strep throat and was starting on antibiotics. I knew that she was handling everything fine at home, but I felt bad that I wasn't there with him when he wasn't feeling well.

"Hi guys." I wondered where to start. "How are you feeling, Jake?"

"Not so good, Mommy," he said weakly.

"We miss you both so much, but it's only going to be a few more days till we get home."

"More days? Why more days?" Jake said with a scratchy voice.

"Yeah, you've been gone long enough, Mommy," Micah said.

"I'm sorry, but we have big news for you guys," Jon said.

"What?" they said at the same time.

"You have a baby sister now," Jon said.

After a brief pause, Jake said, "Mom, you're not pregnant, are you?"

"No, no, no, you don't understand," I said, laughing. "We adopted a baby girl and she's here with us now. She's officially your sister now. Isn't that the best news?"

There was a pause. "You mean like when we adopted Jasper?" Micah said.

"Yes, just like that," I said.

"She can't sleep on the third floor with us. There's no room," Jake said.

"What's her name?" Micah said, ignoring Jake's complaint.

We laughed and answered, "Sophie."

Micah said, "Why can't you name her something I can remember? I think you should name her Rachel."

"Sorry, buddy," Jon said, "Rachel is your friends Sam and Oliver's little sister. Your sister's name is Sophie. You're going to love her."

"If you say so," Micah said. "Maybe you should name her Reggie, like the baseball player. I can't remember Sosie or whatever you said."

"It's Sophie and you'll remember," Jon said.

"Mom, I thought you were going to tell us that Papa Bear was dead," Micah said bluntly. We laughed nervously and I felt extra guilty.

"I'm sorry if we upset you, Micah. I guess I should have said we have *good* news when we called, shouldn't I?" Jon said.

"Yeah," Micah said, "never mind."

"Papa Bear is just fine, so no need to worry anymore about him," Jon said. "Sorry we had to tell you he was sick."

"Mom, there's a big problem," Jake said. "What if she cries?"

"At night," Micah said for emphasis.

"All babies cry, Jake. I'll take care of her when she cries, don't worry," I said, trying to understand what he was really worried about. "She's been here with us for two days and I still haven't heard her cry yet."

"Two days? Why didn't you bring her home already?" Jake said.

"We had to wait two days for the woman who gave birth to her to sign some papers allowing us to raise her because she wasn't able to. The judge had to decide if Daddy and I would be good parents, which he did today," I said.

"Why couldn't her mom raise her?" Micah said.

"She's very young and already has two little boys, ages one and two," I started to explain.

"Oh no. I can't share my dog with all those kids," Micah said.

"No, you're not getting all of them, just one," Jennifer said. We were laughing too hard to speak.

"Why can't you come home now?" Jake said, clearly not feeling well.

"Because the state of Missouri and the state of Washington have to say it's okay before we can bring her home. They'll probably tell us it's okay to come home on Tuesday."

"When is *she* coming here?" Micah said.

"She'll be coming home with us, Micah," Jon said.

"Are you sure Jasper won't eat her socks?" Micah said.

"I don't think he'll like her socks, but he may like her stuffed animals so you'll have to help her protect them, okay?" I said, laughing.

"Okay, I have a secret hiding place in my room to hide them in. It's a secret compartment."

"Thanks for being so helpful, Micah," I said.

"Mom, where's she gonna sleep?" Jake said.

"In the room across from Daddy's study."

"Awww, she gets that room? That's the good room," Micah said.

"You have a good room," Jon said.

"Mom, we're pretty sure I have strep throat," Jake whined.

"I know, Jake. I'm sorry I'm not there to nurse you back to health. The medicine Jennifer is giving you should help though," I said, still feeling guilty for not being there.

"We love and miss you guys, and we'll be home very soon," Jon said. We wanted to end the call so they could digest this news.

"Bye," both boys said, clearly saving their other comments for our return.

Jon pressed the speakerphone button to end the call. "Wow, that went pretty well. It's a good thing they have a few days to get used to this idea before she's living in their home."

"Yes, their concerns were interesting and funny. I can't wait till they get to meet her," I said.

"I already told my dad that he can be honest with our friends now if for any reason someone calls to congratulate him," Jon said. "He's pretty happy for us and wants to know when the big party is so he can come visit right after Passover."

"I'll get to that party right after I finish the first party next week. We can talk about dates this weekend if you want though, as long as we are talking about April. This is all so overwhelming. March has turned into a crazy month for us but I love it. It's like a dream and I'm afraid that any minute I'm going to wake up."

"Nope, you're awake, and it's really happening," Jon said with love and admiration in his voice. "I can show you our real dream girl if you need proof. There's a little baby girl sleeping in that room, and she's all ours." I wasn't sure who he loved and admired more, Sophie or me.

"I need to call my brother next. Let's try his cell phone. He's with his family in Hawaii on spring break right now," I said.

My brother and his family were all together in a rental car when my brother picked up the phone.

"Hey Mur. It's your sister. How's Hawaii?"

"It's great. I'm surprised to hear from you. What's up? Is Dad okay?" he said with concern in his voice.

"Dad's just fine. I just talked to him to give him our big news."

"What big news?"

I heard my sister-in-law's voice in the background. "She's having a baby," she said in a subdued tone. My sister-in-law had some baby-related disappointments in her life and didn't sound excited.

"Tell Michele she's close. We just adopted a baby girl!" I exclaimed.

"That's great! Congratulations!" my brother said. "Where are you?"

"We're in Missouri. The papers were signed today and the judge ruled that she's absolutely ours as of this afternoon. We've known about this since March 1, but we didn't want anyone to know in case it didn't happen. We wanted the boys to know only when it became official." I knew I would tire of retelling this story to friends and other family members in the next week.

"That's great, Patty. We're all really happy for you both. We'll come by to see her when we get back. Have a great Passover."

"You too. Bye," I said, as another call came in. I clicked to the other line. "Hello?"

"Patty . . ." I couldn't recognize the voice and looked at the caller ID. The call was from our hometown area code, but I didn't know the number and I had no idea who it was. I heard a woman crying and she couldn't speak clearly through her sobs. "Hello? Are you okay? Who is this?"

"It's . . . it's Kim. I can't believe you have a daughter named after your mom." It was my girlfriend from college.

"Hi, Kim. You must have gotten the email that Jon sent out." She was one of the friends I had to apologize to after lying for over a week. Jon had sent a mass email out with a photo of Sophie while I was speaking to my dad. Obviously, people were starting to read it, as Jon's phone started ringing.

"Congratulations. That is such a beautiful baby, and what a story." Kim gushed for what seemed like hours about how much she loved my mom and how this was meant to be. I was delighted to hear from someone who was so enthusiastic for us.

"I just can't get over it. Your mom was the best, and now you have a daughter just like you wanted. I'm so happy for you."

"Thank you, Kim. I'm so sorry we had to lie to you about canceling the party and Jon's dad."

"What are you talking about? I understand why you did it. Don't even think about it. I'm sorry that I couldn't restrain myself from crying. I'm just so happy for you all."

My other line clicked with a call from another friend, and another. We kept this up for several hours while Sophie slept—thank goodness she was tired from her first airplane ride. We tried to keep each call brief since we had so many people waiting for us to call them back and relate the news directly. It was a heartwarming evening.

We got calls and emails from people we hadn't even sent the email to. Seattle seemed like a big city but when it came to good (or bad) news, it spread like it would in a small town.

When the calls from our friends finally slowed down, Jon called his cousin Ina from North Carolina. "You were one of the first on our list, but we haven't been able to get off the phone once I sent the email."

She was delighted to hear the news. Ina had known about our struggles to conceive a baby girl, because she kept us company when we were in Virginia. That seemed like a lifetime ago, and if we had known that this gorgeous baby girl was waiting until March 2002 to come into our lives, we would have skipped all of it.

"I guess all of the scientific fertility work we tried was for a reason," I said after we hung up from our chat with Ina. "If we hadn't tried everything else to get our girl, we might not have appreciated Sophie as much."

After a long moment, he looked at me and we both said, "Nahhhh."

Jon said, "We appreciate her just as much. In fact, I don't think we could appreciate her more."

I wasn't at all sure if our history mattered now that Sophie was with us. I did feel that there was a reason for the struggles we had with pregnancy. We believed that Sophie was destined to be our daughter, and what transpired over the course of several years before her arrival gave us the strength and courage to get through the last few weeks.

I heard Jon say to several people on the phone, "There were times when we thought it wasn't going to happen and we'd be back home empty-handed, but then something magical happened and everything worked out." I was convinced that God wanted us to have Sophie in our family and no matter how hard we tried to get a daughter through different means, he was saving her for us, and we just had to be patient.

The surprise we experienced through our friends' reactions was amazing. Adoption wasn't prevalent in our community, although I knew many couples who were struggling with fertility problems who might have been considering it. We hadn't thought about adoption until six months earlier. It snuck up on us as an option to my continuing ache for a daughter. It was an added benefit that we might have opened up the door for other couples that had not considered adoption, based on what we were hearing.

When Sophie woke up from her nap, Jon went into the bedroom and as he looked at our daughter, he started singing a rhyming song about "Princess Sophie." He congratulated himself when Dan Brown's *The Da Vinci Code* was published a year later and introduced the literary character with the same name. It was the cutest image of them together. Jon still sings that song to her every morning when she wakes up. Even if he is out of town, he calls her in the morning and sings the song to her.

That Friday evening, we went for a stroll down to the hotel lobby and into the nearby shopping village, which was in the heart of Kansas City. Sophie was the perfect angel when we stopped for dinner, napping off and on in her stroller while we ate. Several people came up to our table to congratulate us on our tiny, new daughter and asked her age.

Over the entire enjoyable weekend in Kansas City, as we shopped for more baby clothes and dined, many people commented on how adorable she was. Several were amazed that I looked so thin after giving birth just four days earlier. We would laugh and thank them for their compliments, rather than explaining the details. We had finally told our real story to our family and friends, and that was sufficient for us.

Despite a wonderful weekend in Kansas City, we were aching to go home by Monday morning. It had been ten days since we had been home, and we were tired of hotels and restaurants, no matter how nice they were. We really missed our boys. We had called them many times since Friday evening to see how they were feeling about everything. They mostly wanted to see Sophie, of course, and wanted us to come home.

We called Eleanor and Sheila to find out the status of the ICPC paperwork first thing Monday and learned that it wasn't going to be ready until late Tuesday.

"The lawyers didn't have good news about the ICPC paperwork, but Orson did get the results for us on Sophie's meconium test," Jon said. "It was negative for any drugs or alcohol. Fayth told us the truth and had stayed completely clean the entire pregnancy. Isn't that the best news?"

"Absolutely. I knew Sophie was perfect, but now we have the results to prove it," I said and gave Sophie a hug while she sucked on her bottle in my arms.

Then I had a devious idea. "Why can't we just tell them that we're still in Kansas City and go home today? They'll never know where we really are."

"Are you serious?" Jon said. "Why would you risk losing this child over another twenty-four-hour wait? I know it's hard for you, but be patient just a little while longer."

"I have been more than patient through this whole process. Patience is practically my new middle name," I said. "I'm surprised you even recognize me now that I'm so patient. I just want to take my daughter home."

"I know, I know. The lawyers are doing their best," Jon said. "I'll tell you what. I will tell the pilots that we are going to leave at noon tomorrow and we will just pray that the documents are done by then. If not, we will still fly home at noon. Okay?"

"Okay." I couldn't wait to walk into our home holding my daughter and hugging my boys.

GOING HOME

"It's Tuesday," I exclaimed as I woke up to Sophie's barely audible chirping on the fourth day of our Kansas City excursion. It was our third city and fifth hotel (counting the hospital stay) in twelve days and I couldn't wait to sleep in my own bed.

"You're going to have to get much louder when those boys are around, Princess Sophie," I said as I picked her up out of the bassinet. "This little chirp isn't going to work when we get in that big house with those big, loud brothers."

When Sophie was settled again after her breakfast, I started packing. "I think I'm going to throw away all of these clothes when I get home. I'm so sick of wearing the same ones every day."

"You'll feel better about everything when you get home," Jon said to console me, "and you'll have Jennifer there to help you with the baby."

"I don't want anyone else to care for her. I'm so in love with her that I want to spend every minute with her."

"Don't forget that the boys need you too," Jon said.

"You don't need to remind me of that. I love and miss them so much. In fact, I think Sophie's arrival has made me love them even more for some reason."

"Maybe it's because you now feel complete with a daughter?"

"Yes, maybe that's it," I said. "I'm sure I'll understand everything better when we get home."

"Oh, by the way, I got an email message last night that said Sophie's furniture that we ordered from New York is being delivered today."

"Perfect timing. Everything has worked out so well," I said. "What were we so worried about last week?"

"Ha ha, funny girl," Jon said, chiding me. "You were a completely different person a week ago, remember?"

"Yep, I remember, but it was totally worth it," I said as I lifted Sophie up and planted a big kiss on her tiny cheek. She squirmed in my arms.

Jon called Sheila again about the ICPC paperwork, reminding her that we were expecting good news today. "I haven't heard anything yet this morning," she said. "Let me call again and get back to you."

It was 10:30 a.m. when we started downstairs to check out of the hotel. We were going to leave Kansas City at noon, no matter what.

"We won't step into Washington State until we land so we have four extra hours for this paperwork to be completed," Jon said. "They may be waiting for us with guns out on the tarmac when we land in Seattle, but we're going," he joked.

"Are you really worried about this, Jon? Maybe we should wait."

"No, I'm confident the lawyers will get this done. We'll be fine," he said, squeezing my hand. "Let's keep moving."

We arrived in our limousine at the Kansas City private aviation terminal at 11:40 a.m. The pilots walked out and started to load the luggage. I felt a little guilty about getting on the plane without the legal documents in place. I was definitely not the kind of person who broke the law or even bent the rules. When I was working at Microsoft, I used to feel guilty about calling in sick, even if I *was* sick. We had gone through so much to get this far, and I didn't want to risk anything. I started to get nervous.

"Jon, maybe we should stay in Kansas City one more day."

"No, let's let them load the plane and then we'll sit for a few more minutes before taking off. I'm sure the pilots have to file the flight plan and check everything out anyway," Jon said as we climbed into the cabin.

His phone rang. I looked at his face for an indication of who was calling. He mouthed, "It's Eleanor. Okay, great. Will you send me some email as soon as it's done? I'm having trouble with my cell phone," he said to Eleanor, knowing that we'd be in the air soon and she'd be unable to reach us for four hours.

"She said the paperwork should arrive at her office by fax anytime now, so I'm sure it's just fine for us to leave," he said after ending the call. "I'll leave my cell phone on until we are out of range just in case."

"Okay. I'll probably worry all the way home."

"Hey, remember that leaving was your idea," Jon said. "Don't make me feel bad about it."

"I'm sorry. I'm just so desperate to get home. You've been great this entire trip and through this massive emotional journey we've taken. I wouldn't have been able to get through it without you, let alone make all the plans and arrangements. You're the best husband I could ask for," I said, kissing him.

"Don't forget that fact when I'm sitting in the King County Jail tonight," he said, jokingly.

I laughed for a moment. Then it struck me that we were again in a nerve-racking situation, even after Sophie became ours. I wondered when would it end and when could we finally relax?

After all that we had been through, I came to the conclusion that the emotional strain of adoption was just as difficult as the physical pain of childbirth. But when I looked at my daughter sitting across from me in her little car seat, I knew that she was worth every minute. What a doll she was and what a blessing. I was so happy to be going home with her and hoped that this legal issue didn't upset me the entire way home.

At 12:15 p.m., the plane was loaded, the door was closed, and we told the pilots we were ready to go. We started taxiing down to the runway and Jon kept looking at his computer for an email message. As the plane made its way around the last corner and I saw the runway ahead of us through the pilot's windshield, Jon received a call.

"Hello?" he shouted into the phone as the engines started to rev up for takeoff. "What? I can't hear you. Really? That's great. We're going home now. Legally. Thanks and good-bye!

"It's done," he yelled to me as the plane sped down the runway.

"I thought she was sending you email?"

"I only told Eleanor to send email. That was Sheila. The deal is done. We can officially leave Missouri," he said as the wheels left the runway and we were lifted into the air. It was amazing timing.

It was just like everything else about the story of our daughter's adoption. Our timing was perfect, our baby was perfect, and in my eyes, our family was finally perfect.

As we flew home with our daughter, we were bursting with love for Sophie. March ended even more happily than it began and our entire family welcomed her into their hearts.

Shortly after we were safely home, Jon called Angela at the FBI to thank her for helping us complete the paperwork so quickly. Again, the phone just rang and rang and rang every time he called the same phone number. It was about a week after we returned home from Missouri when a woman finally answered and promised to find Angela. When she picked up the call, Jon gave her a brief synopsis of our story and thanked her for her help. He told her we might have still been waiting in West Plains for the FBI paperwork without her assistance. He said her voice broke up when she said, "You know, no one has ever called to thank me for anything in the twenty-two years that I have worked here." The call was certainly worth the effort.

EPILOGUE

As I tiptoed into my daughter's dark room at midnight on her ninth birthday, I looked at her peaceful face and wondered where she would be sleeping if she hadn't become part of our family. Would she be the same happy nine-year-old that bounds around the house, singing and laughing? Would she have received the same loving hugs every night before bed and every morning when she wakes up? As I gently swept the hair off her face, I wondered what our home would have sounded like, felt like, and looked like without her delightful presence and positive energy.

As I pulled the sheet and blanket up over her shoulder, I wondered how I ever questioned whether I would have enough love for a third child that I didn't give birth to myself. The sheer delight of watching her grow into a toddler and now a beautiful child had been incredible, but our love for her had grown the most. As I glanced around her room in the dim light, I smiled at the picture of us holding her in the first moments of her life. She was this perfect, sweet baby with everything to look forward to, and we had front-row seats to watch her journey. And as I turned and quietly closed the door to her room, I gave thanks to God for the gift of my daughter for the zillionth time.

The story of our daughter Sophie's adoption is not like most of the adoption stories I've heard or read. We were already parents when we decided to adopt. We were desperate for a child for different reasons than most parents, although I am sure there are people who struggle with the same issues as I had. They are out there, maybe suffering in silence. We were very private about our plans for a third child, so we didn't receive condolence messages from friends and family about the miscarriages or failed fertility attempts. We didn't travel to a foreign country to bring a child home after weeks, or even months, of paperwork and legal bureaucracy. Everything we did was on American soil, and while we had plenty of legal paperwork, the process took only three weeks and didn't require passports. We didn't publicize our birth mother search locally. We were very specific about what we wanted and found our way to an adoption facilitator, who helped us manage the entire process privately.

However, our adoption story did include many of the same hardships we had heard about through other adoptive parents. We have great compassion for couples we know, and those we don't know, who went through adoption experiences even more difficult, or disappointing, than ours. Our story is complicated, occurred in a very short time frame, and most important, had an amazing outcome. Every time I look at my daughter, I am thrilled with the decisions we made. The risks we took were not easy, but the way fate led us to her in March 2002 was rewarding. What an amazing month March was that year.

Why tell this very personal story? Since our daughter's adoption, we have had the pleasure of helping other couples, both friends and strangers, adopt children of their own. Most of those couples had no natural children, were desperate to start their families, and were daunted by the same issues that had frightened us before and during our adoption. Most feared the emotional toll it could take. Some of them also thought that domestic adoption was much harder than international adoption. I have also been approached by several friends who are mothers of boys and, like me, desired a daughter. They wanted to know how we did it, the courage and other resources it took, and if we were happy. It gives me great joy to help others find their dream of having children when pregnancy isn't possible. For whatever reason, guiding others down the adoption path feels like giving back for the joy we have received through our daughter.

Adoption is a gift between two strangers that goes both ways. The birth mother receives the peace of mind that her child will be well taken care of. The adoptive parents receive the privilege and responsibility of raising a child when they might not otherwise have had that opportunity.

When considering adoption, there were so many stressful issues to face, especially for someone like me who worried about *everything*. It seemed like a difficult process legally, emotionally, and logistically. I knew very few people who had adopted a child, and no one in our community really talked about it. I was completely in the dark about adoption. I later realized that I wasted a lot of time wondering where to start. I had always shoved the possibility of adoption on a theoretical shelf labeled "too difficult."

I now believe in adoption completely and so do many friends of mine. I have subsequently discovered many other adopted children and adults that I never knew about—even some good friends who were adopted and never mentioned it. We have joined a community of people who have found incredible happiness through adoption.

My daughter is now a great artist, an excellent tennis player, and loves to play the piano, sing, and dance. She might never have realized her potential in life without the opportunities we have and will continue to expose her to, but we wouldn't have known the joy of her accomplishments and unconditional love without her. Adopting Sophie was one of the best things we ever did for our family, and I want to tell other people aching for a child how wonderful the experience can be, with a little luck and lots of love.

Life is about striving to achieve *all* of your goals. Having a daughter was my dream and I had to do all that I could to make it come true. At first glance, I thought it was selfish, risking the happiness we had with our two boys. But they are in love with their little sister and we all agree our family is better off because of her. The only thing I regretted was not doing it sooner. Throughout the first year of my daughter's life, I asked myself,

"What was I afraid of?" I am delighted I gave myself permission to follow my dream.

Our relationship has reached a point that Sophie recognizes how close we really are as a mother-daughter duo and how wonderful that feels. I often wonder how old I was when I first realized how special my mother really was. I now know that the grief over losing my mother will never completely fade, but having my own daughter to share the kind of love that my mother shared with me is rejuvenating. No one will ever love me like my mother loved me, but the love I feel for Sophie is blissful.

I tell this story of Sophie's adoption so that other mothers, and potential mothers, can stop wondering and start down their own path to happiness. Like giving birth, adoption is an ordinary miracle that takes courage, patience, and a lot of love.

The mother of one of my girlfriends gave Sophie the following poem at her Baby Naming celebration in April 2002, when our family and friends welcomed her into the community. I loved the poem and have found it to be so accurate over the last nine years. Sophie has known she was adopted since the age of five and often asks me to explain it, again, just before bed. I tell her, again and again, that "your brothers grew in my tummy, but you grew in my heart."

Legacy of an Adopted Child

Once there were two women
Who never knew each other
One you do not remember
The other you call mother

Two different lives shaped
To make yours one
One became your guiding star
The other became your sun

The first gave you life
And the second taught you to live in it
The first gave you a need for love
And the second was there to give it

One gave you a nationality
The other gave you a name
One gave you the seed of talent
The other gave you an aim

One gave you emotions
The other calmed your fears
One saw your first sweet smile
The other dried your tears

One gave you up
It was all that she could do
The other prayed for a child
And God led her straight to you

And now you ask me through your tears
The age-old question through the years
Heredity or environment
Which are you a product of?

Neither my darling, neither
Just two different kinds of love.

ABOUT THE AUTHOR

Patty Lazarus is an author, blogger, and mother of two sons and a daughter she adopted at birth in the United States. After spending nine years as an Account Manager for Microsoft, she left to focus on raising her children and became actively involved in their schools and several Seattle-area charities as a board member and fundraiser. Patty lives in Washington State with her husband and three beautiful children, and enjoys golf, tennis, and traveling with her family.

18000839R00146

Made in the USA
Charleston, SC
11 March 2013